AUSTRALIA
MOMENTS IN HISTORY

AUSTRALIA
MOMENTS IN HISTORY

FROM CAPTAIN COOK TO THE 21ST CENTURY

VICTOR SWAIN

NEW HOLLAND

FOR MY GRAND-DAUGHTERS, STEPHANIE AND MONICA

AUTHOR'S NOTE

The following pages are not a history of Australia, for the author is not qualified to write such a work. Perhaps it would be appropriate to describe this book as a 'potted history', presented in an easily readable form, and intended to provide glimpses of the totally fascinating story of one of the newer members of the community of nations; and of a peaceful and proud people who have fashioned their own distinctive culture and lifestyle in a land that is like no other place on earth.

Only minor changes have been made to this reprint edition. Several new episodes have been added to reflect events that have occurred since publication of the previous edition.

CONTENTS

THE EARLY YEARS

FEDERATION

THE TWENTY-FIRST CENTURY

PREFACE

The choice of 'The Great South Land' in the 1770s as the site of Britain's new convict settlement was indeed fortunate. For the early British settlers had stumbled upon a vast and unexploited (according to Western thinking) island continent.

For many of the settlers, however, it was a forbidding environment; unlike the Aboriginal people, they had not learned to adapt to the land. The centre was arid, with large desert areas, and almost devoid of waterways. The northern regions were subject to annual dousings of monsoonal rains and occasional cyclones. At other times, the continent would be in the grip of severe drought.

Gradually, however, as more convicts and immigrants swelled the population, the land was explored and then, where possible, made productive. Large areas became grazing lands or were ploughed to cultivate wheat and other grains. Pastoral industries steadily developed to provide a sound base for Australia's nineteenth-century economic development.

Gold, copper and tin were discovered during the 1850s, heralding the twentieth-century discoveries of Australia's vast mineral wealth. Significant deposits of petroleum products, both onshore and beneath the seas, reduced to a large extent Australia's dependence on imported oil, and provided power for the expansion of the country's manufacturing and transport industries, as well as for domestic needs.

Australia's enormous natural wealth did indeed justify the 'lucky country' appellation, which was current at the time of the bicentenary in 1988. (*The Lucky Country* is the title of the best-known book by Australian writer and academic Donald Horne (1921–2005).) But if any review of the first two hundred years of Australia's European settlement is attempted, one should also take into account the non-material factors that contributed to Australia's good fortune.

Two significant factors were inventiveness and adaptability. The early explorers and pioneers were, in a host of ways, innovators, for they were far removed from the 'mother country' and in many respects were dependent upon their own resources. It was they who, despite the generally inhospitable conditions, opened up the country to establish the great wool, wheat, beef and other pastoral industries which laid the foundations for Australia's future economic prosperity and independence. The nation's ability to survive in difficult circumstances was amply demonstrated during the 1850s gold rushes, when thousands of native-born Australians and newly arrived immigrants managed to live and work at the diggings under conditions that today would be considered intolerable.

Then there was the resolute courage and determination of the early explorers and pioneers. Who can fail to be moved by the supreme courage of Sir Douglas Mawson (see pp. 234-7) when, in 1912, he found himself alone and in dire circumstances in the wastes of Antarctica? Perhaps this fine and unassuming man in some way drew his inner strength from the many tales of steadfastness and determination demonstrated by so many of the nineteenth-century pioneers.

The various military conflicts in which Australian troops have been involved have also spawned innumerable accounts of courage and tenacity on the part of Australia's soldiers, sailors and airmen, and women service volunteers, especially during the two world wars.

As we reflect on Australia's recent history, we should also think of the achievements of the early administrators, the legislators and the civil servants who laboured—not always to everyone's satisfaction—to regulate the economy and society in a constructive manner in keeping with the Australian way of life. Their work found expression in many ways, especially towards the end of the nineteenth century, as the six colonies and the territories struggled to mould the desires and aspirations of the independent and widespread communities into a unified whole.

That the new nation grew and prospered, despite inevitable bickering and disagreements, is testimony to the fundamental belief of the Australian people in the paramountcy of their particular way of life. This conviction was strengthened by Australia's unquestioning participation in the two world wars, and the terrible sacrifices that resulted. The Anzac tradition and the bonds of mateship that emerged from the tragic Gallipoli campaign in 1915, and the battlefields of France and Belgium, will forever continue as a reminder of the true Australian spirit.

Particularly during the second half of the twentieth century, Australians made significant contributions to medical and scientific knowledge and to industrial 'know-how'. These achievements prompted Donald Horne (see p.17) to think of Australia as 'the lucky country'. In 1990 Robert Hawke, then Australia's prime minister, coined the phrase 'the clever country' when launching the 1990 election campaign.

In the decades since the end of World War II, Australia has become a true multicultural society. Nineteenth-century Australians were predominantly of Anglo-Saxon heritage, but in the post-war years there has been a strong immigration mix of peoples from Europe, the Mediterranean lands, the Middle East, Asia and elsewhere. Many facets of Australian life have been affected by the admixture of the cultures, customs and languages of these later arrivals. That the nation has been able to absorb the influx of these diverse peoples is testimony to the readiness of Australians generally to share their heritage with those who similarly value democratic freedoms and the rule of law.

Australians can look back with a sense of pride at the achievements of the years of European settlement and at the same time face the challenges of the years ahead with the confidence of those ever ready to 'have a go'.

IN THE BEGINNING

Most Earth scientists now believe that planet Earth first formed about 4.6 billion years ago, in the form of a gaseous cloud resulting from a supernova explosion. Matter then crystallised, and by about 4.5 billion years ago rocky outcrops had begun to form.

Earth's moon was also formed around this time, probably as the result of a collision between a giant asteroid and Earth.

CONTINENTS

Between 900 million and 600 million years ago, during a series of Ice Ages, the Earth's landmasses formed a gigantic super-continent named Rodinia. By about 250 million years ago Rodinia had broken up. Another super-continent named Pangea evolved and straddled a large part of the Earth's surface. Pangea lasted about 100 million years before splitting into two: a northern part, comprising what is now North America, Europe and Asia; and a southern part, named Gondwana (Gondwana is a Sanskrit name meaning 'Land of the Gonds'). When Gondwana began to break up about 184 million years ago, India, Madagascar and Africa parted from the super-continent, followed by New Zealand and New Caledonia about 90 million years ago. Australia broke away from Antarctica about 30 million years later, followed by Africa around 30 million years ago. About 10,500 years ago the rising seas flooded Bass Strait, separating Tasmania from mainland Australia.

LIFE ON EARTH

The Pilbara region in the northern part of Western Australia rose above the sea about 3.5 billion years ago and was one of the Earth's first landmasses. Life in the seas probably developed at approximately the same time.

There is evidence to suggest that around 2.5 billion years ago there was a significant increase of oxygen in the Earth's atmosphere, thus creating a much deeper ozone shield. This allowed various organisms in the ocean to exist in shallow water and on land. By about 480 million years ago the first backboned fish had developed.

Evidence of the first land plants exists from around 450 million years ago, and by 300 million years ago all major plant families had emerged except the flowering plants (angiosperms), which emerged about 120 million years ago, before Gondwana began to break up.

Dinosaurs roamed the Earth around 210 million years ago, and birds appeared about 60 million years later.

HUMAN BEINGS

Humans, classified as part of the animal kingdom, first evolved about 2.3 million years ago from the family known as hominids. The genus 'man' (*Homo sapiens*, meaning 'wise man') first appeared in Africa approximately 160,000 years ago; then, at a later period, migrated northwards to Europe and eastwards through the Indian subcontinent, spreading to northern latitudes about 50,000 years ago and to the lands now called Thailand, Cambodia, Laos, Vietnam, Malaysia, Borneo and Indonesia. The tide of humanity travelled mainly by land, having as yet little or no seafaring experience. *Homo sapiens* were part of the second migration of hominids out of Africa, being the forerunners of modern humans.

THE UNKNOWN LAND TO THE SOUTH-EAST

Eastwards from Java, the Indonesian island linking to Sumatra, lies a series of smaller islands extending towards the larger island of Timor. When these lands were first occupied, the seas were lower, hence there were many small islands which provided 'stepping stones' towards the then unknown land to the south-east.

Yet the coastal dwellers of the southern lands of what is now Indonesia would have been well aware of the existence of a landmass to the south-east. Evidence of this would have been the smoke that periodically drifted to the north-west from bushfires naturally started by lightning strikes or periodic burn-offs. The coastal dwellers would also have noted the seasonal flights of birds migrating to and from the unknown land, and from New Guinea, which was then joined to Australia by a land bridge.

THE FIRST OCEAN VOYAGE

Aboriginal Australians think of the Dreamtime as the period of creation of the world and spiritual beginnings of their people. Many Aborigines believe that their ancestors came from across the sea, a belief now shared by most scientists.

We can only speculate as to the type of craft that the first successful ocean voyagers used on their perilous first journey across the Timor Sea towards the unknown land to the south-east. Quite possibly rafts or canoes made from bamboo would have been used, for bamboo, having an outer coating of silica, is very buoyant.

Wind and tide would largely have determined the precise landfall of the world's first ocean voyagers. It may well have been the Kimberley coast to the south, though Arnhem Land and the Cape York Peninsula could also have been the site of the first human footprints on Australian soil.

EARLY AUSTRALIANS

The Willandra Lakes region in western New South Wales has proved to be a rich source of skeletal remains of early Australians. The earliest skeleton, comprising a skull and limb bones and known as 'Willandra Lakes Hominid 50', is at least 35,000 years old, and quite possibly much older.

It has been estimated that by about that time most of the main ecological areas in Australia were occupied. Possibly as many as 1 million people had populated the continent by the time the Europeans first settled in Australia in 1788.

ABORIGINAL CULTURE

Over a period of probably more than 50,000 years the Aboriginal people developed a highly sophisticated culture. They had no need for agriculture as we know it, for their hunting, fishing and food-gathering skills ensured an adequate supply of food. (The nineteenth-century European explorers frequently testified to the Aboriginal people's ability to locate water and to their highly efficient foraging methods.) The constructive use of fire produced many benefits and added to their food supplies.

Available evidence points to the fact that the Aboriginals, by skilfully adapting to the land and to the prevailing climatic conditions, were able to fashion an existence that was both socially acceptable and spiritually satisfying.

Writing in his journal during his 1770 voyage along Australia's east coast in the barque *Endeavour*, Lieutenant (as he then was) James Cook made some trenchant observations concerning the Aboriginal people he encountered during his expedition. He wrote:

> *'From what I have said of the Natives of New-Holland they may appear to some to be the most wretched people upon Earth, but in reality they are far more happier than we Europeans. They live in a Tranquility which is not disturb'd by the Inequality of Condition: The Earth and sea of their own accord furnishes*

them with all things necessary for life, they covet not Magnificent Houses, Household-stuff &.ca, they lie in a warm and fine Climate and enjoy a very wholesome Air, so that they have very little need of Clothing and this they seem to be sensible of, for many to whom we gave Cloth &.ca to, left it carelessly upon the Sea beach and in the woods as a thing they had no manner of use for. In short they seem'd to set no Value upon any thing we gave them, nor would they ever part with any thing of their own for any one article we could offer them; this in my opinion argues that they think themselves provided with all the necessarys of Life and that they have no superfluities.'

COOK TAKES POSSESSION

Cook made three voyages of exploration. On the first of these, from 1768 to 1770, after observing the transit of the planet Venus across the Sun, he circumnavigated what is now New Zealand, then crossed the Tasman Sea. At Latitude 38° South, land was sighted at what proved to be the south-east corner of New Holland, as Australia was first known. (The Dutch had charted much of the western half of Australia in the seventeenth century and had named the continent after their homeland.) Cook named a nearby headland Point Hicks (after the lieutenant who had made the sighting), changed course to the north-east and sailed northwards, charting Australia's entire eastern coast.

On 22 August 1770, on tiny Possession Island off the northern tip of the Cape York Peninsula, Cook raised a flag and ceremonially took possession of eastern Australia in the name of his sovereign, King George III.

Paying gracious tribute to the explorers who had preceded him, Cook wrote in his diary:

'Having satisfied my self of the great Probability of a Passage, thro' which I intend going with the Ship, and therefore may land no more upon this Eastern coast of New Holland, and on the Western side I can make no new discovery the honour of which belongs to the Dutch Navigators; but the Eastern Coast from the Latitude of 38° South down to this place I am confident was never seen or visited by any European before us, and Notwithstand[ing] I had in the Name of His Majesty taken possession of several places upon this coast, I now once more hoisted English Coulers and in the Name of His Majesty King George the Third took possession of the whole Eastern Coast from the above Latitude down to this place by the name of New South Wales, together with all the Bays, Harbours Rivers and Islands situate upon the said coast ...'

Cook's passengers on the *Endeavour* included gentlemen of the Royal Society and their assistants, one of whom was a botanical draughtsman...

SYDNEY PARKINSON

Until the camera was invented, to depict any scene or object it had to be hand drawn, painted, carved, sculptured or otherwise represented.

In Australia, of course, Aboriginal people had been developing their unique art forms for many thousands of years.

The first European artist to record the Australian scene pictorially was Sydney Parkinson.

Born in Scotland, he went to London about 1767, where his skill as a botanical artist came to the notice of a wealthy member of the Royal Society, Sir Joseph Banks. Banks duly employed the young artist, who was then aged about twenty-two, and in the following year included him in his team of 'scientific gentlemen' to accompany Lieutenant

James Cook on the first of his three voyages of discovery to the South Pacific in the *Endeavour*. Parkinson was the expedition's botanical draughtsman, and when the topographical draughtsman, Alexander Buchanan, died at Tahiti, Parkinson shouldered Buchanan's duties. On the voyage he completed more than 1300 drawings and sketches, and in addition compiled vocabularies of words and expressions used by the Tahitian and New Holland natives.

Parkinson was the first European artist to make authentic portraits from direct observation of Aboriginal Australians, and the first to draw or sketch Australian flora, fauna and landscapes.

Much of Parkinson's work survives. The British Museum in London has some eighteen volumes of his plant drawings, of which eight volumes, comprising 243 drawings, are of Australian plants. There are an additional three volumes of zoological subjects.

Sydney Parkinson died at sea in 1771 on the return voyage to England. He was a gentle and industrious man, and a very talented artist.

SOUTH SEAS EXPLORATION

Cook's 1768–70 voyage of exploration was preceded by some cat-and-mouse activities on the part of the five seafaring and trading European nations—France, Spain, Holland, Portugal and Britain—which had their covetous eyes on the South Seas.

During the early 1520s the Portuguese had produced a map of Australia's eastern seaboard, and for 300 years thereafter numerous expeditions had touched upon various parts of the extensive Australian coastline. In a few instances they had clashed with Aboriginal people. The French, Spanish and Dutch had also briefly visited Australia's west coast in the course of voyages to the East Indies. There is ample evidence, as we shall see, that France in particular had territorial designs on the Australian continent.

In the 1760s there were both French and British expeditions to the South Seas. During the next decade they were followed by the Spanish, who sent expeditions in 1772 and again in 1774.

In 1772 the French had made a landing on the continent's west coast, at Dirck Hartog Island, on the western side of Shark Bay. (Dutch explorer Dirck Hartog named the island after himself during a three-day stay in 1616.)

THE FOUNDING OF MODERN AUSTRALIA

In 1786 the British government appointed Captain Arthur Phillip, a naval officer and part-time farmer, to command an expedition to Botany Bay, there to establish a penal settlement. (Botany Bay had been discovered by Cook in 1770. During his voyage along Australia's east coast he named the bay after two members of his party—Joseph Banks, the aristocratic young president of The Royal Society; and David Solander, the expedition's botanist—who had spent a week there collecting plant, bird and animal specimens which were then not known to European science.)

The decision to transport convicts to New South Wales was primarily taken in order to provide some relief in the overcrowded English prisons, although thoughts of the strategic advantage of a presence in the South Pacific also doubtless influenced the minds of the government in London.

In May 1787, the First Fleet, comprising two naval vessels—Phillip's flagship HMS *Sirius* and HMS *Supply*—together with nine merchant ships, departed from Portsmouth. After eight months, during which period forty-eight people died, the fleet arrived at Botany Bay in January 1788. Unimpressed with the location as a suitable settlement site, Phillip explored the coastline northwards in the *Sirius* and soon happened upon what he described as 'the finest Harbour in the world', with a deepwater inlet into which flowed a freshwater stream. He named the place Sydney Cove (after Lord Sydney, the British Home Secretary, who had recommended the establishment of a penal colony in New Holland).

Six days later, as the remainder of the fleet was preparing to depart for Sydney Cove, two French frigates sailed into Botany Bay. After overcoming his astonishment, Phillip made a courtesy call on the French commander, Jean-François de Galaup, Comte de la Pérouse, and learned that the two vessels were equipped for a scientific and exploratory expedition. Phillip may well have speculated as to whether there was another motive behind the French presence in New Holland waters.

When this piece of news eventually reached London, the British government may also have speculated—as historians have done ever since—as to the course of events had the First Fleet arrived at Botany Bay to find the French established there and the Tricolor flying from a flagpole.

THE FLEDGLING COLONY

The First Fleet's complement, which disembarked at Sydney Cove on 26 January 1788, numbered approximately 1473, which included 443 seamen and 753 convicts and their children. A flag was ceremonially hoisted, the marines fired a salute and all present gave three cheers. The colony of New South Wales had been formally established.

The colony's first governor, Captain Arthur Phillip, proved to be a dignified and zealous leader, determined to wrestle with the daunting task that confronted him.

Shelter was an immediate priority, for the settlers were initially accommodated either in tents brought up from the First Fleet's holds or in makeshift timber and thatch dwellings. The Governor himself had to make do with a leaking canvas tent.

Few of the convicts had any tradesman's experience, the majority being skilled only in thieving and other petty crimes usually undeserving of such a harsh punishment as transportation. Many were ill, dispirited and disgruntled after the long voyage, for transportation had removed them to a strange and apparently inhospitable land at a time when the unaccustomed summer torments of heat, high humidity and the ubiquitous flies discouraged any form of manual labour.

SURGEON JOHN WHITE

When the First Fleet arrived at Botany Bay in 1788, many of the total complement of men, women and children were in poor health after the eight-month (over 15,000 nautical miles) voyage from England. But for the skill and care of the expedition's chief surgeon, John White, there would undoubtedly have been more than forty-eight deaths during the protracted journey.

Once established in the colony, Surgeon White and his assistants initially faced acute medical problems. There were outbreaks of scurvy and dysentery, food was severely rationed and there was little suitable accommodation for the sick. But within a year a hospital had been built and there was a marked improvement in the settlers' health.

Like some members of the medical profession, White was a keen naturalist. He found time to accompany Governor Phillip on two journeys of exploration, using the expeditions to gather floral specimens and to make sketches of fauna encountered on their travels. This material he sent to England, together with the journal he had kept after joining the First Fleet. The journal, together with sixty-five engravings from his specimens, was published in 1790 under the title *Journal of a Voyage to New South Wales*. The book was a great success—there were later German, French and Swedish translations.

As the infant colony's critical food situation persisted, White was amongst several officers who fished at night to supplement the rations. He also participated in the erection of the signal station at South Head. From there the Second Fleet was sighted in June 1790, its arrival placing additional medical strain upon White and his staff. About 759 men, women and children were landed, some dying, others seriously ill. Despite the lack of medicines and adequate hospital facilities, the surgeon and his assistants nursed more than half the voyagers back to health.

The situation was repeated in September 1791 with the arrival of the Third Fleet. At one time about 600 newly arrived sick convicts were being cared for. By 1792, a total of 436 deaths had been recorded.

White, now suffering the effects of continual strain, applied to the home government for leave in England. Whilst awaiting a decision, he maintained his natural history studies and continued to send specimens and drawings to England. In this he was assisted by Thomas Watling, a convict who was also a skilled artist.

In 1793 White was granted 100 acres (40 hectares) of land (where the Sydney suburb of Leichhardt is now located), which he called Hamond Hill Farm. He was later granted a further 30 acres (12 hectares) with water frontage at what is now known as White Bay.

Also in 1793 White's first child was born illegitimately to a convict, Rachel Turner. The lad later went to England as a member of his father's household. He joined the Royal Engineers, fought at Waterloo, and in 1823 returned to Sydney to be reunited with his mother, who had meanwhile married a prominent settler, Thomas Moore.

The good doctor's leave application was duly granted and he sailed from Sydney at the end of 1794, leaving the colony a far healthier place than it had been. Deaths from all causes in 1794 totalled only fifty-nine.

White later elected not to return to New South Wales, and from 1796 to 1799 he served as surgeon on various ships. At about this time he married and fathered a son and two daughters. He then had a number of shore-based appointments until being superannuated in 1820 at the age of sixty-three.

Surgeon John White died in England in 1832, aged seventy-five. He was an honourable member of an honourable profession.

THE SETTLEMENT GROWS

Voluntary manpower was critically short in the new settlement, with officers and men alike being more interested in self-advancement than in acting as gaolers and policemen. Nevertheless, construction work began slowly to alter the landscape, as buildings fashioned from locally available timber and stone took shape.

Initially, foodstuffs were sufficient to provide adequate rations, thanks to Phillip's insistence in provisioning the First Fleet to the maximum extent, despite the British government's lack of interest and tardy support. At the Cape of Good Hope, Phillip had also made purchases of seeds, plants, poultry and other necessities.

Despite this preparedness, in July of that first year Phillip was forced to send the *Sirius* back to the Cape to replenish the government store. Early in 1790 Phillip once again had to send his flagship to the Cape on a repeat mission. (Later that year a disaster occurred when the *Sirius* was wrecked off Norfolk Island whilst on a voyage to China.)

By 1792 conditions had improved for the settlement's population of 3000. The Second Fleet's arrival in mid-1790 had brought much-needed provisions and stores. But there was also news of the loss of the store ship *Guardian*, which had sunk after striking an iceberg off the Cape of Good Hope.

The convicts who arrived with the Second Fleet were accompanied by 500 officers and men of the newly commissioned New South Wales Corps, under the command of Major Francis Grose. One of the Corps' officers, Lieutenant

John Macarthur, was later to leave an indelible mark on the pages of Australia's history (see pp. 34–36).

By June 1791 Phillip had established a satellite settlement at Rose Hill, some 28 kilometres west of Sydney Cove, where more fertile soil and good pastures had been found. A plan for the town was drawn up and buildings constructed, including a barracks and a house for the Governor. The place was subsequently renamed Parramatta, an Aboriginal name with two meanings: 'the head of the river', and 'the place where eels lie down'.

Towards the end of 1791, Phillip resigned when increasing ill health began to take its toll. He had survived four years of hardship, frustration and incessant criticism. History was to regard him as a good governor who strove to lay the colony's foundations despite the most arduous circumstances.

Phillip departed for England in December 1792. He took with him an Aboriginal man named Bennelong, whom the military had captured in 1789. Bennelong had proved friendly and soon adapted himself to European customs. He readily wore the clothing given to him and developed a liking for liquor and European food. A hut was built for him on the eastern side of Sydney Cove, which is now known as Bennelong Point. (The Sydney Opera House now stands on the site.)

Bennelong was presented to King George III in London. In 1795 he returned to Sydney aboard the same ship (the *Reliance*) as did Phillip's successor, Governor Hunter. Bennelong settled on land granted to him by Phillip, living there until his death on 3 January 1813.

Phillip had perceived that the future wellbeing of the colony depended upon the introduction of a class of free settlers who would employ the readily available convict labour. The 'home' government was not unsympathetic to this view, and by the time of Phillip's death in 1814 increasing numbers of Britons were responding to the challenge and opportunities that Australia presented.

In addition to convicts and free settlers, there were also the emancipists: convicts who had been pardoned or whose sentences had expired. One emancipist was Simeon Lord, who had been sentenced to seven years transportation for thieving. By 1798 he had established himself as a trader in seal skins, whale oil, coal, and in commodities required in the Pacific Islands.

JOHN MACARTHUR

John Macarthur was one of the most outstanding, and most ambivalent, of New South Wales' early personalities.

As a man he was arrogant, contemptuous, vengeful, uncompromising, intolerant and humourless. One is left with the impression that he was only at peace with himself when in his family circle with his devoted wife, Elizabeth, and their children.

Yet it was his vision, determination and restless energy that were largely responsible for the founding of Australia's wool industry, an industry that was to bring immeasurable economic and social benefits to the country. (Wool was Australia's principal export earner from the 1820s until the 1960s.)

Twenty-two-year-old Macarthur, along with his wife and their baby son, arrived at Sydney Cove with the Second Fleet on 28 June 1790. Macarthur was a second lieutenant in the newly-commissioned New South Wales Corps. Like other members of the Corps, it was not long before Macarthur was engaged in various non-military activities intended to increase his personal finances and influence.

Thus, he was soon embroiled in a series of minor disputes, resulting in a reprimand from Governor Phillip, and thereafter haughtily withdrew from social occasions at Government House.

By 1792 Macarthur was based at Parramatta as the regimental paymaster, a financially beneficial appointment. A year later he became the unpaid but influential Inspector of Public Works.

In 1793 a 100-acre (40-hectare) land grant, together with a gift of stock from his commanding officer, enabled Macarthur to commence farming on good-quality soil near Parramatta. Swift clearance of the land earned him to acquire another 100 acres. By the following year he was selling produce profitably to the government store.

Macarthur was promoted to the rank of captain in 1795. In the following year, after a dispute with Governor Hunter, Macarthur resigned as Inspector of Public Works. A further series of altercations followed, culminating in a disagreement with Hunter's successor, Governor King. As a result, King decided to send Macarthur to England to face a court martial.

Macarthur took with him selected fleeces from his own flocks. These greatly impressed representatives of the English wool trade, and prompted Macarthur to propose to the British government a scheme for significantly increased production of wool in New South Wales. Macarthur's proposal gained official approval, and he was awarded a special grant of 5000 acres (2025 hectares) of prime land in the settlement, with the promise of another similar grant if the scheme proved successful.

After being formally censured by the authorities, Macarthur was able to secure approval to resign his commission and return to New South Wales. He arrived back in Sydney in 1805 and was allocated thirty-four convicts by Governor King, to work the 8500 acres (3442 hectares) he then possessed.

The next twelve years were, for Macarthur, a period of increasing turbulence. A far-reaching disturbance occurred in 1808 with Governor Bligh, which was to trigger Bligh's deposition, arrest and return to England in 1810 (the outcome of Macarthur's dispute with Bligh is referred to on p. 43). Macarthur departed for London several weeks ahead of Bligh in order to defend his actions.

Macarthur remained in England until 1817. By then he was running short of money and becoming increasingly in debt. Nevertheless, he devoted his time to the study of English wool processing and made a visit to the Continent to investigate farming methods and viticulture. He returned to Sydney towards the end of 1817.

By the time Commissioner Bigge arrived in 1819 to investigate the settlement's affairs (see pp. 51–3), Macarthur was grazing some 6000 sheep, including 300 prime merinos. He exerted his influence to direct Bigge's thoughts towards his vision of greatly expanded wool production in the settlement, and the introduction of new capital.

After Bigge's report had been officially approved, Macarthur claimed the additional 5000 acres (2025 hectares) he had been promised in 1804. The fresh land at Cowpastures was later incorporated into Macarthur's Camden Park estate, which then comprised over 60,000 acres (24,300 hectares) of the settlement's best land.

Macarthur's wool was now selling in England at record high prices. In 1822 his contribution to the wool industry was acknowledged in London when the Society of Arts awarded him two gold medals.

In 1824 Macarthur's vision for the Australian wool industry took more tangible form with the incorporation of the Australian Agricultural Company. This scheme prospered initially, despite some local resistance.

In the following year Macarthur was appointed to the new Legislative Council, despite a dispute with Governor Darling over the council's composition. Notwithstanding emerging doubts as to his mental stability, in 1829 Macarthur was again appointed to the newly reformed Legislative Council. He was removed from that body in 1832 by Governor Bourke due to his eccentric behaviour.

John Macarthur died on 11 April 1834 at Camden Park, aged sixty-six. He was survived by his wife and six of his eight children.

By his words and deeds Macarthur worked incessantly towards the establishment of a landowners' aristocracy, which was to exert a powerful influence over the course of future development in New South Wales.

THE CONVICTS

The number of convicts sent to Australia from 1788 to 1868, when transportation to all colonies ceased, totalled approximately 160,000, of whom about 25,000 were women.

Transportation to New South Wales and Van Diemen's Land (Tasmania) ended in 1853. However, convicts were sent to Western Australia from 1852 to 1868 (see pp. 93–4) to meet a labour shortage.

Men and women convicts were sentenced to transportation for a variety of offences, the most common being theft, burglary and pickpocketing. Most of the convicts were first offenders. The usual sentence was seven years, but longer terms were sometimes handed down. About a quarter of the male convicts were sentenced to transportation for life.

During the early years of settlement, the majority of convicts were employed by the government. The men were given a variety of occupations, usually as labourers on public works, road construction and on buildings. Many became agricultural workers. Most of the female convicts became domestic servants.

Under the assignment system, which was used extensively after 1789, convicts were allocated to free settlers as servants, the government stipulating the quantities of food and clothing to be issued to the assignees. No convict was allowed to be paid.

Convicts who became repeat offenders after arrival in Australia received a variety of punishments, the most serious for men being flogging or transportation to Port Arthur in Van Diemen's Land, Norfolk Island or other harsh penal settlements. Death sentences were even handed down on rare occasions.

A convict who behaved well could be granted a 'ticket-of-leave', which entitled him or her to be paid for work, and to choose their own employer. Pardons, both absolute and conditional, were also granted, the latter requiring the convict to remain in Australia until his or her sentence expired.

Both the British government and the colonists benefitted from the transportation system. The former needed an inexpensive way to dispose of felons, whilst the latter welcomed the source of low-cost labour.

Successive governors, from Macquarie onwards, made changes to the convict system. Governors Brisbane and Darling made the sentencing laws harsher, whilst Lieutenant-Governor Arthur introduced a system of regulated punishments for convicts sent to Van Diemen's Land.

From 1819, male convicts were confined during weeknights in the newly built Hyde Park Barracks, where Governor Macquarie was able to exercise some degree of control over them. Women convicts were placed in the Female Factory at Parramatta, constructed in 1821, and in the Cascades Factory at Hobart, these institutions being intended to protect the females from prostitution.

RAGS TO RICHES

Many of the convict women served out their sentences as domestic servants. But there were some who, by their own efforts and determination, were able to aspire to a better life.

In London in 1786, Esther Johnston, then aged about fifteen, was sentenced to seven years transportation for stealing a small quantity of silk lace. A daughter, Rosanne, was born to her whilst she was in Newgate prison awaiting a transport ship.

During the long voyage to New South Wales, Esther attracted the attention of Lieutenant George Johnston, an officer with the First Fleet's marines. Upon arrival at Sydney Cove, Esther became Johnston's de facto wife. A son, George, was born to them in 1790, and two days later mother and son accompanied Johnston on transfer to Norfolk Island.

The family returned to Sydney in 1791. Two years later, Esther's sentence expired. By then Johnston had been granted land at Bankstown, where he grew wheat and stocked cattle. In 1809, Esther was granted in her own name 570 acres (231 hectares) of adjacent land.

In 1811 Johnston was tried in London for his part in the rebellion against Governor Bligh. His properties were ably managed by Esther during his absence. After he was acquitted, Johnston returned to the colony and, at Concord in November 1814, his marriage to Esther was celebrated by the Reverend Samuel Marsden (see pp. 42–3). Upon his death in 1823, Johnston's Annandale estate passed to his wife for the term of her natural life.

Esther died in 1846, aged about seventy-five, at her son's Georges River property. She had risen from convict degradation to social respectability during the rough-and-tumble of the settlement's early days. She was deeply devoted to her husband and children—always behind, but never in front of, the man who had helped her rise from the filth and squalor of the transport ship to a life of acceptance.

MARY REIBEY

In 1790 a 'youth' was arrested in England and charged with horse stealing. At the trial it was discovered that the youth, who had been dressed as a boy, was in fact a girl. She was Mary Reibey (née Haydock), then a thirteen-year-old. She was convicted of felony and sentenced to seven years transportation.

Mary arrived in Sydney aboard the *Royal Admiral* in 1792, and was assigned as a nursemaid to the household of Major Francis Grose, commandant of the New South Wales Corps. Two years later she married Thomas Reibey, who was then employed by the East India Company, and who had also been on board the *Royal Admiral*.

Thomas Reibey became a free settler and acquired property on the Hawkesbury River, where he farmed and established a grain-carrying business. Later he moved the business to Macquarie Place, in Sydney's centre, and there began trading in general merchandise. He also began dealing in coal, timber and wheat along the Hawkesbury River system and in the Hunter region. Later he became involved in trading with the Pacific Islands, China and India. He died in 1811 after a long illness, and was survived by Mary and their seven children.

In addition to the demands of motherhood, Mary had managed a hotel and had actively assisted her husband in his numerous trading activities. She became accepted by the new emancipist society, and proved that she could hold her own in the hard school of overseas trading. She became a favourite of Governor Macquarie.

In 1816 Mary put up for sale all of her properties, her husband's ships and their seven farms on the Hawkesbury River. In 1820, in company with two of her daughters, she travelled to England to revisit her family and friends and the scenes of her childhood. Returning to Sydney the following year, Mary resumed her business activities and was responsible for the construction of many fine buildings in Sydney's business centre. She gradually divested herself of her business activities, and was able to retire on the income from her various investments. She died in the Sydney suburb of Newtown in 1855, aged seventy-eight, survived by her three sons, each of whom became prominent in the world of commerce and trade. (There are streets named after the Reibey family close to Circular Quay and at Newtown.)

In addition to her devotion to her husband and family, and to her successful career as a forthright businesswoman, Mary Reibey took an active part in local religious affairs, in education (she was a governor of the Free Grammar School) and in charity fundraising. A convict of humble beginnings, she became a legend in her lifetime.

EARLY COASTAL EXPLORATION

Two navigators who made a significant addition to the settlement's knowledge of the continent were George Bass (who was the surgeon on the *Reliance*) and the *Reliance*'s master's mate, Matthew Flinders. The pair, who became lifelong friends, first sailed about 17 nautical miles south of Sydney and explored the upper reaches of the Georges River. They were accompanied by Bass's servant, a boy named William Martin. The three somehow crowded into a tiny boat named the *Tom Thumb*, which was less than 3 metres long.

In 1798–99, Flinders and Bass explored the coast further south and established, by circumnavigation, that Van Diemen's Land (Tasmania) was separated from the mainland. The stretch of water separating the island from the mainland was subsequently named Bass Strait.

In 1802–1803 the intrepid explorers embarked on a year-long circumnavigation of the continent, this feat providing important information for both Sydney and London as to the extent of the landmass.

Flinders subsequently wrote of his experiences in his book *Voyage to Terra Australis*, in which he first advocated the name Australia. In 1817, after Governor Macquarie took up the name in his dispatches, it was officially adopted.

From 1817 to 1822, Captain Phillip Parker King, son of the settlement's third governor, Philip Gidley King, continued the work of surveying the Australian coast, charting those regions which Flinders and Bass had been unable to explore. As a native-born, Phillip Parker King was one of the few whose work was recognised in England. He was made a Fellow of the Royal Society and was promoted by the Admiralty to the rank of Rear-Admiral. He died in Sydney in 1856.

VINEGAR HILL

In 1800, Governor Hunter received information that groups of the settlement's Irish convict population, by then numbering well over 1000, were planning an insurrection in protest against floggings ordered by magistrate Reverend Samuel Marsden. The festering resentment came to a head in 1804 when some 300 of the Irish convicts were confronted at Vinegar Hill, west of Parramatta, by a detachment of the military. Within a few minutes nine of the Irish were dead and their leader, Philip Cunningham, lay wounded. Cunningham and eight other leaders were later hanged. Others were flogged or sent to the penal settlement at Coal River, later named Newcastle.

THE REVEREND SAMUEL MARSDEN

A man of God who became a rival of John Macarthur, the Reverend Samuel Marsden was born in 1764, the son of a blacksmith. He was appointed by the British government as assistant to the Reverend Richard Johnston, Anglican chaplain to the colony. Both men arrived at Botany Bay with the First Fleet.

Marsden, like Macarthur, became a personality during the settlement's early period. But unlike Macarthur, he did not leave an enduring mark on Australia's history.

Marsden was a pious man who craved association with the settlement's most influential figures. He devoted his time variously to spiritual matters; to his religious duties; to the affairs of the British and Foreign Bible Society, the London Missionary Society and the Church Missionary Society; to a Sunday school which he opened in 1797; to several colonial appointments, including the magistracy; to his mission to the Maoris, which he tenaciously pursued during seven visits to New Zealand between 1814 and 1837; and to his various personal interests, especially farming. Like Macarthur and others, Marsden was amongst the first in New South Wales to experiment in sheep-breeding at his property west of Parramatta, which, by 1827, had grown to well over 5000 acres (2025 hectares) and was well stocked with cattle, poultry and pigs in addition to his flocks of sheep.

Whereas Macarthur was developing the Spanish merino breed, Marsden's main sheep interest was in the Suffolk strain. A suit made from Spanish merino wool so impressed his monarch, King George III, that Marsden was presented with merinos from the royal Windsor stud. However, his contribution to the development of the wool industry in Australia, and to sheep breeding and wool technology, cannot be compared to that of Macarthur.

Marsden had been appointed to the magistracy in 1797 by Governor Hunter. It was not long before he became notorious for the severity of his sentences—500 lashes was not unusual, and on one occasion 1000 were ordered. Such extremes, however, may not have indicated a sadistic trait in his character. Rather, the harshness has been attributed to his piety, his detestation of sin and his passionate belief in the need for personal salvation.

In 1810, after returning from leave in England, Marsden was promoted as the settlement's senior chaplain.

Marsden, never above ingratiating himself with those in authority, enjoyed cordial relations with Governor King, and was praised by Governor Bligh. But he found himself at odds with Governor Macquarie, whose sympathy for the emancipists and association with ex-convicts ran contrary to Marsden's view of the penal settlement as principally a place of correction.

In 1810 Marsden declined an invitation to become a trustee of the Parramatta turnpike road because the other appointees were affluent ex-convicts. This aroused Macquarie's ire and a running feud developed between the two, with particular acrimony arising from a disagreement in 1818 over the treatment of prisoners.

Marsden's activities diminished during his declining years, but he continued to minister to the sick and needy. He died at Windsor, in Sydney's north-west, in 1838 and was buried at Parramatta. He was seventy-three.

THE RUM REBELLION

The heated conflict that had arisen between the choleric Governor Bligh and the irascible John Macarthur came to a head in 1808, several weeks after a shipment of 8000 gallons of rum and other spirits had arrived in Sydney from the Cape of Good Hope to supplement the well-established trading activities of the New South Wales Corps. Not surprisingly, the whole affair came to be known as the Rum Rebellion, rum and other spirits being the principal commodities used as the recognised medium of exchange (although other produce, such as tea and sugar, was also accepted by the Corps).

The Corps was subsequently ordered back to England in disgrace. Its commander, George Johnston, and John Macarthur were both found guilty by courts martial in London. Bligh himself was rewarded with promotion to the rank of vice-admiral, and subsequently retired into obscurity. History would judge that his undoubted loyalty as an officer and his talents as a navigator were overlaid by a violent temper and a vitriolic tongue.

JOHN PIPER

Through the influence of his uncle, eighteen-year-old John Piper secured a commission as ensign in the newly-formed New South Wales Corps. He arrived in Sydney in 1792 at a time when the fledgling colony was facing a severe food shortage. The light-hearted and irrepressible Piper quickly became a social success and a close friend of John Macarthur.

Probably as a consequence of an indiscreet love affair, resulting in the birth of a daughter, Sarah, young Piper applied for a posting to the primitive convict settlement at Norfolk Island. In 1795 he was promoted to the rank of lieutenant and transferred back to Sydney. Two years later he departed for England on leave, then returned to the colony in 1799 with the rank of captain.

By that time, with the bitter struggle between Governor King and the New South Wales Corps raging, Piper felt obliged to side with his friend Macarthur. Both were placed under arrest, the governor deciding that Piper should face a local court martial. Piper duly apologised and was acquitted, much to King's disgust.

Now without the support of either King or Macarthur, the latter having been sent to England to face trial, Piper was again posted to Norfolk Island where he was to remain for six years. He became the island's acting commandant in 1804 when the colony's lieutenant-governor, Foveaux, departed on prolonged sick leave. Piper proved a mild and tolerant governor, gaining the respect and goodwill of the convicts.

Piper's sojourn on Norfolk Island enabled him to avoid becoming enmeshed in the Rum Rebellion and the subsequent fall of Governor King in 1808. He also found solace through a romantic involvement with the daughter of a First Fleet convict, fifteen-year-old Mary Ann Shears, who had spent all her years on the island. She was to remain with Piper for the rest of his life.

Piper brought Mary Ann with him on his return to Sydney in 1810, and in the following year the couple left for England, together with their two small sons and Piper's first daughter, Sarah. Ever sensitive to the changing times, Piper resigned his commission and applied for the vacant post of naval officer in Sydney. He was successful and again returned to the colony in 1814. Two years later, by which time two more children had been born, he married Mary Ann by special licence.

The exuberant and charming Piper was now in a position of considerable influence as chief customs officer, harbour master and head of the water police. Furthermore, as he received 5 per cent of all monies collected in lieu of a salary, his annual earnings in the expanding colony soon increased to the considerable sum of £4000.

Piper's new-found wealth enabled him to entertain on a lavish scale and to become a man of property. He bought what is now known as Vaucluse House, a fine sandstone building with a magnificent view westwards of Sydney Harbour. In 1816 he built an official residence on land granted to him at Eliza Point, now named Point Piper. The property cost £10,000, and Piper named it Henrietta Villa. Accessible by road or by water, the sumptuously decorated residence, which also had magnificent views of Sydney Harbour, became the centre of Sydney's social activity.

The upswing in Piper's fortunes continued for the next ten years. He became a close friend of Governor Macquarie, and in 1819 was appointed a magistrate. By 1825 he was chairman of the Bank of New South Wales (now Westpac). He was a committee member of the Australian Agricultural Company and president of the Scots Church Committee. He owned land in the Sydney suburbs of Woollahra, Vaucluse, Petersham, Rose Bay, Neutral Bay and Botany Bay, as well as farmland in Van Diemen's Land (Tasmania) and Bathurst. He was generous to a fault, freely lending money to his friends without security.

The pendulum of Piper's fortunes finally began to swing the other way. He resigned as chairman of the Bank of New South Wales in 1827 when Governor Darling ordered an inquiry into the bank's affairs. Piper was later suspended from his position as Naval Officer when a deficiency of £12,000 of the bank's funds was discovered. Further investigation revealed that the department's accounts were in a chaotic state, that customs duties had not been properly collected, and that Piper had extended long-term credits to his friends. Carelessness and an inherent lack of business acumen, rather than any intentional dishonesty, had been the cause of his downfall. Piper was dismissed. He attempted to drown himself, but was rescued.

Piper was now forced to sell his city properties and his farms at a time of depressed land prices. Nevertheless, he succeeded in settling his debts to the government and in satisfying his creditors.

Piper was able to retain his Bathurst property, Alloway Bank, and it was there that he retired at the age of fifty-four. An adjoining property fronting the Macquarie River was made over to him by William Charles Wentworth (see pp. 55–6) in part settlement for the purchase of Vaucluse House.

With these Bathurst properties Piper began life anew. He actively farmed, became a magistrate and an important figure in Bathurst's affairs. He spent three years building a 'miniature mansion', and there entertained his many guests, including governors Darling and Bourke.

But Piper's Alloway Bank activities did not prosper, and by 1832 he was selling the remainder of his Sydney properties. He was one of many who were adversely affected by the 1838 drought, and was eventually forced to mortgage the Bathurst properties. At the instigation of his friends, notably W.C. Wentworth, the Macquarie River property was reassigned to provide security to the devoted Mary Ann Piper.

John Piper died in obscurity at Bathurst in 1851, aged seventy-eight. He was survived by his fourteen children and by Mary Ann, who had borne all but one of his children. She lived on in Bathurst for another twenty years.

VAN DIEMEN'S LAND

Van Diemen's Land (Tasmania) was discovered in 1642 by the Dutch explorer Abel Janszoon Tasman during the first of his two voyages to the South Seas. Tasman claimed the land for the Netherlands and named it after Anthony Van Diemen, the Dutch governor-general at the time. Then, having found nothing of commercial interest to the Dutch East India Company, Tasman continued on his voyage, discovering New Zealand and other lands in the South Pacific.

The next explorer to touch the shores of Van Diemen's Land was a Frenchman, Marion du Fresne, who, in 1772, reached Frederick Henry Bay and there came into armed conflict with local Aboriginal people.

In 1803 Governor King despatched a military party to Van Diemen's Land, firstly in response to growing fears of French intentions to establish a settlement on the island's east coast and to proclaim Britain's rights to the territory; secondly, to find another outlet for the growing tide of convicts; and thirdly, to develop whatever trading opportunities could be found.

In the following year, a stronger force of marines, together with some settlers and convicts, were sent to the new settlement, there establishing the future town of Hobart. A settlement was also established at Port Dalrymple, the port at the mouth of the Tamar River on the north coast of Van Diemen's Land. (The port was named after Alexander Dalrymple, an explorer in the pay of the British East India Company. Both the Royal Society and the East India Company had suggested that Dalrymple should lead the proposed expedition to the South Seas, but the British Admiralty preferred to appoint Lieutenant James Cook.) It was regarded as one of the harshest of the penal settlements.

Van Diemen's Land achieved a degree of independence from New South Wales in 1825 when the Lieutenant-Governor, George Arthur, assumed full control of the island. A Legislative Council was appointed in the same year. By then Hobart had become the island's administrative and trade centre, with sealing, whaling and pastoralism accounting for the island's principal sources of revenue. Convicts made up more than half of the population.

When Governor Arthur arrived in 1824 there were over 12,000 white people living on the island. By 1853, when transportation to the colony ended, the population of Van Diemen's Land's had grown to approximately 68,000.

LACHLAN MACQUARIE

By 1810 the British government still viewed New South Wales as little more than a faraway prison and perhaps something of a deterrent to French interests in the South Seas. Thus, the colony's governors were left mainly to their own devices in formulating administrative, economic, financial and security policies, with little in the way of realistic guidelines.

The settlement provided minimal commercial advantage to offset its maintenance costs to the British exchequer, and it soon became apparent that there was need for someone to resolve the settlement's administrative problems and to determine a fresh and purposeful course for its future. Fortunately, that someone was available.

Governor Lachlan Macquarie had several advantages when he took office on 1 January 1810 as the fifth governor of New South Wales. Firstly, unlike his four predecessors, who were each naval captains, Macquarie was an army man. Secondly, he brought with him his own regiment, with whom he had served overseas, to replace the discredited New South Wales Corps. Thirdly, he was a well-educated Scot, a disciplinarian yet a compassionate man, ever loyal to his king and country. And fourthly, he was conscious of the need to implement, to the best of his ability, the British government's instructions, notwithstanding that in many cases such instructions had been formulated by men with little or no experience of colonial administration and which, in many instances, were based upon second-hand or unreliable information.

Whilst progress had been made during the rule of his predecessors, Macquarie quickly noted a range of undesirable practices and a lack of discipline in the settlement, mostly stemming from the self-interest of the New South Wales Corps. He also became aware of deficiencies in the settlement's administration, and of the absence of policies directed towards economic development on sound and progressive lines.

Part of the problem lay in the inescapable fact that the settlement was hemmed in by the Nepean and Hawkesbury river systems to the north, by the Blue Mountains to the west, and by the Illawarra escarpment and the Shoalhaven River (and other river systems) to the south-west. But in 1813, the colony's development was to change dramatically, for after more than a decade of unsuccessful probing, a route to the west was found across the Blue Mountains by 35-year-old Gregory Blaxland, an English settler who farmed at the foot of the mountain barrier; by Lieutenant William Lawson, aged thirty-nine, who had been an engineer with the New South Wales Corps until resigning his commission in 1811; and by 23-year-old William Wentworth, a 'currency lad' (as men born in Australia were nicknamed). Blaxland had perceived that a route westwards might be found by scaling the ridges rather than the numerous gullies that had thwarted so many previous attempts to cross the heights.

Macquarie acted quickly by ordering the construction of a road along the route and through the present Victoria Pass. With the extension of the road, the town of Bathurst (located 205 kilometres west of Sydney and named after the then Secretary of State for the Colonies) was established in 1815. The fertile grazing lands of the western plains were soon occupied, whilst to the north productive farming country in the Hunter Valley was later discovered and opened up.

With the availability of an ample convict labour supply, Macquarie was able to embark upon an extensive building program. New roads and bridges were constructed, and schools, hospitals, government facilities and military barracks built. Many of these buildings still survive as a monument to Macquarie's initiative and to the architects who designed them. One of these civil architects was a controversial figure of undoubted ability ...

FRANCIS GREENWAY

Francis Greenway came from an English West Country family of builders and architects. He was in private practice as an architect in Bristol when he was found guilty of forgery and sentenced to death, the sentence later being commuted to transportation for fourteen years. He arrived in Sydney in 1814 and was followed by his wife, Mary, and their three children.

Greenway used his professional training to obtain a degree of freedom and to set up in private practice. When Governor Macquarie sought his advice concerning Sydney's Rum Hospital, then being built, Greenway's radical proposals were to involve a long list of costly changes.

A tactless, arrogant but gifted man, Greenway was soon given a ticket-of-leave (see p. 54), and in 1816 was appointed to a salaried position as civil architect and assistant engineer.

Greenway devoted the next twelve years to the design and construction of various buildings in Sydney, Parramatta and other districts. St Matthew's Church in Windsor is regarded by many as his masterpiece, although there have been subsequent alterations to the original building. Another church designed by Greenway, St James's in King Street, Sydney, is considered to be one of the finest Georgian buildings of the period.

Despite his abrasive character and the enmities he constantly aroused, Greenway survived mainly because of Governor Macquarie's patronage and tolerance of his behavioural quirks. He was also unfailingly supported by his wife, who bore him five sons and two daughters.

Francis Greenway, a genius of his time, died at the age of sixty at the Hunter River property granted to him by Macquarie. His grave is unmarked.

COMMISSIONER BIGGE'S REPORT

Despite the general goodwill that Macquarie's enlightened governorship generated, he had soured relationships with some of the settlement's leading figures, notably John Macarthur, the Reverend Samuel Marsden, Ellis Bent (the Judge Advocate) and Bent's brother Jeffery, who, in 1814, was appointed Judge of the Supreme Court of New South Wales.

Friction also developed when Macquarie, who saw no reason to deny former convicts the rights and opportunities of normal citizenship, began inviting to his dinner table selected emancipists who had proved themselves as acceptable members of society by their good conduct and self-advancement. Macquarie's action enraged the exclusives (the settlement's 'nobility', led by John Macarthur, who vigorously rejected the notion that former convicts should be allowed to occupy positions of responsibility). The exclusives' mounting hostility was to manifest itself in 1819 during the wide-ranging inquiry that the British government decided should be conducted into the transportation system and into the settlement's affairs generally, and its future development.

The Colonial Office in London decided that Commissioner John Bigge, a 39-year-old former chief justice of Trinidad, should be appointed to travel to New South Wales to report on the colony's affairs and to make recommendations. He arrived in Sydney in 1819 and was cordially welcomed by Governor Macquarie. The inquiry lasted seventeen months.

It was not long before Bigge and Macquarie crossed swords. John Macarthur, not surprisingly, had sought to influence Bigge towards his views regarding the importance of wool to Australia's future economy, the need for a land policy directed towards the creation of large holdings (but limiting grants to ex-convicts), and to the desirability of encouraging the investment of British capital.

As the difficulties, animosities and frustrations of his governorship mounted, Macquarie made several requests to be relieved of his responsibilities. In 1821 his resignation was finally accepted, and in the following year a substantial crowd gathered at Sydney Cove to bid him an affectionate and grateful farewell. When Macquarie arrived in London he was received with kindness by the Secretary of State for the Colonies, Earl Bathurst.

Bigge's three-part report was published during 1822–23. He was critical of certain features of Macquarie's administration, though in some instances his accusations were later judged to be unfair and based upon incorrect information.

Commissioner Bigge also expressed dislike over certain liberalising features of Macquarie's administration: his leniency towards convicts, and his encouragement of local manufacturing of some coarse textile goods in competition with similar goods available from English manufacturers. Bigge opposed the introduction of trial by jury, although he agreed with the emancipists' arguments concerning the restitution of their legal rights. Bigge also opposed the abolition of land grants to emancipists and favoured restrictions on ticket-of-leave holders and the granting of pardons.

Bigge was also concerned about the burden placed on the colony's finances by the continuing influx of convicts—over 2500 male and female convicts had arrived during a five-month period in 1819–20—and he was particularly critical of what he regarded as extravagance in Macquarie's public works construction program.

Macquarie, deeply distressed by the tenor of Bigge's report, responded by sending to the Colonial Secretary a long defence of his eleven-year administration. Bathurst replied with assurances that the government recognised that he had done much towards laying the foundations of a sound economy for New South Wales.

Most of Bigge's recommendations were subsequently accepted by the government, and Macquarie's successor, Sir Thomas Brisbane, was instructed accordingly.

It was later judged that most of Bigge's opinions were soundly based. It came to be recognised that Australia's future lay firmly in wool production, and to this end there was agreement that convicts should be transferred from Sydney in order to provide a source of labour to the pastoralists.

THE COLONY AT THE END OF THE MACQUARIE ERA

Notwithstanding the strictures of the Bigge report, the fact remained that during Macquarie's tenure the human population of New South Wales more than trebled, whilst cattle and sheep numbers increased approximately tenfold. Land under cultivation expanded more than fourfold. Fertile lands to the west of the Blue Mountains and to the north had been opened up for farming and grazing. Many new towns had been established, new roads constructed, and some fine buildings had arisen in Sydney and Parramatta. By the end of the Macquarie era, free settlers and emancipists made up the greater part of the population of New South Wales. Throughout his governorship, Macquarie, despite fierce opposition from Macarthur and other exclusives, had demonstrated his humanity by steadfastly supporting both settlers and reformed convicts.

From about the end of the Macquarie era it is possible to discern the emergence of a multi-strand pattern in Australia's population. There were those convicts who became ticket-of-leave men and women. There were also the emancipists (see p. 33). They became eligible for land grants. Then there were the 'currency lads and lasses'—men and women who had been born and had grown up in Australia, some of whom were resentful of the land grants made to various monied immigrants. The exclusives made up yet another group—the socially elite and powerful, who were initially led by John Macarthur (see pp. 34-6), and who sought to exclude former convicts from positions of rank and power.

When Macquarie took the helm in 1810, New South Wales was in poor shape, a badly administered convict settlement. At the end of his term, New South Wales was an undeniably prosperous, expanding colony with a sizeable population of free people, their numbers steadily growing with the arrival of immigrants.

History has judged Macquarie more kindly than did the Colonial Office of his time. Such actions as his public support for the emancipists, and the substantial expenditure on public works that he authorised, were not in accord with London's policies or Bigge's interpretation of them. But later generations have viewed the Macquarie era as one of enlightenment and progressive development. The turbulence that preceded him, and the hostility of those leading figures around him who created conflict in pursuit of their ideals and ambitions, undoubtedly caused Macquarie considerable stress from which there was little respite.

It has been said of Macarthur that he was the 'father of Australia's wool industry'. The accolade accorded to Macquarie that he was 'the father of Australia' is equally appropriate.

In London, Macquarie was unable to escape the strictures of the Bigge report. He was granted a modest pension but denied a title. In poor health, tired and disillusioned, he retired to Scotland, where he died in 1824.

WILLIAM CHARLES WENTWORTH

William Charles Wentworth, one of the small party that had made the first crossing of the Blue Mountains in 1813, became something of a personality on the Sydney scene in the years after Macquarie's departure. He was of unusual pedigree—the son of a surgeon, D'Arcy Wentworth, and his convict wife, Catherine Crowley. D'Arcy, who had been charged four times in England for highway robbery, had purchased land in the Parramatta area and became involved in trading enterprises with the Pacific Islands markets.

D'Arcy sent his two sons, William and D'Arcy, to England to be educated. Returning in 1810, William was incensed to find that his father was excluded from upper-class society because of his convict background, even though he had agreed to travel to New South Wales as a colonial surgeon.

In 1817, William again travelled to England to study law, returning to Sydney in 1824. By that time his father's farming and commercial interests had made him a wealthy man. His native-born son, now a flamboyant, charismatic and forthright figure, was soon quarrelling with Macarthur, one of the leaders of the landed gentry faction. Wentworth, who was a strong supporter of the landowners and graziers, used every opportunity to attack the government for its attitudes towards civil liberties and the oppression of the individual. He also had strong empathy with the first and second generations of native-born settlers, who came to regard Australia as their country and were proud to call themselves Australian. A newspaper *The Australian*, which Wentworth founded in conjunction with a student friend, Robert Wardell, became the main platform for his campaigns.

Wentworth was, however, placed at a disadvantage by having, as it were, one foot in Australia—his birth place and the scene of his struggles on behalf of those he perceived to be debarred from their rights and privileges—and the other in England, where he had been educated.

His most significant achievements were the successful campaigns for the introduction of trial by jury in criminal cases, which came into practice in 1833, and his unrelenting support for the emancipists in their struggle against the exclusives. He was also prominent in the campaign for self-government in New South Wales, a measure of which was finally achieved in 1843 when the British government agreed to the popular election of two-thirds of the Legislative Council (see p. 90).

In 1862 Wentworth finally left the Australian scene for England, where he died ten years later. In Sydney, the government accorded him the colony's first state funeral, his ashes having been brought from England to be interred in Sydney near Vaucluse House, his beautiful harbourside residence.

UNLOCKING THE LAND

In 1818 the Surveyor-General, John Oxley, led an expedition to investigate the sightings made in 1813 by Blaxland, Wentworth and Lawson to the west of the Blue Mountains. The party discovered and named the Namoi, Peel, Apsley, Macleay and Hastings rivers, crossed the Liverpool Plains (east of Coonabarabran and to the north of the Liverpool and Warrumbungle ranges), then followed the Hastings River to its estuary, 407 kilometres north of Sydney. Oxley named the place Port Macquarie, where a penal settlement was established shortly afterwards.

Further north, in 1823, Oxley discovered another river and again named it after the governor of the day, Sir Thomas Brisbane. In the following year another convict settlement was set up, this time at Moreton Bay, at the mouth of the Brisbane River.

In 1827 Allan Cunningham, who was a botanist as well as an explorer, investigated the country north of the Hunter Valley and discovered the fertile pastures known as the Darling Downs. Cunningham also found the pass, which was named after him, through which there is easy access to the port of Brisbane.

Meanwhile, in 1824, Hamilton Hume and William Hovell had set out with a small party, including six convicts, to explore the region south-west of Sydney. They came upon the Murrumbidgee River, crossed the Australian Alps and finally, eleven weeks later, reached Corio Bay (on the western side of Port Philip).

Hamilton Hume was also a member of an 1828 expedition, led by Captain Charles Sturt, during which they discovered a major river. They were unable to determine its course, however. As was customary, they named the river after the governor of the day, Darling.

The following year, Governor Darling sent another expedition, again led by Sturt, to the Murrumbidgee to determine whether that river flowed into the Darling. They discovered that in fact the Murrumbidgee joined a westward-flowing waterway, which proved to be Australia's longest river. Sturt named it the Murray. From near its headwaters, and for the greater part of its course westwards, it was later to form the boundary between New South Wales and Victoria.

Sturt and his party continued downstream, past the confluence with the Darling River (near the present city of Mildura on the New South Wales–Victorian border and a little to the east of the present South

Australian border) and, eventually, despite some hostility from Aboriginal people on the river's banks, were able to rejoice at the sight of seagulls and the salty tang of sea air. The ocean was nearby! The Murray, they found, drained into Lake Alexandrina and beyond to the Southern Ocean at Encounter Bay.

Sturt's second expedition established the fact that the majestic Murray was inaccessible for most ocean-going vessels, and laid to rest the theory that the westward-flowing rivers drained into a vast inland lake.

THE MURRAY RIVER

The Murray River, Australia's principal waterway, is some 2570 kilometres in length. One of its tributaries, the Darling, is slightly longer, but its source is usually considered to be another river, probably the Severn. The two rivers have a combined watercourse length of 3750 kilometres.

The official source of the Murray is on the side of a hill near Mount Pilot in the Australian Alps, some 32 kilometres south of Mount Kosciuszko. There are some, however, who claim that the river really begins further downstream at Limestone Creek, whilst others consider the junction of the Swampy Plain and Indi rivers to be the true source. There are also other theories.

The fact is that from this area—remote and rugged country inhabited by wild horses—the Murray flows northwards and then to the west into Lake Hume, before resuming its course westwards, passing between the twin cities of Albury and Wodonga. The broadening river then continues in a westerly direction past Echuca, then north-westwards to Mildura. Along this section of its course, in the vicinity of Balranald, the Murray is joined by the Murrumbidgee River. Beyond Mildura, and close to Wentworth, it is joined by the Darling.

The Darling comprises a series of rivers, some in New South Wales and flowing in a generally north-westerly direction, others with their headwaters in Queensland and flowing south-westwards. East of Bourke these rivers combine and become the Darling River, which then flows into the Menindee Lake east of Broken Hill. The Darling then takes a generally southerly course until it flows into the Murray.

From Wentworth the Murray River continues westwards into South Australia and to the town of Morgan, where its course follows a southerly direction past Murray Bridge. It then flows into Lake Alexandrina and the Southern Ocean.

The Murray provides on average just over half of South Australia's total irrigation, stock, domestic and industrial water supply.

Aboriginal people have many names for the Murray: Ingatta, Moorundie, Goodwarra, Parriang-ka-perre, Tongiwillum and Yoorlooarra are some of them.

The river first became known to European settlers during Hume and Hovell's 1824 expedition from south-west of Sydney to Corio Bay (near to present-day Geelong). Hume named the river after himself, but it was six years later that Sturt, after travelling down the Murrumbidgee in a whaleboat, came upon 'this broad and noble river' and named it after the then British Colonial Secretary.

Today, the river system faces serious environmental problems. Some believe that a reduced capacity and drying up of groundwaters is due to over-extraction of water over decades of irrigation use, combined with the effects of climate change. There is some controversy over this theory; however, what is indisputable is that years of agricultural use of the surrounding lands has led to large amounts of waste in the river system. Waste management strategies and campaigns have been implemented in many towns along the river to rectify the problems.

PROTECTING THE COAST

In the 1820s, rumours persisted that the French, their ambitions having been thwarted by the establishment of colonies in New South Wales and Van Diemen's Land, were turning their attention to the continent's west. In 1826, therefore, small military bases were set up at Westernport (east of Port Philip Bay in Victoria), at King George Sound (overlooked by the present city of Albany in Western Australia) and on the far north coast at Melville Island (close to present-day Darwin). The intention of these moves was to secure, at least temporarily, the whole Australian landmass as British territory. But during the latter part of the nineteenth century the colonies again held fears of foreign intrusions arising from reported French and German activities off the Australian coast.

AUSTRALIA FELIX

In 1836 Surveyor-General Major Thomas Mitchell set out to investigate much of the river country that Sturt had explored seven years earlier. He was profoundly unimpressed by what he saw. But moving from the Murray River in the direction of the present city of Hamilton (in south-west Victoria), he came upon, in the region south-west of the present Grampians National Park (north of Hamilton), rich pasture grasslands of a quality that delighted his jaundiced eye. He named the area 'Australia Felix' ('felix' is Latin for happy or fortunate). He wrote of his discovery: '... just such land as would produce wheat during the driest seasons, and never become sour even in the wettest.'

Continuing southwards towards Portland Bay, Mitchell encountered another surprise when he came upon two pastoralists who were bringing sheep and cattle across from Launceston in Van Diemen's Land to feed on the rich pastures bordering the Glenelg River. They were two of the sons of a determined English migrant named Thomas Henty ...

THE HENTY FAMILY

Thomas Henty was a farmer and banker. He and his wife, Frances, had eleven children, three of whom died in childhood. They were a close-knit family. The couple and their remaining seven sons and a daughter were to participate in events which, in an unexpected way, were to shape their lives.

Henty had established a reputation as a horse and sheep breeder in Sussex, England, where he had a farm. He had acquired merino sheep from King George III's flocks, which in turn had been gathered from Saxony and Spain. (It was to Henty that the Macarthur family came in the 1820s when they were seeking quality merinos for New South Wales.)

Farming prospects in England at that time were poor, and it was this that prompted Henty to decide upon emigration to either New South Wales or Van Diemen's Land. Then, in 1827, he heard news of Captain Stirling's discoveries at the Swan River in Western Australia, and of the British government's plan to settle the area (principally to forestall possible French designs on the territory) by granting land to free men on the basis of the value of property brought into the colony. Henty calculated his land entitlement as 34,160 hectares.

That was enough for the Henty family. New South Wales and Van Diemen's Land were forgotten, and they prepared to send a vanguard party to Australia. In 1829 a vessel, the *Caroline*, was chartered and on board went men from their Sussex village of Tarring, about 150 precious merinos clad in flannel coats as protection against the cold, and a full range of stock, together with farm implements and seed. The Hentys' eldest son, 29-year-old James, a merchant and banker, and his brothers Stephen and John, were in charge of the party. It was almost like a military operation.

Unfortunately, the Hentys had not done their homework properly, for land at the Western Australian settlement proved to be of very poor quality: 'sand, sand and sand everywhere'. (Perhaps the Hentys were parodying Samuel Taylor Coleridge's verse from 'The Rime of the Ancient Mariner'.) However, James was able to acquire some land on the Swan River that was sufficiently fertile 'to keep the stock alive'. But after two summers (the harvest having failed during the second summer) and fruitless exploration of land in the interior, James proposed to his father that an appeal be made to the British Colonial Office that they be granted acreage in Van Diemen's Land in exchange for the Swan River grant.

In 1830 the British government promulgated new regulations designed to prevent colonial land falling into the hands of speculators who would not improve the land; and to limit the dispersion of population into areas that were difficult to administer. This news prompted Thomas Henty to sell his Sussex property and to depart for Van Diemen's Land. He and Frances, together with three of their four remaining sons, Francis, Edward and Charles, sailed at the end of 1831 in the *Forth of Alloway*. Their third-eldest son, William, was left behind to complete his law studies and to act as an intermediary with the Colonial Office.

Whilst awaiting a decision from London on the appeal, James transferred his capital to Launceston, then Australia's third oldest city (after Sydney and Hobart), located nearly 200 kilometres north of Hobart, and moved there with his wife. In 1832 they were joined by James's parents, Thomas and Frances, and by his brothers Edward, Charles and Francis Henty.

However, the Colonial Office rejected the Hentys' appeal, putting them in a difficult situation, for land was now available to the highest bidder and the Henty's capital had been diminished by expenditure in Western Australia. Thomas Henty therefore petitioned Governor Arthur in Hobart, setting out their circumstances and requesting land in lieu of the Swan River grant. This request was again rejected by the British government.

The Hentys meanwhile turned their eyes across the waters of Bass Strait towards the considerable areas of unoccupied land in the Portland Bay district of New South Wales (later Victoria). They were aware of the British government's policy of denying occupation of New South Wales land far removed from Sydney, but nevertheless a fresh petition was prepared, applying for unspecified land across Bass Strait. The petition was taken to London by James, who had become established as a successful trader and wished to further his activities in England.

When this petition was also rejected, James made a specific application to the Government for 8100 hectares at Portland Bay. Pending a decision, he wrote to his father advocating occupation of the land, even though this would be risking official censure.

Thomas Henty, determined to explore all avenues open to him, embarked in his own little vessel, the 57-ton schooner *Thistle*, to deliver a full cargo of goods to Fremantle and to make a survey of the mainland's south coast and the Swan River. On his return, Henty, now in agreement with James's proposal, sent Edward in the *Thistle* to Portland Bay to carry out the survey. He was followed a month later by Francis, who brought with him the future state of Victoria's first merinos.

In London, meanwhile, the government informed James that whilst it could not agree to his request that the Hentys be granted undisturbed rights of settlement should the district ever become a permanent colony, the Secretary of State (the Earl of Aberdeen) was 'not prepared to say that Mr Henty's pretensions to any land <u>actually brought into cultivation and surrounded by a proper fence</u> [these words were underlined by the Earl himself] would not be favourably looked upon by His Majesty's Government at a future period'. Here, at last, was a loophole which the Hentys were able to exploit.

In Launceston, the energetic and intelligent Charles Henty, later to become managing director of the Bank of Australasia, persuaded his father to allow his brother Edward to proceed to Portland Bay. Edward and two of his other brothers duly sailed in 1834 and began 'squatting' (see p. 68) in the Portland Bay area. Thomas Henty's troubled mind was put at rest the following year when he received James's news from London.

Hearing from Major Thomas Mitchell of the fine country to the north, the Henty sons wasted no time in taking his advice and, in 1837, established a station in the rich plains to the west of Hamilton.

In Sydney, Governor Bourke was aware of the Hentys' presence in what is now western Victoria, but took no action over their unauthorised land use due to his preoccupation with the claims of John Batman, John Fawkner and the squatters of the Port Philip Association (see p. 94). In 1839 Bourke's successor, Governor Gipps, ordered the resident magistrate at Geelong to investigate the Hentys' situation. The magistrate reported that '... Mr Henty has fenced in a vast quantity of ground ...', which was what Lord Aberdeen had stipulated. A survey of the new town of Portland was made shortly afterwards and included Stephen Henty's house and garden and all the fenced areas around the Bay.

The Hentys now made a last effort to get on the right side of the law by petitioning the government for compensation over the Henty property at Portland when the new town was laid out, or, alternatively, that they be allowed to purchase the land which had been fenced. They resented having to bid at auction in 1840 for blocks of land they had pioneered.

In London, a new Secretary of State, Lord Stanley, conscious of Lord Aberdeen's ruling on cultivated and fenced lands, allowed the Hentys pre-emptive rights over the lands they had developed, and granted compensation. This decision was binding on Governor Gipps, but it was not until 1849 that the Hentys received final settlement. Thus, the Henty family's twenty-year saga was finally resolved.

Thomas Henty, who became a magistrate at Launceston, died there aged sixty-four.

Of the seven sons, three—Stephen, Edward and Francis—pursued successful careers in the new colony of Victoria. Stephen became a Member of the Legislative Assembly from 1856 to 1870. Edward, Victoria's first settler, was also a Member of the Legislative Assembly, from 1856 to 1861. Francis devoted himself exclusively to the management of the Merino Downs station and took no part in public life.

John made several unsuccessful attempts at farming in western Victoria before returning alone to Western Australia, where he died aged fifty-five.

Of the three sons who initially remained in Tasmania, Charles actively concerned himself with banking and sat in the House of Assembly from 1856 to 1862. William, a solicitor, followed his family to Australia and took a prominent part in the Portland Bay affairs, but never went there. He was Colonial Secretary from 1856 to 1862, then returned to England where he died aged seventy-three.

James, who initially ran a successful business as a merchant and exporter, played a prominent part in Launceston's affairs before being declared bankrupt in 1846. He sailed for England two years later, then returned in 1851 to Melbourne where he established his own business, James Henty & Co. He became a member of the Victorian Legislative Council and held a number of public offices. He died in Melbourne aged eighty-two, having outlived all his brothers.

EDWARD EYRE

In 1838 another of the early explorers, Edward Eyre, was also proclaiming the virtues of the same fine country the Hentys had occupied, though he had been mainly occupied exploring the region from the newly established city of Adelaide to the province's eastern border.

Eyre was again exploring in 1839, this time to the north of Adelaide and eastwards towards the Murray River. He found nothing but barren, inhospitable and mostly waterless country south-west of the Grampian range.

In the following year, Eyre set out from Fowlers Bay (between Ceduna and the head of the Great Australian Bight) on the journey for which he is best known, a survey to test the possibility of a stock route across the forbidding Nullabor Plain to the Swan River settlement in Western Australia.

His original plan was to use drays backed up by a coastal cutter to transport the expedition's equipment. However, he subsequently decided 'to force a passage almost alone', taking with him his overseer, John Baxter, an Aboriginal boy named Wylie (who had been with Eyre two years earlier when he drove sheep and cattle overland from King George Sound to Perth), two other Aboriginal people, and several pack horses. The small party set off westwards on 25 February 1841.

Two months later, with most of the horses now left behind and the last of their carefully stored water finished, the party was in dire straits. Their plight was temporarily relieved, however, by the discovery of some water from a 'well'. But disaster then struck when the two Aboriginal people shot Baxter and made off into the night with most of the remaining provisions. The faithful Wylie had refused to take part in the attack.

Eyre, Wylie and the remaining horses now continued on, followed at a distance by the two Aboriginals. After several days of forced marching, both men now near to collapse, they chanced to find a new source of water. There they rested for several days, eating only the flesh from one of the horses they had killed.

Continuing slowly westwards, the two men eventually came to a bay (near the present town of Esperance) where a large sailing ship was anchored. Eyre and Wylie were invited aboard and remained on the vessel for twelve days, gradually recovering from their ordeal. They then continued their journey to King George Sound, where the loyal and courageous Wylie was reunited with his family.

Eyre returned to Adelaide by sailing ship and was later awarded the Royal Geographic Society's Gold Medal in recognition of his remarkable journey.

LUDWIG LEICHHARDT

In 1842 Ludwig Leichhardt, a German university student who had developed an interest in exploring the Australian continent, arrived in Sydney. Two years later he led an expedition from Moreton Bay (near the mouth of the Brisbane River) to Port Essington (east of Darwin).

In 1848 he led another small expedition, which included two Aboriginal people, with the ambitious intention of crossing the continent from east to west. Departing from the Darling Downs (to the west of Brisbane) they headed westwards but were never heard of again. Various attempts to unravel the mystery of the party's disappearance have proved fruitless.

THE END OF TRANSPORTATION

The last convicts to be assigned to New South Wales and the settled parts of Van Diemen's Land arrived at Sydney Cove on 18 November 1840.

Despite the rigours and injustices of the transportation system, it is unlikely that Australia would have developed as it did had convicts not been available as an essential source of labour.

A sign of the changing attitude towards transportation was the fact that convicts were at no time transported to the fledgling colony of South Australia.

Western Australia, realising that the availability of convict labour in New South Wales was to a considerable degree attributable to the prosperity in the east, petitioned the British government to commence transportation to the colony there. Some 10,000 male convicts were duly sent to Western Australia from 1852 until the end of the era of transportation in 1868. By that time, almost 160,000 male and female convicts had served their sentences in Australia, many of the sentences being for what would today be regarded as venial offences.

Transportation had undeniably done much to solve the problem of Britain's overcrowded gaols. Equally, the rapid developments in Australia's east, which occurred from about 1820 onwards, undoubtedly resulted from the availability of a continuing supply of convict labour.

Some convicts, when their sentences expired, opted to return to Britain. Many, however, decided to remain, the more enterprising of them becoming prosperous and influential members of Australian society.

SQUATTERS

As the explorers gradually probed the continent's secrets, in their wake came the land-hungry. Most were squatters (people who occupied Crown land), and most of the squatters were ex-convicts. Usually they purchased a flock of sheep, a few cattle, one or two horses and perhaps a cow. Mostly they occupied land outside the settled areas, pausing only when they found pasture land and adequate water. There they would 'squat' and establish a run or station, eking out a living in usually harsh and lonely conditions. In the pastoral districts, cattle and sheep stealing, and other unlawful activities, were common.

Squatting was illegal until 1836 when the practice was officially recognised and the squatters attained some degree of respectability.

Whilst most of the squatters were ex-convicts, there were some who were migrants. And whilst they were predominantly hard and determined people, there were some squatters who did not conform to the usual pattern ...

CAROLINE NEWCOMB AND ANNE DRYSDALE

Caroline Newcomb emigrated to Australia in 1833 on medical advice. She became governess to the children of John Batman (see p. 94), who, in 1836, settled on the north bank of the Yarra River (the site of present-day Melbourne), having moved from Launceston. Batman brought with him his wife and seven daughters. A son, John, was born shortly afterwards. As the children's governess, Caroline would have been fully occupied.

Early in 1838, Caroline went to stay with a medical practitioner, Dr Alexander Thomson, who had land at Kardinia on the Barwon River (near present-day Geelong) and was one of the leaders of the early pastoral society in the area.

There she met another immigrant, Anne Drysdale, who had arrived in 1840. Anne had had a Scottish upbringing and was no stranger to farming. (One of Anne's brothers was to become the great-grandfather of the well-known artist Sir George Russell Drysdale.)

Caroline and Anne soon became close friends, for although they differed in temperament they had much in common: each woman was energetic, well-bred and deeply religious.

With Dr Thomson's help, Anne was able to acquire a 10,000-acre (4050-hectare) licensed run at Boronggoop (near present-day Geelong). She and Caroline then decided to go into partnership as squatters. The arrangement worked well. They improved the property and built a home, putting a piano in the parlour and constructing a fine garden and gravelled paths. At Boronggoop they acquired many friends. On a visit to the two squatters, the Reverend J. Dunmore Lang (the radical Presbyterian minister and historian) declared that the establishment had 'a rare domestic character'. (The Boronggoop station was subdivided by the government in 1852 and subsequently sold.)

In 1843 the partners expanded their interests by acquiring the Coryule run, an 800-acre (324-hectare) property on the Bellarine Peninsula. Five years later they secured the freehold of the property. It was there, in 1849, that they built the Coryule homestead, which still stands today. It was designed by Charles Laing, a well-known Melbourne architect. The old-world charm of the township named Drysdale grew up around their property. Anne Drysdale died there in 1853, aged sixty-one.

Caroline continued to run the Coryule property after her partner's death and to take an active part in local affairs. In 1861 she married the township's Wesleyan minister, the Reverend James Dodgson, who had arrived from Britain four years earlier.

Caroline died in 1874, aged sixty-two, and was buried beside Anne Drysdale at Coryule (their remains were later moved to Geelong).

Perhaps the most remarkable aspect of the relationship between the two women was that they were so unalike in temperament. Anne Drysdale, coming from a secure family background, had a natural dignity, a cheerful disposition, a quiet tolerance of others and a single-minded determination to achieve her objectives. Caroline Newcomb, lacking a stable home life, had grown up to be self-reliant and assertive. She developed a strong personality and a quick temper. As well as her partner's companionship, Anne came to rely upon Caroline's forthright character, initiative and determination. Both derived great strength from their religious convictions, and it was Caroline who supervised their daily devotions

THE MYALL CREEK MASSACRE

In 1838 an event occurred that highlighted the tensions that sometimes surfaced, especially in the bush, between Aboriginal people and the white settlers. The event was the massacre at Myall Creek (west of Inverell, in northern New South Wales), which resulted in the murder of twenty-eight Aboriginal people by twelve whites, eleven of them ex-convicts. Seven of the whites were executed for the crime which, apart from being an horrific indictment of the settlers' disdain for the native inhabitants of the country, served as an example of the manner in which the Aboriginal people were continually losing land they steadfastly maintained was theirs.

CONTROLLING THE LAND

From the earliest days of settlement, land was acquired by grants, some of which were made to ex-convicts. These grants were usually free of charge, save for a quit rent (a small amount paid by a freeholder in lieu of services).

From the 1820s onwards, land became a vexed issue. The British government regarded the sale of land as an important source of revenue, not least to fund immigration schemes.

Various methods, including the 1831 Ripon Regulations, were proposed with a view to controlling the sale and occupancy of land, but these either met with powerful resistance or proved administratively unworkable.

Opposition came from both the established landowners and the squatters. The latter maintained that by their own unaided efforts they had brought into use vast areas of hitherto unoccupied and usually poor-quality land, and that accordingly they should have unrestricted title to their runs. They contended that they had made a very significant contribution to the colony's economy.

It was to be many years before workable arrangements were made to control and survey Crown lands outside the settled areas, and to devise appropriate leases and rents.

Squatting was widespread by 1833. The immense efforts of the squatters had been responsible for opening up vast areas of New South Wales. One ex-convict, for example, despite broken dray shafts and other misfortunes, successfully drove 12 000 sheep along a little-known route to his employer's run in the colony's north. It took him a month. Another squatter spent over five months taking two herds of cattle and over 2000 sheep to his Clarence River property. He was assisted by only a handful of inexperienced ex-convicts.

The authorities initially could do little or nothing to control the surge into the interior and the illegal occupation of Crown lands. Nor could they stop unauthorised grazing, stock stealing and the periodic outbreaks of lawlessness. The lands had not been properly surveyed, or not surveyed at all. Nor, in the more remote regions, were there police to enforce whatever regulations might be made.

During the period of Richard Bourke's governorship, from 1831 to 1838, the governor proved reluctant to attempt to control the squatters, recognising the increasing prosperity that their activities were bringing, as well as the welcome inflow of both capital and migrants. He was also aware of the harsh conditions that most of the squatters had to endure: primitive living conditions, loneliness, occasional intrusions by unfriendly Aboriginal people and, at night, the ever-present threat of dingo attacks. And at times there were problems of insufficient stockfeed, especially during the five-year drought, which lasted from 1837 to 1841.

The squatters—most of whom had, in effect, made something out of nothing—not unnaturally began agitating for security of land tenure. In 1844, Sir George Gipps, who succeeded Bourke as Governor, introduced regulations designed to purchase land which the squatters had occupied for five years or more and then requiring them to pay an annual licence fee. This move was opposed by the squatters, many of whom contended that they had made a considerable investment in improvements on their runs, and should therefore not be ejected from their properties.

A political struggle of some magnitude had now developed, and it was to be many years before the issues were resolved. At a time when New South Wales was in the grip of a severe recession, the squatters—or rather, the graziers, as they had become—were supported by members of the labouring class in Sydney and in other towns. With urban unemployment high, the townspeople perceived that the revenue Gipps intended raising from the graziers would be used to promote subsidised emigration from Britain, thus increasing significantly the size of the urban labour force, with a consequent reduction in wage rates and a deterioration in working conditions.

The graziers also received backing from another quarter, the larger English woollen goods manufacturers, who stressed to the British government the unemployment and economic problems that would arise should there be a serious interruption of supplies of wool from Sydney.

The upshot was that Gipps' proposals were discarded. In 1847 legislation was passed that gave the graziers fourteen-year leases with the option of buying their land on reasonable terms.

The squatter movement had spread west and north from Sydney, and when the fertile lands became available, farming and grazing properties were established in the Port Philip district and as far away as Mitchell's 'Australia Felix' (see p. 60). It was estimated that by the late 1840s the newly claimed lands were running well over five million sheep.

FREDERICK BRACKER

The wool industry produced many expert wool men, one of whom was a German who became a Queenslander.

Frederick Bracker was born in Germany about 1798, the son of a farmer. In 1828 he sailed from Hamburg for Australia with approximately 300 stud sheep selected from the Silesian flock of Prince Esterhazy. The prince was a member of the aristocratic Magyar family, which produced numerous Hungarian diplomats, army officers and patrons of the arts.

Bracker's intention was to deliver the sheep, then to return to Germany. But in Australia the Aberdeen Co., which had purchased the sheep, offered him charge of the Rosenthal sheep run near Warwick on Queensland's Darling Downs. Bracker accepted.

Bracker managed Rosenthal until 1849. In the previous year he had leased another property at nearby Warroo, on which he ran 30,000 sheep. The property soon developed a reputation for its fine-quality merinos.

In 1843 Bracker married in Brisbane. The couple had four sons and five daughters.

Bracker became noted not only for his hard work and skill as a wool grower, but also for his hospitality, quaint manners and old-fashioned mode of dress. Many aspiring young squatters received their initial training under Bracker's supervision at the Rosenthal and Warroo properties. It became customary for anyone proposing to settle in the area to go to Bracker for advice.

Bracker was also an innovator, being responsible for introducing the first steel roller mill which was driven by horse power. He was also the first Queensland grower to produce flour from his own wheat.

The explorer Ludwig Leichhardt (see p. 67) visited Rosenthal in 1846, when Bracker gave him a horse and twenty-five wethers to augment his supplies. Leichhardt also visited the property during the following two years, in 1848 bringing some mules that had been broken in on Bracker's property.

It was Bracker who suggested the introduction of Rambouillet sheep to improve the short-stapled wool of the Negretti Spanish breeds. And when scab broke out in the area, it was Bracker who proposed dipping the sheep to counteract the disease. He also successfully experimented with lucerne as a feed crop, and ran a herd of Shorthorn cattle.

Frederick Bracker was one of Queensland's best wool men. He died at Warroo in 1870, aged seventy-two.

IMMIGRANTS

By 1840, and for several decades to come, it was not convicts who crowded the Australia-bound ships; rather, it was Britain's unemployed, particularly from the northern industrial regions, and the land-hungry free settlers who sought passage to the colonies. They were attracted by the perceptions, which increasing publicity had created, of a new and wholesome lifestyle 'down under', and the talk of readily available arable land to anyone with modest capital. The 1850s gold rushes (see pp. 119–22) added momentum to the exodus from Britain.

In the ten years from 1831 to 1841, nearly 100,000 free immigrants made their way from Britain to the Australian colonies. By 1850 the number of immigrants had doubled. The 1861 census showed that Australia's white population was in excess of 1.1 million (including some 24,000 Chinese, many of whom had been attracted to the goldfields during the 1850s).

By the middle of the nineteenth century it was evident that a significant change had occurred in the 'mix' of Australian society. The formerly convict-dominated population had been transformed by the influx of free settlers into a liberal, middle-class society. There were also the emancipists, many of whom came to regard Australia as 'their' country as thoughts of their pasts receded in memory.

The seeds of the future Australian nation had been sown as well as the culture and unique lifestyle of its people.

By 1871, when Australia's white population had increased to over 1.6 million, nearly 60 per cent of the population had been locally born. Ten years later, in excess of 2.3 million were counted. By 1901 the population had grown to 3.7 million.

The immigrants were many and various, and they, like the convicts, were to make a significant contribution to Australia's rapid development during the first half of the nineteenth century and beyond. Amongst them were a couple who were to prove their willingness to 'have a go' in the best Australian tradition ...

THE WYNDHAMS

George Wyndham, who was educated in England at Harrow and Cambridge, met his wife, Margaret, in Italy in 1825. Margaret was a teacher and had founded a school in Brussels. The couple were married there in 1827. George was then aged twenty-six.

The Wyndhams immediately decided to emigrate to Australia and to devote themselves to experimental farming. Taking with them some cattle and Southdown sheep, they arrived in Sydney at the end of 1827 and secured land in the Hunter Valley. They named their property Dalwood.

George Wyndham's initial crops were wheat, maize, mustard, caster oil, hemp, tobacco, millet and cape barley. Then he planted a vineyard, concentrating mainly on cabernet, shiraz and hermitage grapes. Some 140 years later, some of the shiraz vines were still bearing quality grapes, and were said to be the world's oldest wine-producing vines. Dalwood wines have won prizes both in Australia and overseas.

The economic crisis and depressed farming prices during the 1840s prompted the Wyndhams to move away from their farm. In 1845, leaving a caretaker at Dalwood, the Wyndhams set out from the Hunter on a long and hazardous journey north-east through largely untravelled country across the Great Dividing Range. George had with him his large family, some cattle and horses, rifles and ammunition, three covered wagons and a handful of trusted ex-convict servants. They took little food, for their intention was to live off the land.

One of the covered wagons was used by Margaret and their twelve children. Their stores were packed in another, and the third wagon contained the kitchen stove and utensils used by the cook to prepare the party's meals.

For three years they travelled slowly across the rugged New England plateau towards the Richmond River and the present-day town of Casino. George normally rode ahead with the cattle, deciding upon their route and selecting campsites. Hostile Aboriginal people were an ever-present danger.

Land in the Richmond River area proved of indifferent quality, so the party and their cattle moved westwards to the rich black soil of the plains. There, in a hut built by George, Margaret gave birth to their thirteenth child, a son.

The Wyndhams' herds had increased significantly during the long journey and did well on the western plains. George's venture had finally proved a success, and having survived the depression he was able to leave the new runs and vineyards to be managed by his eldest sons and to return to the neglected Dalwood property with Margaret, the younger children and the wagons. With prices generally improving, George was then able to devote much of his time to blending the wines that were to make the Dalwood name famous.

CAROLINE CHISHOLM

In 1839 a lady of immense compassion arrived in Sydney. She was to leave an indelible mark on the history of her time, and for the work she was inspired to do for the lonely and destitute assisted-immigrant women and girls who had arrived from Britain. This was at the beginning of a period of economic depression and rising unemployment.

Married at twenty-two, Caroline Chisholm had spent six years with her Army-officer husband in India, where she reared two sons and founded a school for the daughters of European soldiers.

Suffering ill health, Captain Chisholm was advised to take sick leave in another country. Australia was decided upon. The family then endured eight months in the sailing ship *Emerald Isle* in grossly overcrowded, uncomfortable and unhygienic conditions.

Arriving in Sydney Town in 1839, Caroline was appalled to find numerous undernourished, ragged and unmarried girls existing in squalid circumstances, many without shelter or employment.

After settling in a house at Windsor, on Sydney's outskirts, Caroline lost no time in petitioning the Governor to provide accommodation for the girls. Her pleas initially fell on deaf ears, but eventually she obtained use of a former barracks and founded The Caroline Chisholm Female Immigrants' Home. Supported by voluntary contributions, the hospice, and an attached employment registry, became home for as many as ninety-six women.

Caroline soon became a familiar figure on the wharves, meeting each immigrant ship and somehow managing to provide food and shelter for the girls and young women who the British authorities continued to send to the overcrowded colony.

In 1840 Caroline was faced with a distressing dilemma when her husband was recalled to duty in India. A third son had been born to them at Windsor and, after much heart-searching, Caroline decided to remain in Australia to continue her philanthropic work.

For the next twenty-six years Caroline devoted herself selflessly to the cause she had espoused. Employment for the immigrants was her main concern. To meet this problem she wrote hundreds of letters to leading country people to enlist their support. Employment agencies were established in Parramatta, Campbelltown and Liverpool. Others were set up in country centres.

A newspaper appeal for money, bullocks and drays enabled Caroline to set off on her first journey into the bush with sixteen girls. Sleeping in the open and seeking food from isolated farms along the way, the girls eventually found work and a home away from the misery of their conditions in Sydney.

Caroline continued to frequent the dirty, muddy Sydney streets and to campaign for official action to settle families on the land.

By 1842, seven country centres had been established for the women, and others were to follow.

The success of Caroline's activities in settling immigrants in country areas steadily became apparent. Two years later her direct involvement in the work she had begun no longer became necessary.

Caroline's restless mind now turned to what she considered to be the root of the problem—the British government's emigration policy.

In 1845 Captain Chisholm retired and left India to rejoin his family in Australia. Together, he and Caroline spent the next year travelling throughout New South Wales collecting information from immigrants to form the basis of the reforms she considered so necessary in England. One aspect of the immigration problem was that many of the would-be settlers were either unhealthy or of bad character.

By now a legend in New South Wales, Caroline and her husband decided that they must confront the British government directly. The couple accordingly sailed for England with their three children.

The next five years were exceedingly busy for the Chisholms. Two further children were born to Caroline, yet she and her husband found time to attend many meetings, to present their proposals to government committees and to travel extensively in Britain. In 1849 she founded The Family Colonisation Loan Society, with committees throughout Britain and agents in Australia. The society's main functions were to provide passage money for intending emigrants, and to assist them in obtaining employment on arrival in Australia. Many influential people, including the famous novelist Charles Dickens, gave strong support to the society.

Captain Chisholm returned alone to Australia in 1851, acting without salary as the society's agent.

Caroline had never forgotten the dreadful shipboard conditions that she and her family had experienced in 1838 on the *Emerald Isle*. Her agitation in Britain now resulted in the passing of the Passenger Act of 1852, which went a long way towards improving conditions for travel by sea. A new vessel was named the *Caroline Chisholm* in 1853.

By the time Caroline returned to Australia in 1854, more than 3000 emigrants had been sent out by The Family Colonisation Loan Society.

Grants from the Victorian government and private subscriptions provided the Chisholms with much-needed money to continue their work.

After touring the goldfields in 1854, Caroline was instrumental in arranging for shelter sheds on routes to the diggings, and these were built during the following year.

In 1857 Caroline suffered ill health and had to travel to Sydney for treatment. Although weakened by illness, she still found time to give public lectures and to open a girls' school.

In 1866 the Chisholms finally left Australia. The British government granted Caroline only a very modest pension, forcing the family to live in humble lodgings in London.

Caroline died in 1877, and her devoted and supportive husband some months later. They were buried in the same grave, the headstone inscribed simply 'the emigrant's friend'.

A reproduction of Caroline Chisholm appeared on the $5 bank note issued on 29 May 1967 by the Reserve Bank of Australia

ABORIGINAL AUSTRALIANS

The British government's official policy towards the Aboriginal people, as given to Captain Cook and subsequently repeated in despatches to various governors, was to treat them with friendliness and kindness. Aboriginal people were to be recognised as the original occupiers of the land.

Despite these exhortations, the first century of European settlement in Australia was marked by periodic conflicts and outbreaks of violence between the settlers and the Aboriginal people. The settlers, whenever they came into contact with Aboriginal people, rarely questioned their own rights to usage of the land for their own purposes, and in many cases considered they had something of a duty to instruct Aboriginal people in the virtues of British civilisation.

The Aboriginal people's attitude in response was frequently to assert that they had their own civilisation, and accordingly, as Captain Cook discovered, that they had little or no use for most of the articles that the Europeans usually offered as expressions of friendship, or for the strange and seemingly impractical customs and lifestyle that the newcomers followed.

As we have noted, Aboriginal people did not till the soil in order to grow crops, neither did they engage in husbandry. Their highly developed skills as food gatherers, hunters and fishers meant that they had no need to practise farming and pastoralisation as did the Europeans. As a consequence, they were generally a nomadic people, roaming over large areas in order to obtain their food requirements and a few other essentials.

Not unnaturally, therefore, Aboriginal people regarded the Europeans as invaders, and were usually deeply resentful of the intrusions into their tribal lands. Given these conflicting attitudes, it was not surprising that there were periodic hostilities. At times Aboriginal people expressed their resentment by stealing the Europeans' goods, by spearing them to death and harassing them in other ways. The Europeans, frequently misunderstanding the Aboriginal people's attitude to their presence, sometimes responded with violence. Disgraceful episodes such as the Myall Creek massacre (see pp. 70-1) unfortunately resulted.

However, there were also many instances of friendship, cooperation and humanity ...

YURANIGH

In 1845 Sir Thomas Mitchell, Surveyor-General of New South Wales, led his fourth and last expedition to explore extensive areas of hitherto unmapped country in central Queensland. Despite a shortage of supplies and periodic threats from Aboriginal people, the twelve-month expedition returned to Sydney without serious incident or loss of life.

Amongst Mitchell's twenty-nine men was an Aboriginal man named Yuranigh, whose outstanding bush skills and loyalty made a deep impression on the leader. Mitchell was also impressed with Yuranigh's negotiations with the Aboriginal groups that followed the party.

In his journal of the expedition, Mitchell made no less than ninety references to Yuranigh, writing of him on one occasion:

'He has been my guide, companion, counsellor and friend on the most eventful occasions during this journey of discovery. His intelligence and judgement rendered him so necessary to me that he was ever at my elbow whether on foot or on horseback. Confidence in him was never misplaced. He knew well the character of all the white men of the party. Nothing escaped his penetrating eye and quick ear.'

After returning to Sydney with Mitchell, Yuranigh became a stockman before rejoining his tribe. He died in 1850 at Molong in central New South Wales, where his grave still remains, marked by carved trees in the tradition of Yuranigh's Wiradjuri people. It is the only known place where Aboriginal and European burial symbols may be seen at the same site.

Mitchell later paid for a headstone at Yuranigh's grave. Restored in 1900, it is made from Molong marble and bears the inscription:

'To Native Courage, Honesty and Fidelity. Yuranigh, who accompanied the Expedition of Discovery into Tropical Australia in 1846, lies buried here according to the Rites of his countrymen and this spot was dedicated and enclosed by the Governor General's Authority in 1852.'

JAMES MORRILL

At about the same time as Mitchell's expedition was taking place, there occurred off the Queensland coast an episode that illustrated the readiness of Aboriginal people not only to befriend a distressed white man, but also to adopt him as one of their own.

There were only twenty-two survivors from the barque *Peruvian*, on passage from Sydney to China, which was wrecked on 27 February 1846 on the Horseshoe Reef off the Great Barrier Reef. The survivors boarded the ship's jolly-boat and slowly drifted towards the Queensland coast. Amongst them was James Morrill, carpenter's mate on the *Peruvian* and a strong and capable young man.

The castaways were without food, but Morrill did his best to keep them alive by catching fish, which they ate raw. Despite his efforts there were only five survivors when the little boat finally made a landing near Cape Bowling Green, a short distance from present-day Townsville.

Taking an Aboriginal bark canoe, which the castaways found on the beach, the shipwright, Morrill, set off in search of help. He was never seen again.

It was not long before some Aboriginal people appeared. They befriended the four remaining survivors, but notwithstanding their assistance, the apprentice boy, White, succumbed to his castaway ordeal.

There were several nomadic tribes in the area, one of which now adopted the *Peruvian*'s master, Captain Pitkethley, together with his wife. These Aboriginal people lived and hunted in the Cape Cleveland area (a little to the north of the survivors' landing point), but despite their help and friendliness both the captain and his wife died after about two years.

The remaining survivor, Morrill, was adopted by another tribe, which frequented the area between the Burdekin and Black rivers and the Mount Elliott district to the south of Townsville (part of the area is now the Mount Elliott National Park). Morrill was generally well-treated by the Aboriginal people and stayed with them for seventeen years, adapting readily to their customs and way of life.

By 1861 pastoralists had established properties in northern Queensland, resulting in some contacts between the settlers and Morrill's Aboriginal tribe. Despite his acceptance by the tribe, Morrill retained a strong desire to return to his own people.

On 25 January 1863, Morrill and some of the Aboriginal people were kangaroo hunting when they came to the out-station of a sheep property. Morrill, then aged thirty-nine, washed himself as thoroughly as possible and very tentatively approached two of the station hands, crying in a language he had almost forgotten: 'Don't shoot, mates, I'm a British object!' He was recognised as a white man, and reluctantly parted from the Aboriginal people who had accepted him for so long.

Morrill was fêted upon his arrival in Brisbane. He later accepted an appointment with the Department of Customs at Bowen (on the coast between Mackay and Townsville), where his special knowledge of the local tribes and their language resulted in a period of peaceful cooperation in the area. In 1864 he accompanied the explorer George Dalrymple on an expedition northwards to open up the port of Cardwell (north of Ingham), and later that year married a domestic servant employed by the police magistrate at Bowen.

In 1865 Morrill was skipper of the coastal vessel *Ariel* carrying the first cargo of bonded goods to the newly established settlement at Cleveland Bay, later to become the city of Townsville. But by this time his health had begun to be affected by the privation of years of wanderings with the tribes. He died on 30 October 1865, mourned by his new wife, his friends and the many Aboriginal people from nearby districts who attended his funeral.

EDMUND KENNEDY

Two years after the shipwreck of the *Peruvian* there occurred another incident in Queensland which illustrated not only the resentment that some Aboriginal people showed when the white man intruded into their domain, but also the readiness of a devoted Aboriginal man to befriend a European, even when threatened by his own countrymen.

In 1848 Edmund Kennedy, who had been second-in-command of Sir Thomas Mitchell's 1845 expedition into the interior of tropical Australia, decided to lead an expedition from Rockingham Bay (between the present Queensland cities of Townsville and Cairns) to Cape York. Included in the party was an Aboriginal man, Jackey Jackey, who soon acquired a reputation for hard work, honesty and outstanding bushcraft.

Various setbacks encountered on the way north prompted Kennedy to leave the main party at Cape Weymouth and to make for Cape York with three of the white men and the faithful Jackey Jackey.

When one of the reduced party accidentally shot himself, Kennedy decided to leave him in the care of the other two white men and to press ahead with Jackey Jackey.

Within about 32 kilometres of their destination they encountered some apparently friendly Aboriginal people, to whom they gave fish hooks and a knife. Shortly afterwards, the Aboriginal people returned and speared Kennedy to death.

Jackey Jackey buried his leader, then made for the coast under cover of darkness. He was able to attract the attention of a relief ship which was anchored offshore.

Although exhausted and grieving over Kennedy's loss, Jackey Jackey set out with a rescue team to search for the remainder of the expedition. Two men were found at the expedition's base camp, the others having died of starvation.

One of the survivors, William Carron, later wrote a moving account of the events under the title *Narrative of an Expedition, Undertaken under the Direction of the Late Mr. Assistant Surveyor E.B. Kennedy* (1849).

PASTORAL EXPANSION

In the twenty years leading up to 1840 there was a remarkable expansion in the pastoral industry, which was temporarily halted by the severe drought that lasted from 1837 to 1841 (see p. 72).

The search for suitable grazing lands began first in New South Wales, then extended north into Queensland and westwards into Victoria. Pastoral pioneering spread later to the other colonies.

The pastoral expansion, involving the movement of herds of cattle and flocks of sheep over vast distances largely uninhabited by white settlers, gave rise to a new breed of men on the Australian scene—the drovers. They were skilled, determined and courageous pioneers who worked long, lonely hours in conditions that were frequently harsh and discouraging. One such was James Hawdon, who, in 1838, walked unannounced into the streets of Adelaide having overlanded a mob of sheep and cattle from New South Wales. The journey had taken him ten weeks.

A second expansion phase began during the late 1800s and continued throughout most of the twentieth century. This period was characterised by the introduction of large-scale development capital and improved managerial skills.

NAT AND WILLIAM BUCHANAN

Nathaniel Buchanan and his elder brother William epitomised the end of the first phase of pastoral expansion. They had arrived in Sydney in 1837 with their parents and four brothers. Two years later the family were farming in northern New South Wales.

The younger Buchanan established himself as a pastoralist and bushman. He met the explorer William Landsborough and, in 1859, joined him in the search for grazing lands in the river areas of northern Queensland. They were successful and, with capital put up by the Scottish Australian Company, they secured 1500 square miles (3900 square kilometres) of land along the Thompson River (which flows through central Queensland).

Nathaniel married in 1863, taking his bride to the barely established Bowen Downs station. She was the only white woman in the district.

In the following year the restless Buchanan secured land further north, near Burketown in the then undeveloped Gulf of Carpentaria country in far north Queensland. Later, with drought threatening, he sold his share in the Bowen Downs station and went back to New South Wales, before returning to Queensland to manage a station near Emerald.

Over the next fifteen years Buchanan enhanced his reputation as a drover, bushman and explorer, pioneering new stock routes in western Queensland and in the Northern Territory, which were used by subsequent overlanders.

In 1883 Buchanan was the first to take cattle into the Kimberley, crossing the Victoria River country with 4000 head of stock. Concurrently, the Durack family, under the leadership of Patrick Durack, made the memorable 4800-kilometre trek from their Thylungra station in western Queensland to the Ord River (south of Wyndham in far north-east Western Australia) with the loss of half of their cattle and several men. Buchanan's journey took two years and four months. They had pioneered the world's longest stock route, generally following the Duracks' track, as did the gold seekers who flocked to the Kimberley fields in 1886.

Also in 1883, in partnership with his brother William and the Gordon brothers, Nat established the Wave Hill station in fertile but remote country on the Victoria River, about 550 kilometres south of Darwin. Their nearest neighbour was over 300 kilometres distant. Until it was later divided up and sold, Wave Hill was the world's largest cattle station.

Over the next thirteen years, Nat was involved in a number of pastoral and mining ventures, some of which were unsuccessful. In 1896, at the age of seventy, the intrepid pioneer made his last expedition—an unsuccessful search for a route through arid and featureless wastes west of Tennant Creek to overland cattle from the Barkly Tablelands to Western Australia.

Nat Buchanan's physical resilience, survival skills and feats of droving and bushcraft, and his remarkable powers of observation, made him a legend in his lifetime. He died in 1901, aged seventy-five, at a small station near Tamworth. Although the *Bulletin* magazine, in its obituary, claimed that Buchanan had at that time settled more country than any other man in Australia, he died a poor man.

William Buchanan also became one of the Australian pastoral industry's most notable pioneers.

In 1839, William joined his father in leasing the 15,500 hectare property in northern New South Wales where the family first settled on arrival from Ireland. Like his younger brother and many other fit men, William went gold prospecting in 1849, first in Gippsland in Victoria and later at Ophir in New South Wales. He had little success in either area, but noted that the geological formations were similar to those in New England. He was later to claim responsibility for the mid-1850s discovery of the northern New South Wales goldfields, although others made similar claims.

Sheep and cattle were the dominant influences in William Buchanan's life for the next fifty years. He steadily acquired properties, mainly in New South Wales, always seeking to improve his stock with new blood and superior breeds. For a brief period he was in partnership with his brother Nat at the Wave Hill property in the Northern Territory, but otherwise their paths as pastoralists and overlanders did not cross.

The elder Buchanan, who became a wealthy pastoralist, was intelligent and forthright, a man of his word, courteous and respected by those who worked for him. He was a fine horseman and a skillful bushman. Like his younger brother, he represented the old school, one of the last of the pioneer overlanders and station owners who laid the foundations of the Australian pastoral industry.

William Buchanan died in Sydney in 1911, aged eighty-six.

GETTING THE MAIL THROUGH

In 1834 Joseph Hawdon arrived in Sydney from England and joined his brother, John, who had rented a property near Batemans Bay on the New South Wales south coast. Two years later, Joseph, his friend John Gardiner and John Hepburn, a sea captain, teamed up in successfully overlanding cattle to Port Philip. The three then remained in Victoria, Joseph Hawdon taking up fertile land near Dandenong, east of present-day Melbourne.

It was not just sheep and cattle that had to be brought overland. The enterprising Joseph soon had another iron in the fire when he secured a £1200 per annum contract to overland mail fortnightly to Yass, nearly 300 kilometres south-west of Sydney.

Melbourne had been established in 1835 and had acquired its first post office two years later. At that time mail to and from Sydney was sent by sea. But it was a very irregular service, a fact that provoked irritation in both centres, especially in government and commercial circles.

Until Hawdon accepted the contract, no-one had been willing to overland the mail because of the dangers involved. The absence of an established track was a deterrent, and there were other risks—the threat of attacks by Aboriginal people and bushrangers, as well as periodic floods and bushfires.

Hawdon needed an honest and reliable bushman to carry the mail. Earlier, whilst overlanding cattle to Melbourne, a young stockman had plunged into the flooded Murray River to reach three non-swimming members of Hawdon's party who were clinging to a floating wagon in the raging waters. The stockman, John Bourke, rescued the men and recovered the wagon. He was just the man Hawdon wanted to operate his mail contract.

Over a period of three years, young Bourke rode the six-day Melbourne-to-Yass stage (a distance of approximately 600 kilometres). Bullock carts then carried the mail bags from Yass to Sydney, this second stage taking about five weeks because of the slowness of the bullocks.

Despite the problems and dangers, John Bourke delivered the mail regularly, riding—in both directions—a total of about 18,000 kilometres in the process. A coach service took over the mail run in 1841.

The bush mailmen were a hardy breed. They established a tradition of always getting the mail through, come what may. John Bourke was the first of the overland 'posties'.

THE GROWTH OF
NEW SOUTH WALES

By 1824, thanks largely to the liberalising views of Macquarie and his successor, Governor Brisbane, New South Wales was no longer a gaol. It was a colony.

Popular sentiment had resulted in the gradual introduction of democratic processes in Australia. A Legislative Council had been established in New South Wales in 1823 and in Van Diemen's Land two years later, with all members to both councils being appointed. Both councils were enlarged in

1828 to fifteen members. The New South Wales council was again enlarged in 1843 to thirty-six members, of whom twenty-four were elected. Only six of the elected members were from the Port Philip district. This decision caused considerable irritation, since it allowed the established New South Wales members to outvote their Port Philip brethren when it suited them, especially over financial matters.

The seven-year term of Governor Darling, who succeeded Brisbane, was noteworthy mainly for the strengthening of the administrative services in New South Wales. Darling, who tended to side with the larger landowners, was not a popular figure, and was followed in 1831 by a progessive and fair-minded administrator in the person of Richard Bourke, a kindly but firm soldier. The emancipists soon discovered that they had the ear of the new governor, who was to preside over the colony's destiny for a seven-year period. Juries in civil trials were introduced during Bourke's stewardship; housing, postal services and hospitals were improved; and the British government was persuaded to grant assisted passages for female emigrants.

Perhaps Bourke's most significant achievement was to convince London that the people of New South Wales had achieved a sufficient degree of responsibility to be able, to a large extent, to manage their own affairs.

It was during the 1820s that the economy of New South Wales became stabilised, based increasingly upon wool exports, especially the fine, long-staple varieties. With its expanding population, Australia served as an outlet for both British goods and surplus capital. By 1839 the value of imports was more than double that of exports; the banks were overflowing with cash; and loans were readily obtainable.

By 1828, when the first census was taken, the white population of New South Wales numbered 36,598, of whom rather less than half were convicts. By the time of the 1841 census the population had increased to 130,856. Ten years later the flood of immigrants had swelled the population more than threefold, to 437,665.

The expanded urban population during the 1830s necessitated improved roadways and the construction of bridges. Francis Greenway, the convict architect (see p. 50), had left an indelible mark on the Sydney scene with his designs for many fine buildings. Now another expert in stonework, but not a convict, contributed to the needs of his time ...

DAVID LENNOX

David Lennox arrived in Sydney from Scotland in 1832. He was already a master mason, having worked on many bridges in Britain over a period of twenty years.

In Sydney, Lennox was first employed on stone cutting but was soon appointed to the Roads Department. He became Superintendent of Bridges in 1833.

Lennox's first bridge was built at Lapstone Hill, west of Sydney at the foot of the Blue Mountains. This impressive sandstone structure (named Lennox Bridge by Governor Bourke) remains the oldest bridge still standing on the Australian mainland. It is beside the present Great Western Highway and is still to be seen from a well-defined walking track.

For the next eleven years Lennox built stone bridges in and around Sydney. He always employed convict labour, and had a reputation as a kindly taskmaster who recommended mitigation of sentences for those who were not troublesome and who proved to be hardworking.

Lennox subsequently transferred his activities to Melbourne, where, as Superintendent of Bridges for the Port Philip District, he built fifty-three bridges over a period of nine years. The best known of these was his largest—a single-arch structure over the Yarra River. This bridge was replaced after thirty-five years to provide for increased traffic.

Lennox retired in 1853, returning to Sydney two years later, where he settled at Parramatta in a modest house of his own design.

Lennox's outstanding skill was responsible for solving many of the technical bridge-building problems of the time. He became a legend in his lifetime. It is fortunate that some examples of his work still remain to be admired.

WESTERN AUSTRALIA

Western Australia's early history was characterised by hesitancy, uncertainty and disappointment. The first white settlement was actually a whaling station at King George Sound, near present-day Albany, which was established in 1824. Fears of the French establishing a colony on the continent's western side prompted the British Colonial Office to despatch Captain James Stirling in 1827 to investigate the Swan River area. Stirling was impressed by the strategic and commercial significance of a settlement there, and two years later Captain Charles Fremantle formally took possession of the territory in the name of his sovereign. A few weeks later, Stirling returned as the settlement's first governor. He was accompanied by a party of free settlers, military personnel and administrative staff. At an appropriate ceremony the British flag was raised, and the new town was named Perth, after the Scottish hometown of the then Secretary of State for the Colonies, Sir George Murray.

Little was achieved during the next two years. The Aboriginal people in the area proved hostile and uncooperative, the land was of poor quality and the summer heat distressing. Some small communities had settled in various locations between Perth and Cape Leeuwin, but nowhere was progress made towards prosperity. Immigrants continued to arrive, misled by irresponsible and inaccurate reports. Stirling went to London in 1832 in an attempt to obtain financial support, but was rebuffed. The Henty family (see pp. 61–6) were amongst those who were disillusioned by conditions in Western Australia.

Stirling was also disillusioned. He resigned from the governorship towards the end of 1837 and departed for London at the beginning of 1839.

Within a few years it had become clear to the colonists in Perth that an influx of labour was necessary if development was to take place. Well aware that the rapid strides that had been made in New South Wales resulted largely from the availability of ample convict labour, the Perth colonists, in 1847, successfully petitioned London to recommence the transportation system and to begin sending convicts to Western Australia.

The arrival of convicts, an increasing influx of free immigrants and capital, and a number of initiatives taken by the British government marked a turning point in Western Australia's fortunes. Within twenty years the white population had increased to 20,000, one half of whom were convicts. The colony's economy benefited from exports of timber from the south, wool from grazing lands opened up in the north, and from whaling products. Ten thousand male convicts made the journey to Western Australia before transportation was finally stopped in 1868.

THE PORT PHILIP DISTRICT

In the late 1830s the lure of reported fertile lands brought an influx of overlanders and squatters to the Port Philip District. In 1834 the Henty family (see pp. 61–6) had crossed from Launceston to Portland Bay with stock, seeds and plants and were soon settled in fertile country on the plains at Muntham, about 15 kilometres east of the present-day town of Casterton (352 kilometres west of Melbourne).

In 1835 John Batman and a small party had crossed Bass Strait, entered Port Philip Bay and reached a river, which the local Aboriginal people called the Yarra Yarra. There, amidst fine grazing land, Batman came to a place that he judged to be suitable for a village. It was the site of present-day Melbourne. With the Aboriginal people in his party acting as interpreters, Batman entered into negotiations with the local Aboriginal chiefs and concluded a 'treaty' which involved the granting of 100,000 acres of land bordering on Port Philip Bay to Batman in exchange for assorted goods, clothing and flour.

He also negotiated a similar 'treaty' involving lands on either side of the Yarra Yarra River.

Returning to Van Diemen's Land, Batman sent Lieutenant-Governor Arthur in Hobart an account of the negotiations and of his plans to move stock to the Port Philip Bay lands. Arthur passed on this information to Governor Bourke in Sydney, who unhesitatingly declared any such 'treaties' concluded with Aboriginal people as null and void.

By 1840 there were over 10,000 white people in the Port Philip District. The authorities in London, recognising the need for a new colony, appointed a magistrate, Captain William Lonsdale, to administer the settlement. Then followed the appointment of a man who appeared to be something of a round peg in a square hole. He was destined to become the first lieutenant-governor of the colony of Victoria ...

CHARLES LA TROBE

The squatters of the Port Philip District were hard, blunt men, intolerant of delay and vociferous in their demands. Into this widely dispersed community, in January 1839, was propelled as superintendent a man who must surely have been one of the British Colonial Office's most unlikely choices as an administrator during the nineteenth century.

He was Charles La Trobe, and he brought with him a wife, their daughter, two servants and a prefabricated cottage, 'Jolimont', which he arranged to be erected on a little hill with a view of the Yarra Yarra River, in the clean air of the eastern hills.

Not far distant was the straggling little township of Melbourne, with a population of about 6000; its dirty, smelly streets lacked drainage or sewerage and had few buildings. The area was administered from Sydney, where Governor Gipps controlled all land sales and official appointments. All revenue for the district, little though it was, went into the coffers of the New South Wales government.

The Colonial Office's appointees to senior administrative posts were usually men with a military or naval background, men schooled in discipline and with administrative and organisational experience. La Trobe had none of these attributes.

He was born in London in 1801 and educated in Switzerland. Both his grandfather and his father were ordained clergymen, and Charles was undoubtedly destined for the ministry. In fact, he taught briefly at a church school in Manchester, then in 1824 returned to Switzerland to become tutor to a family at Neuchâtel. During his three years there he became a noted mountaineer, a pioneer member of the Alpine Club and the author of two books on his climbing experiences. The young La Trobe usually dispensed with guides and porters during his frequent expeditions to the mountains and high passes.

For two years, from 1832 to 1833, La Trobe travelled in the United States and Mexico, and soon afterwards published two more books on his experiences. During his visit, he met the American author Washington Irvine, who published an account of their travels together through the American prairies.

On his return to Switzerland, La Trobe stayed with a Swiss Councillor of State, Frederic Auguste de Montmollin, who had a country house near Jolimont, a tourist resort in the Neuchâtel district. There he became engaged to one of Montmollin's daughters, Sophie. They were married at the British Legation in Berne in 1835.

Then occurred a strange twist in La Trobe's career. The British government, perhaps influenced by his writings or by his family's connection with the anti-slavery movement, invited him to visit the West Indies and to report on measures to be taken before granting freedom to emancipated slaves. Having completed this assignment, La Trobe was appointed in January 1839 as Superintendent of the Port Philip District.

The quietly-spoken, well-educated, cultured and gentlemanly La Trobe very soon became involved in the community's enormous and turbulent difficulties. Land claims and the lack of qualified surveyors were a constant problem, for the rich western and northern lands had been occupied illegally by pioneering squatters who had migrated from New South Wales and Van Diemen's Land. These men were well-organised and forthright, and they quickly made known their grievances.

A long drought occurred from 1838 to 1840 and had serious repercussions. The depression of 1841 followed and led to a crisis in industry. The rampant land speculation in and around Melbourne declined, and British investors began withdrawing their money. Several of the banks failed and there were widespread bankruptcies. Relief work for the escalating unemployed became an urgent necessity.

Furthermore, throughout the 1840s the free settlers maintained their unrelenting demands for separation from New South Wales. There were other pressing problems—the totally inadequate allocations of funds for urgent public works was one; another was the convict problem, for whilst a decision had been taken in 1840 to cease transportation to the mainland colonies, convicts continued to arrive. La Trobe was known to oppose the sending of convicts to Port Philip, and criticism of him on this score desisted when, in 1849, he refused permission for a shipload of convicts to land, sending the human cargo on to Sydney in defiance of the Colonial Office's instructions.

When a 36-member Legislative Council was formed in Sydney in 1843 (see p. 90), only six seats were allocated to the Port Philip District. This was an absurd situation, for upon contentious issues such as funding and separation the Port Philip representatives were, as has already been noted, invariably outvoted by the Sydney members.

In 1846 La Trobe was shouldered with another burden when, for four months, he was required to act as lieutenant-governor of Van Diemen's Land after the colony's governor had been peremptorily dismissed.

The continuous criticism and non-stop invective in the press failed to put La Trobe off his stride. Ever sensitive to his obligation to take instructions from Sydney, he fostered and enjoyed a very cordial relationship with Governor Gipps, who was both mentor and friend. La Trobe's quiet and diffident manner caused him to be thought of as timid and weak, whereas in fact he assiduously endured the long hours of deskwork which his official duties involved. His indecisiveness can largely be explained by his inexperience in administrative matters and colonial procedures. Sydney was a three-week journey distant, so inevitably he sometimes had to procrastinate whilst decisions were forthcoming.

Despite the undoubted stresses and strains of his position, the indefatigable La Trobe enjoyed the simple pleasures of family life and of contact with those individuals and organisations, both religious and cultural, that had his patronage. He delighted in horseriding and in visiting pastoralists in their homes. Doubtless thoughts of the Swiss mountains crossed his mind periodically, for he took every opportunity to explore 'this strange, capricious land' to which he had been sent. On occasions when he and his family were staying at their summer cottage at Queenscliff, on the Bellarine Peninsula, he would customarily leave at four in the morning and ride the 32 kilometres to Geelong to catch the morning steamer in order to be at his Melbourne office desk in good time.

In January 1851 La Trobe was appointed Victoria's first lieutenant-governor, with an Executive Council of four. He now had considerable powers but was handicapped by the inexperience of the officials appointed to his government. Whilst the separation issue with New South Wales had been finally resolved and he was no longer dependent upon Sydney, La Trobe's Executive Council was to become a battleground between the squatters and the radical and urban forces.

Later that year gold was discovered at Ballarat (113 kilometres west of Melbourne), and the resultant turmoil presented La Trobe with a series of immense problems. Large numbers of able-bodied men in the colony went to the diggings at one time or another, and thousands from elsewhere in the country and from overseas migrated to the goldfields near Ballarat, Bendigo and Omeo. La Trobe was in no position to control the demand for leases, nor to adequately maintain law and order. Inexperience led him to impose a monthly licence fee permitting the search for gold. This impost aroused the ire of the diggers, for few of them had the money to pay. The decision in January 1852 to increase the fee to £3 per month led to a vigorous protest from the diggers. The government was forced to back down. Friction then developed between La Trobe's Executive Council and the Legislative Council, the latter refusing to vote money for any purpose connected with the discovery of gold. La Trobe's preference now was for an export levy on gold, but this was not approved by the Legislative Council.

Wearied by the persistent problems and his own isolation, La Trobe tendered his resignation in December 1852. But it was over a year before his successor arrived. In deference to his replacement, La Trobe did not implement any new policies, but during 1853 there was a greater degree of cooperation between the two councils and a steady improvement in his government's control of the new colony's affairs.

In ill health, La Trobe's wife, Sophie, preceded him to Europe. Just before departing himself in May 1854, La Trobe received news of Sophie's death in Switzerland. As his homeward-bound ship passed through the Port Philip heads he poignantly noted in his diary: '14 years, 7 months and 6 days since I first entered here.' He was to have a sad homecoming.

History and present-day Victorians have judged La Trobe more kindly than did the colony's people during his years in their midst. That he made mistakes during his stewardship is not disputed. That he was thrust into a wild frontier society without the qualifications or experience necessary to the time is also without question. But he kept the colony's government functioning and maintained the rule of law during very difficult times. Those were important achievements.

It was La Trobe who commissioned Dr Ferdinand von Mueller to lay out Melbourne's Royal Botanic Gardens. He was also associated with the establishment of the Royal Melbourne Hospital and with the founding of the University of Melbourne and, later, with the La Trobe University and the La Trobe Library.

In 1855 La Trobe married his late wife's widowed sister. In retirement, failing eyesight prevented him from writing an account of his Australian experiences, but the carefully preserved documents he intended using were entrusted to the Public Library in Melbourne.

Four years after his return to England, La Trobe was appointed a Companion of the Bath. It was a further six years before he was awarded a modest pension. He died in England in 1875, aged seventy-four.

His family erected a memorial to him in Neuchâtel, where he had met his first wife and where she lived briefly on her return from Australia.

JAMES HARRISON

Before he emigrated to Australia, James Harrison had been an apprentice printer in Glasgow, Scotland. Later he worked in London as a compositor, and was subsequently employed with a publishing and bookselling firm. He arrived in Sydney in 1837 and worked for a short time on the *Literary News*. He was later employed on the staffs of the *Monitor* and the *Sydney Herald*.

In 1839 Harrison joined one of the first settlers in the Port Philip District, John Fawkner, who in the following year commissioned Harrison to establish and edit the *Geelong Advertiser*. Three years later Harrison had acquired sufficient funds to enter into a partnership with John Scamble to buy the paper. The two then produced a sister paper, the *Geelong Almanac*.

By now Harrison was an influential and fearless journalist. He advocated broad and forward-looking policies, aligning himself during the 1840s on the side of the Port Philip squatters in their fight for secure leases. Later he acquired Scamble's share of the *Geelong Advertiser*, which became a daily in 1850, and also published a number of maps and magazines.

Harrison's influence spread during the 1850s in the newly constituted colony of Victoria. He became a member of Geelong's first town council, then was elected to the Legislative Assembly during 1859–61. Financial difficulties forced him to sell the *Geelong Advertiser*, although he remained the paper's editor. By 1865 he founded another newspaper, the *Geelong Register*, but again his financial situation compelled him to sell, and he was appointed editor of the influential Melbourne newspaper, the *Age*.

Harrison was an inventor as well as a highly regarded journalist, and it was this other interest that caused his periodic financial embarrassments. He was fascinated by the commercial prospects of refrigeration. On one occasion, whilst washing down his printing press with ether, he observed the cooling effect caused by the liquid. The innovative Harrison then set about designing a machine that compressed ether, and used the technology to make the world's first mechanical refrigeration system, which was installed in a brewery at Geelong, Victoria, and patented in 1854.

He returned to London in 1856 to patent both his process and his apparatus. A London manufacturer used Harrison's designs to produce improved refrigerating machinery. One of these machines was shipped to Harrison's works near Geelong. The output of three tons of ice per day far exceeded the Geelong district's needs, so Harrison transferred his equipment to Melbourne, where production was stepped up to more than 10 tons daily. He then built an ice-making plant in Sydney, but before long the company there was sold.

Harrison now turned his attention to marine refrigeration, for there was an obvious potential for the export of frozen meat. Harrison's success was commemorated by a gold medal awarded to him at the 1873 Melbourne Exhibition for demonstrating the feasibility of keeping meat frozen for months at a time. A trial shipment to England of beef and mutton was arranged, but the experiment proved unsuccessful due to inadequate machinery and lack of experience in chilling the meat to the correct temperature. (Shortly afterwards, an American refrigeration company devised the right equipment and techniques that made the shipment of chilled foodstuffs a feasible proposition.)

After a further visit to Britain, Harrison returned to Australia as a columnist for the *Age*, then finally settled with his family at Point Henry, on the outskirts of Geelong. He died there in 1893, aged seventy-seven. Three years later, as a result of a public subscription, a tombstone was erected at his grave, the inscription including the words '... one soweth, another reapeth'.

KEEPING COOL

Electricity began to come into general use in Australia in the 1890s. Domestic refrigerators became available in the early 1920s. In the days before these modern amenities, the population had to find other methods of trying to keep cool.

In fact, Australia's resourceful bush people had long since found ways and means of keeping food and water cool. Constructing a below-ground cellar was one method, whilst another was its variation, the 'half-cellar', which was partly underground and open at both ends, allowing cool draughts to flow through. Cool rooms with thick mud-brick walls and insulated roofs were quite common and well-suited to storing meat that had been salted in a barrel and left in brine, or boiled and preserved in sugar soap.

Another method was to dig a hole in the ground, allow it to be filled with roof water, then suspend in it a cloth-covered crate containing bottles and jars.

Meat was frequently placed in a sealed sugar bag and hung under a verandah or in the middle of a tree. Similarly, using the principle of evaporation, water kept in a canvas bag and hung on the verandah would soon become delightfully cool if there was a breeze, even though the water might taste of whatever had previously been in the bag.

The explorer Sir Thomas Mitchell is sometimes said to have invented the canvas waterbag after noting that Aboriginal people carried water in kangaroo skins. The principle still remains in use today by some outback motorists who suspend a canvas waterbag at the front of their vehicles.

A similar cooling principle was used for the 'Coolgardie safe', which originated during the gold rush days in Western Australia in the 1890s. The safe was a timber cabinet, usually having two or three compartments and covered with closely woven hessian. From a dish of water on top of the safe, wet strips of canvas, or wicks, would transport moisture by capillary action to the surrounding hessian curtain, the hem of which rested in a tray (so that the water could be recycled). Water evaporating from the hessian would absorb the surrounding heat, thus keeping cool the interior of the safe. The legs of the safe would usually be placed in tins of water to keep ants away.

The Coolgardie safe was in fact a variation on the age-old way of keeping a tent cool in hot weather by hanging a hessian curtain over its entrance, then throwing a bucket of water over the hessian.

Ice chests eventually became commonplace, but initially the problem was to procure the ice. In 1839, and for the following twenty years or so, lake ice was brought by steamer from the United States, but the wastage in transit was high, as was the resultant cost of the ice.

Thanks to James Harrison's mechanical refrigeration process (see p. 99), ice soon became available in the capital cities at a fraction of the cost of the imported American ice. By the 1890s ice chests were in common use, with ice being available at a reasonable price.

Bush people usually prevented milk from turning sour by scalding it over a pan of boiling water, then cooling it in a container suspended in the 'well', or in a stream if there was one nearby. Butter in a container was also kept cool by immersion in water.

During the 1870s Thomas Mort developed a system for supplying the Sydney market with refrigerated country milk, supplying farmers with a small portable refrigerator.

Soon after the conclusion of World War II, the 'Silent Knight' range of electric refrigerators, made by Sir Edward Hallstrom's company, heralded the appearance in Australian households of the (almost) indispensable 'fridge'.

SOUTH AUSTRALIA

Adelaide was founded in 1837 by a British group keen to take advantage of the fine lands on the southern coast, which had been discovered by explorer Charles Sturt when he reached the mouth of the Murray River in 1830 (see pp. 58-9).

An advance party, led by Colonel William Light, was sent out in 1836 to select a site for the settlement. In the following year the city of Adelaide (named for Queen Adelaide, William IV's consort), was founded, with its wide and symmetrical street grid, and it remains an eloquent tribute to Light's original plan. In 1838 the British government appointed Captain John Hindmarsh as the colony's first governor. Five years later the settlement's population exceeded 15,000.

As already mentioned, South Australia was the only Australian colony that did not have convict origins. From the outset it was populated by free immigrants, who brought with them the culture and customs of their British and European homelands.

South Australia's economy received a welcome boost when copper was discovered in 1844 at Kapunda, some 79 kilometres north of Adelaide. The discovery attracted miners from Britain, mainly from Cornwall and Wales, who brought with them their traditional copper-mining skills. In the following year there was another copper discovery in Burra, 86 kilometres north of Kapunda. By the late 1840s there were 5000 people at Burra. The output from the mines there represented three-fifths of the copper exported from South Australia. To the west, at Moonta on the Yorke Peninsula, there was yet another important copper discovery in 1861.

These were Australia's first successful underground mining operations. The mines continued to operate until 1877, although some open-cut mining was resumed in 1971. As a result of the copper mining boom the colony became Australia's principal exporter of minerals.

In addition to the Cornish and Welsh miners, people of other nationalities were attracted to South Australia, notably German settlers who arrived in Adelaide in 1838–39 seeking freedom and peaceful surroundings to practise their Lutheran way of life. Some settled in the Barossa Valley, north-east of Adelaide and now one of Australia's principal wine-producing areas. Others were attracted to the Adelaide Hills, south-east of the city, and settled in the Hahndorf and Mount Barker areas.

A building boom in the late 1870s converted Adelaide into a prosperous city.

RIDGWAY NEWLAND

Apart from the Welsh and Cornish miners, there was another group that arrived in South Australia in the first part of the nineteenth century. They were pioneers of a different kind, and they were intent on a quite different mission.

In England in 1817, 27-year-old Ridgway Newland was ordained as a Congregationalist minister. Twenty-two years later, when the Colonial Missionary Society decided to sponsor a settlement in South Australia, Newland was selected to lead a group of thirty colonists. He was accompanied by his second wife and their eight children.

The group went immediately to Encounter Bay, in South Australia where the Murray River meets the Southern Ocean, and where a large area of land had been acquired. With commendable energy Newland and his party set about constructing houses to form a small settlement which they named Yelki. The group was both innovative and versatile—from the local clay they made jars and the favoured milk dishes used at that time, whilst whale bones were crushed and sent to the potteries in England.

Livestock did not prosper on the coast, but crops did. Within two years Newland was able to inform South Australia's governor that the local Aboriginal people were becoming as adept as the immigrants in sowing and reaping their crops of wheat, oats and barley. The settlement soon became self-sufficient.

Newland opened his first chapel at Encounter Bay in 1846. Further places of worship were built in succeeding years. But Newland did a great deal more than attend to the spiritual needs of his community. There was no other pastor in the south, so it was not unusual for him to ride long distances to minister to isolated settlers. On a number of occasions he walked the 80 kilometres to Adelaide carrying a bundle of necessities and wading across three rivers on the journey.

In due course Newland was appointed a Justice of the Peace. He became active in local affairs, chairing meetings and always encouraging debate. He had the ability to influence public opinion to his way of thinking, but without offending others' points of view or in any way limiting discussion. He was also a district councillor and an active campaigner for the construction of roads and bridges.

On a return journey from Adelaide in 1864, the coach Newland was travelling in capsized and he was fatally injured. He was seventy-four years old.

Ridgway Newland was a fine man and an inspiring Christian leader. The little Colonial Missionary Society community had made a useful contribution to their adopted country.

RIVER TRADE

In 1850 the South Australian government, desirous of promoting river trading, offered a £4000 bonus 'to be equally divided between the first two iron steamers ... to successfully navigate the waters of the River Murray ... to at least the junction of the Darling.'

The challenge was quickly taken up by two men: Francis Cadell, the Scottish-born son of a wealthy ship builder and mine owner, who at that time was engaged in the Australian coastal trade; and William Randell, who had been brought up on the banks of the Murray, working first in his father's flour mill, then as manager of the family's grazing interests.

It is here that two ladies enter upon the scene. One was *Lady Augusta*, a Mississippi-style paddle-steamer, which Cadell had built in Sydney and sailed to South Australia. The other was the *Mary Ann*, a steamer constructed by William Randell and his brothers Thomas and Elliott with the help of local tradesmen.

On 25 August 1853, the *Mary Ann* set off from the South Australian town of Mannum, north of Murray Bridge, with William Randell at the helm. Ten days later the *Lady Augusta* set off in hot pursuit, with Cadell at the wheel and the South Australian Governor, Sir Henry Fox Young, and his wife, Lady Augusta, on board.

For almost three weeks the two paddle-steamers raced neck and neck, boilers at full pressure. Snags and obstacles were somehow avoided. With Swan Hill in sight, the *Lady Augusta* finally forged ahead, enabling Cadell to claim victory and his £2000 share of the prize before returning to his starting point, Goolwa, near the river's mouth. But the government denied Randell his share on the pretext that his vessel did not comply with certain regulations.

Randell, more concerned with river trade prospects than with gratuitous publicity, continued as far as Moama (near Echuca), some 1700 kilometres from the river's mouth. The South Australian government belatedly granted Randell £600 for his efforts. The public's response to this modest handout was to 'pass the hat around', providing Randell with a £400 testimonial.

Over the next eight years, Cadell, Randell and others continued their exploration of the upper reaches of the Murray and its main tributaries, the Darling and the Murrumbidgee. River trade rapidly developed and thrived over the next thirty years, then declined as the twentieth century approached.

In 1886 the Victorian government induced two Americans, the Chaffey brothers (see p. 138), to come from the United States to establish an irrigation settlement. But their imaginative schemes were not entirely successful due to the settlers' lack of confidence in their projects. Notwithstanding, the Chaffey brothers' proposals were to result in significant benefits to farming, particularly the dried fruits and wine industries in the southern colonies.

River trade was always at the mercy of the periodic floods and droughts which significantly affected the river's navigable water levels. To control the loss of water to the sea during times of flood, it became clear that a system of locks and weirs was necessary. Eventually, thirteen locks on the Murray and two on the Darling eliminated some of the uncertainties of river navigation, although numerous unseen tree snags were an ever-present hazard on various stretches of the rivers.

The construction of a railway line to Melbourne gave a boost to trade through the port of Echuca, but it was the flexibility and reliability of road transport that was to diminish the Murray's importance as an artery of trade.

If there is some controversy over the Murray's present-day source, so also was there some disagreement over the river's other end—the Mouth. Most of the early steamer captains refused to attempt the treacherous and shifting sandbars that marked the narrow entrance to Lake Alexandrina from the Southern Ocean. A few attempted the feared passage. However, Captain George Johnston, who Cadell brought from Scotland in 1852, was on board the *Lady Augusta* when it safely negotiated the Mouth on its maiden voyage from Sydney. Johnston then regularly negotiated the Mouth for thirty-six years.

But in 1879 the *Queen of the South*, with Captain Johnston in command, was caught by the Mouth's shifting sand. Cargo, including a grand piano, was jettisoned. Eventually, with the help of a favourable tide, the lightened steamer managed to get through. Other vessels retrieved some of the cargo, including the grand piano, which was found floating in Lake Alexandrina.

Cadell was active on the Murray for several years after the race, but his own business, the River Murray Navigation Co., failed in 1861. In 1864 he undertook work in New Zealand. He was back on the Murray two years later; then in 1870 returned to New Zealand, began whaling and for a time was engaged in trading with the Islands. He disappeared in the Dutch East Indies in 1879.

With the 1853 race over, William Randell continued to work the river, first extending the *Mary Ann*'s hull, then mounting another hull alongside with the paddle-wheel between the two hulls. In 1858, with the redesigned vessel now named the *Gemini*, Randell succeeded in navigating the Murrumbidgee River to beyond Hay, a distance of 420 kilometres from the Murray junction. In the following year he tackled the Darling River, penetrating as far as Bourke, some 1500 kilometres from the junction. He then added another 100 kilometres to his journey by reaching Brewarrina, where further progress was blocked by rapids. Two years later, in 1861, and with the help of floods, Randell took the *Gemini* as far as Walgett, a distance of 1760 kilometres from the Murray junction and 2570 kilometres from the sea.

Randell, who had married in 1855, then engaged in various activities until 1899, when he handed over his business affairs to his son. Whilst living at Wentworth, he had been a Justice of the Peace in New South Wales, and was later a JP in South Australia. He was a member of the South Australian House of Assembly from 1896 to 1899. In failing health he moved to North Adelaide in 1910, and died there the following year, aged eighty-seven.

Cadell and Randell, and their paddle-wheeling ladies, earned an enduring place in the pioneering history of the Murray River.

COBB & CO.

In 1853, the same year as the Murray River race was held, another form of transport was finding its way into the pages of Australian history, and in doing so became a national icon. In America it was Wells, Fargo & Co. In Australia, Cobb & Co.

There were several American stagecoach makers—Adams & Co. was one—that updated and improved on the European version of the horse-drawn passenger carriage, but it was Wells, Fargo & Co. that subsequently caught the imagination of the Hollywood scriptwriters. So perhaps it was fitting that Freeman Cobb was an American. He remained on the Australian scene for just three years and one month, but that was time enough for his name to be perpetuated in the Australian story.

Cobb, in fact, was an employee of Adams & Co., operating coaches in California and Central America during the Californian gold rush days. In 1853 he arrived in Melbourne in company with a Wells, Fargo & Co. manager with the intention of starting an Australian branch of the firm. Several other American coach drivers and carriers arrived shortly after, obstensibly with the intention of capitalising on opportunities presented by the Victorian gold diggings. But neither Adams & Co. nor Wells, Fargo & Co. became established.

Cobb and three of the other Americans, however, seized on the opportunity and set up their own coaching firm. They used two 'Concord' thoroughbrace coaches, which Cobb had had shipped to Melbourne. Bad weather and the rough roads caused their venture to be abandoned but, undeterred, Cobb and his partners established 'Cobb & Co.' with financial assistance from an American entrepreneur.

For nearly two and a half years the firm, despite competition and without a mail contract, operated profitable passenger services, first from Melbourne to Port Melbourne and then to Castlemaine. Later, other routes in Victoria were opened. Cobb & Co. soon established a reputation for efficiency and reliability.

In May 1856, Cobb and his partners announced that the business had been sold to another American syndicate. Cobb departed for America a few days later, never to return to Australia's shores. One of the other partners also went back to America, whilst the third stayed on and settled in Victoria. There were a number of ownership changes in subsequent years as the business expanded and new routes were opened.

The great virtue of the Cobb & Co. coaches was that they were so light a team of horses could pull them across most creeks and out of almost any bog. At one time the firm controlled over 11,000 kilometres of mail coach routes and owned several stations, hundreds of coaches and 30,000 horses. By the mid-1870s it was possible to travel by Cobb & Co. from northern Queensland to South Australia, or on any of the thousands of kilometres of inland routes which connected to the main system.

Coaches continued to operate in Australia until the 1920s. Although the original partners had long since left the business, the Cobb & Co. name lived on and coaches continued to dominate the transport industry until August 1924, when the last Cobb & Co. coach ran from Yuleba to Surat in Queensland. It was the end of an era.

The final verse of Henry Lawson's poem 'The Lights of Cobb and Co.' conjures up images of the Cobb & Co. days:

Swift scramble up the sidling where teams climb inch by inch; Pause, bird-like, on the summit—then breakneck down the pinch; By clear, ridge-country rivers, and gaps where tracks run high, Where waits the lonely horseman, cut clear against the sky; Past haunted half-way houses—where convicts made the bricks— Scrub-yards and new bark shanties, we dash with five and six; Through stringy-bark and blue-gum, and box and pine we go— A hundred miles shall see tonight the lights of Cobb & Co.!

THE RAILWAYS

During the 1850s, other forms of transportation entered upon the Australian scene. In 1850 work began on the first planned railway line in Australia—the 125-kilometre route to Berrima, in the Southern Highlands south-west of Sydney.

In 1854 Australia's first steam-hauled train ran from the centre of Melbourne to Port Melbourne, a distance of 4 kilometres. In the same year, a 12-kilometre horse-drawn railway was opened from the South Australian town of Goolwa (the last port on the Murray River before it flows into the Southern Ocean) westwards to Port Elliot (a town midway between Goolwa and Victor Harbor).

In 1855 a line was opened from Sydney westwards to a station near to Parramatta, a distance of about 20 kilometres.

The first trains, apart from those pulled by horses, were drawn by steam locomotives. But if the method of propulsion is not the criterion, and a railway is thought of as a public service of vehicles using rails, then it could be said that Australia's first railway began operating in Van Diemen's Land as early as 1836.

It was a very odd affair. The railway was the brainchild of Captain O'Hara Booth, Commandant of the Van Diemen's Land settlement, who addressed the problem of transporting people from Hobart Town to Port Arthur. The normal route to Port Arthur was the sea passage around stormy Cape Raoul, likened by some to rounding Cape Horn.

There were no steam engines available at that time, but Captain Booth had an ample supply of another form of power—manpower, provided by the convicts under his command. His solution was to build a 7-kilometre railway line across the Tasman Peninsula. Passengers would cross the water to Norfolk Bay, then travel (from the site of the present-day town of Taranna) on the railway across the Peninsula to Long Bay (the present-day Oakwood). A further 5 kilometres by land or sea along the coast would bring them to Port Arthur, thus making the journey from Hobart Town somewhat longer but invariably less arduous than the Cape Raoul route, although not without some degree of excitement.

The line was built by convicts in 1836. Somewhat crude carriages with cast-iron wheels, each carriage having two double seats, ran on wooden rails cut from gum trees. Poles, on which convicts pushed or pulled, extended from the back and front of each carriage. There was a halfway stage where there was a change of convicts to haul the fare-paying passengers.

Considerable exertion was required to pull these rough vehicles up the several gradients, but when they came to downhill stretches the convicts would jump on the carriages and enjoy the helter-skelter ride. Speeds of up to 65 kilometres per hour were reported on some downhill sections, and it was not unknown for carriages to leave the rails on these sections, spilling passengers into the bush. But it seems that the railway was preferred to the rough sea passage round Cape Raoul.

The line remained open until 1877, and the innovative Captain Booth duly entered the history of railways in Australia.

In 1883, New South Wales and Victoria were first linked by rail at Albury, the border town on the Murray River. Four years later Victoria and South Australia were joined by rail, and in the following year New South Wales and

Queensland were linked. But it was not until 1917 that the completion of the railway line between Port Augusta and Kalgoorlie linked Western Australia with the east.

The spread of the railways came at a high price, for the colonies decided upon various gauges for their tracks. New South Wales elected to have the 4 foot 8½ inches (143 centimetres) gauge (which was the standard in Britain); whilst Victoria opted for 5 foot 3 inches (160 centimetres). South Australia chose the same gauge as Victoria, but also laid some tracks with the narrow 3 foot 6 inches gauge (106 centimetres). This was also the gauge decided upon by Queensland.

The folly of this lack of foresight soon became apparent to rail travellers between Sydney and Melbourne, passengers being required to change trains at Albury, which had what was at the time the world's longest platform (with a different gauge track on either side). Passengers had to transfer themselves and their baggage from one end of the platform to the other (involving a long walk), for the rolling stock from each of the colonies could go no further.

It was not until 1970 that the first freight train crossed the continent direct from east to west on the 4 foot 8½ inches (143 centimetres) standard-gauge Sydney-to-Perth line. This line includes the world's longest dead straight section of railway track, 475 kilometres in length, which crosses part of the 1000-kilometre width of the totally flat and almost waterless Nullarbor Plain.

BURKE AND WILLS

In 1857 the Royal Society of Victoria, a progressive institution, put forward a proposal that the Australian interior should be explored by making an overland journey from Melbourne to the north.

An expedition, more elaborate than any previous Australian expedition, was quickly organised and a leader chosen. He was Robert O'Hara Burke, an Irish soldier who had migrated to Tasmania in 1853, had become a police inspector in Melbourne and had then been transferred to the Victorian goldfields. The expedition was financed jointly by the Victorian government and by public subscription.

In August 1860 the expedition set out from Melbourne, farewelled with the good wishes of a large crowd. The party comprised fifteen men, twenty-three horses and twenty-seven heavily laden camels. Their objective was to find a transcontinental route through hitherto largely unexplored country.

Two months later an advance party had reached Menindee (approximately 107 kilometres south-east of present-day Broken Hill), where their first depot was established. Rather than wait for the remainder of the expedition, the impetuous Burke decided to press ahead accompanied by his second-in-command William Wills, and by William Brahe (the foreman), John King (who was in charge of the camels), four assistants and several camels. It was arranged that they would rendezvous with the main party at Cooper Creek, some 640 kilometres to the north. The advance party duly arrived there four weeks later and established a depot at nearby Innaminka (in northern South Australia).

Burke, aware that John Stuart's expedition from Adelaide would also be heading for the north coast, then decided to make a forced march to the Gulf of Carpentaria accompanied only by William Wills, John King, the expedition's surveyor, and one of the assistants, Charles Gray. They departed on 16 December with six camels and a horse. By mid-February 1861 they had reached the banks of the Bynoe River, only a few kilometres from the sea. But it was to be their northernmost point, for intense tropical storms and an impenetrable swamp prevented further progress.

After a day's rest they reluctantly set out on the return journey to the Cooper Creek depot. Nearing their immediate destination, Charles Gray died from exhaustion. Four days later, Burke, Wills and King reached the depot to discover warm ashes from a fire and a note indicating that the depot party, having waited for eighteen weeks and with some of the men beset by illness, had decided to return to Menindee. They had departed about eight hours before the arrival of Burke, Wills and King. However, they had buried some provisions at a spot marked on a coolibah tree by the inscription:

DIG

3 ft. N.W.

Apr. 21 1861

Some days later, the depot party, led by one of the foremen, William Brahe, met up with the main party, which had been moving slowly northwards under William Wright's leadership. Brahe and Wright then decided to return to the Cooper Creek depot, where they found the area of the food cache apparently undisturbed, although they did not verify whether the provisions had been taken.

Meanwhile, after two days rest but still weak from their ordeal, Burke, Wills and King had made the fateful decision to return by following the Cooper to the Strzelecki Creek and the Flinders Ranges towards the Mount Hopeless station in South Australia (so named by Edward Eyre), instead of travelling by the Menindee route. But after several days they were again overcome by exhaustion and despair. They ate the last of their poor-quality rations. Some friendly Aboriginal people kept them alive with gifts of fish and a type of seed cake, then for a further month they wandered slowly towards their objective until they could go no further. First Wills and then Burke died.

John King was the only one to survive, cared for by the friendly Aboriginal people. Nearly three months later he was found by Alfred Howitt, who was in charge of one of the four relief expeditions that had been organised. Although extremely weak, King was able to direct Howitt and his men to an Aboriginal shelter where they found Wills's remains. They found Burke's body three days later. Both of the dead explorers were buried where they lay. At the end of the year, Howitt returned to Cooper Creek to recover their bones and return them to Melbourne.

The tragedy of Burke and Wills had been written large in the annals of Australian exploration.

TELEGRAPHY

The technology of the 1850s brought an entirely new method of communication to Australia when, in 1854, the first telegraph line was opened between Melbourne and the outlying Williamstown—a distance of 17 kilometres. Within a few weeks, the first electric telegraph in Sydney had been opened.

In 1862, in the same week as the bleached bones of Burke and Wills were brought to Adelaide, the explorer John Stuart, his body in a grossly emaciated condition, and unaware of the disaster that had overtaken Burke and Wills, slowly made his way into the South Australian town of Clare, some 136 kilometres north of Adelaide. He and his small party had been the first to successfully complete the south-north transcontinental crossing and to return.

Stuart's great feat inspired thoughts of an overland telegraph line to link Australia with the rest of the world. Within ten years that dream had become a reality.

The first overseas telegram had been sent from England to France in 1850 after a submarine cable had been laid beneath the English Channel. By 1866 an operative cable was in use across the Atlantic Ocean. Two years later there was a telegraph cable reaching to Bombay. In 1869, by which time Darwin (then known as Palmerston) had been established as a permanent town, the British–Australian Telegraph Company mooted the idea of extending the cable to Darwin, hence an overland line could be laid to Port Augusta (322 kilometres north of Adelaide).

The South Australian government immediately realised the commercial benefits of this proposal. There was also the advantage of prompt communication with Port Darwin, for at that time the South Australian government was responsible for administration of the Northern Territory, with communication between Adelaide and Darwin possible only by the coastal sea route—a journey that usually took six to eight weeks.

Accordingly, the South Australian government concluded an agreement with the British–Australian Telegraph Company. But conditions were written into the agreement—one being that the overland line should be completed by 1 January 1872; another imposing a late penalty of £100 a day (a lot of money at that time) for every day over the agreed completion date. The South Australian government now had just fifteen months to complete the mammoth task of stringing the telegraph line over 3000 kilometres of harsh and trackless territory.

In 1861–62, as we have noted, John Stuart, at the third attempt, had succeeded in crossing the continent northwards from Adelaide. One of the main problems he encountered was water—or the lack of it. Another was the sheer logistics of the telegraph undertaking. Poles, wire, insulators and other equipment, together with supplies for the working parties and feed for the animals, had to be transported from Port Augusta into the semi-desert. Equipment and supplies for the northern party, which was to work southwards from the tiny settlement of Port Darwin, had to be sent by the long sea route from Adelaide.

The first pole at Port Darwin was planted with due ceremony on 15 September 1870. Work began on the following day. From the south, the first section of the route was relatively easy. The arid and difficult terrain of the central section was eventually completed on schedule. But it was the northern section that was to cause a major problem, for no-one had thought about 'the Wet'. (In northern areas, the annual wet season lasts from approximately the end of November until the middle of April.)

The rains arrived on schedule in November, transforming the land into a sea of mud and the rivers into raging torrents. The linesmen sank to their knees in the mud, which would not support the poles. Bullocks and horses were finding it increasingly difficult to work in the soggy conditions, and were unable to forage for themselves. Clothing and equipment became saturated, whilst men and beasts were tormented by flies, particularly blowflies and mosquitos. Many of the men suffered from dysentery, and all from 'prickly heat'. The flour, full of weevils and tiny grubs, was mostly inedible. The heat, the enervating humidity and the almost continuous rain made conditions unbearable.

Small wonder, then, that in March 1871 some fifty-six of the northern party voted to go on strike.

In April the rains ceased and work resumed at full speed. But in London, the British–Australian Telegraph Company's directors, unsympathetic to the severe problems which beset the South Australian government, invoked the time-delay penalty and threatened to route the telegraph line through Queensland.

Whilst the arguments were going on, the southern and northern lines were finally joined on 22 August 1872. Celebrations were duly held in Adelaide, Sydney and London to mark the end of Australia's communications isolation.

Meanwhile, fate intervened. For the British–American Company's submarine cable to Darwin, laid beneath the Timor Sea, had gone dead! Unable to restrain his glee, the South Australian Treasurer sent a message to London referring to the interruption in the working of the Company's submarine cable and to the contractual penalty clause which now applied. The fault in the cable was repaired and the service restored on 21 October 1872, but the London company had no choice but to pay up for their breach of the agreements.

And so, despite the immense difficulties, the Overland Telegraph Line was completed. Some 36 000 ironwood poles had been planted over a distance of 3177 kilometres in mostly unexplored terrain and in conditions that were never good, and frequently appalling.

It was never going to be possible for the South Australian government to complete the work in the contractual time. In the event, the job was done in a little over two years. It was a mighty achievement by men possessed of outstanding courage and tenacity.

THE DISCOVERY OF GOLD

The finding of gold in Australia triggered a succession of gold rushes. The Victorian gold rush began within a few months of the New South Wales discoveries in the Bathurst region in 1851. Rich finds were made in a belt of country north-west of Melbourne: in the Ballarat area, at Bendigo and nearby Mount Alexander, on the Broken River (north of Shepperton) and at other locations.

Within the next few years gold was found at a succession of places northwards along the length of Australia's Great Dividing Range. In timbered hills north of Brisbane, James Nash discovered the Gympie reefs in 1867 and started one of the wildest gold rushes in Queensland's history.

The various discoveries quickly attracted gold-seekers from far and wide, some from overseas ...

BERNHARDT HOLTERMANN

Bernhardt Holtermann had unsuccessfully prospected for gold during the 1849 Californian gold rush. He arrived in Australia in 1858, where he found that his brother, Herman, had gone to the goldfields. Being unable to secure work in Sydney, Holtermann took a job as steward on a Pacific Islands schooner, then as a waiter in Sydney. Later he met a Polish miner, Louis Beyers, and in 1861 the two decided to go prospecting on the Hawkins Hill site at the Hill End goldfield north of Bathurst.

At first they had little success. In 1868, after a windfall crushing provided some much-needed finance, Holtermann became licensee of one of Hill End's early public houses—the All Nations Hotel in Clarke Street. Shortly afterwards he married Harriett Emmett, whose sister, Mary, married Louis Beyers on the same day.

Holtermann sold the hotel in the following year, then made some unwise business investments and had to resort to ferrying passengers across the Macquarie River to make a living.

In 1871 there were spectacular crushings along the Hawkins Hill line of reefs, and by the following year Hill End had become a boom town. The rapid expansion brought a demand for real estate. The speculators moved in and began staking claims in land around the town, Beyers and Holtermann among them.

By the following year Holtermann was manager of the Star of Hope mine. It was there, on 19 October 1872, that a charge was exploded which revealed a virtual wall of gold and rock—the largest specimen of reef gold ever discovered.

When Holtermann was informed of the find he gave instructions for it to be removed intact. The specimen, which weighed 286 kilograms and came to be known as Holtermann's Star of Hope Nugget, was taken to Hodson's Store where it was photographed by a freelance photographer, Beaufoy Merlin, and his young assistant, Charles Bayliss (the two had earlier established a photographic studio, the A & A Photographic Company, at Hill End).

When the mine company was unable to agree on a price for the specimen, the rock was crushed, yielding 3000 ounces (93.2 kilograms) of pure gold. It meant a windfall dividend for the company's investors.

Holtermann's interest then turned to the commercial possibilities of photography, for Merlin had floated the idea of a comprehensive series of photographs depicting scenes in New South Wales and Victoria, to be sent abroad to encourage emigration.

Merlin died in 1873 when much of the work had been done, the project being completed by Bayliss.

By then Holtermann had built a large house on Sydney's North Shore, complete with a tower containing a stained-glass window depicting Holtermann standing beside the huge Star of Hope nugget. The view from the tower was to inspire in young Bayliss the idea of photographing Sydney's spectacular scenery by the wet plate process, which involved making two negatives, each measuring about 95 by 160 centimetres. At that time, when little was known of the technique of photographic enlargement, these were the largest photographs ever taken using the collodian process.

Bayliss's photographs were duly exhibited overseas and received several awards. Holtermann himself took sets of the photographs to

America and Europe and arranged for their exhibition. From Germany he brought back a consignment of lager beer, being the first to introduce this particular brew to Australia.

In 1882 Holtermann stood for parliament and represented the constituency of St Leonards, on Sydney's North Shore, until 1885. He was then especially interested in promoting immigration and in the development of North Sydney. It was at this time that Holtermann put forward the idea of a 'North Shore Bridge' and offered to contribute £5000 to the project.

Holtermann died in 1885, aged forty-seven. Notwithstanding the massive Hawkins Hill gold find, he is mainly remembered today for the large collection of photographs that he sponsored.

Fortunately, the Merlin and Bayliss plates were preserved by the Holtermann family, providing a unique record of the Hill End goldfields and of New South Wales and Victorian localities at the time.

Events were to prove that a particular date associated with Bernhardt Holtermann gave rise to an unusual coincidence. He was born on 29 April, arrived in Australia on 29 April, and died on 29 April.

THE EUREKA STOCKADE

For the miners and others attracted to the goldfields, conditions were invariably harsh. The working hours were long, sanitation was primitive, and the rudimentary accommodation usually provided inadequate shelter from rain and the cold winter nights. There was little relief from the irritations of summer heat, flies and dust. The authorities were poorly equipped to maintain some semblance of law and order; thieving was commonplace; disputes were frequent; and more serious crimes were often punished by rough justice meted out by the miners themselves.

The introduction of licensing fees was a constant source of irritation to the miners. At the Ballarat goldfields in Victoria in 1854, the miners' antagonism came to a head over the imposition of a monthly licensing fee, especially when they were required to make the payments at a location distant from the main mining centres. Periodic licence checks by the police fuelled the miners' resentment.

The unrest culminated in the formation of the Ballarat Reform League, which put forward a series of demands to the Legislative Council. Towards the end of 1854 a posse of police confronted the Ballarat miners with the intention of inspecting their licences, which the miners had by then refused to carry. Flashpoint was reached when a group of miners burnt down the Eureka Hotel, whose proprietor had been acquitted on a charge of murdering a miner. About 500 miners erected a stockade near the hotel, defying the police and army detachments which had arrived in support.

At daybreak on the following day the troops and police attacked the stockade and soon overpowered the miners. When the dust had settled, twenty-four of the miners lay dead, whilst five soldiers had been killed and another dozen, including a policeman, were wounded.

In Melbourne, some supported the actions of the authorities, whilst others were on the side of the miners, thirteen of whom were tried for treason. Their later acquittal lent support to the popular view of respect for the rights of the individual and abhorrence of the use of undue physical violence when conflicts arose.

In time to come, the blue Eureka flag, with its white cross and five stars, was to become something of a symbol of freedom to the oppressed.

THE LAND BILLS

In 1861, Land Bills were introduced by John Robertson, the New South Wales Secretary for Lands, which opened up Crown land to free selection prior to surveying. Similar legislation was enacted in Queensland and South Australia.

Under the legislation, squatters were able to protect their runs by selecting the best of the land, a process which became known as 'peacocking'. By this means, unscrupulous squatters were sometimes able to secure title to land fronting rivers and creeks, thus denying selectors the use of water for their stock. Another subterfuge which became commonplace was for a squatter to select land in the names of his family, friends or employees (a procedure known as 'dummying').

As a result of the Selection Acts, many of the selectors, a proportion of whom were immigrant families, acquired properties that were unsuitable for small-scale farming. This caused impoverishment for many free selectors, particularly in New South Wales and Victoria. They lacked the capital to improve their land, and were thus squeezed out by the larger and well-established squatters. Disillusionment resulted.

Arising from this situation, few of the selectors gave much thought to soil management. Areas planted with wheat, for example, were steadily enlarged, so that the soil tended to become exhausted, giving progressively lower acreage yields.

By the 1880s, in many areas of New South Wales, Victoria and parts of South Australia, the decaying remnants of timber shacks, brick chimneys, stone walls and broken fences bore testimony to the failure of the experiment in establishing small-scale farming in rural Australia. Success would only come to those with sufficient capital, determination and, most significantly, good land.

The eight-year drought from 1895 to 1903, following upon the 1891–94 economic depression and the succession of bank failures, resulted in difficult times for many of the selectors, as well as for the growing numbers of unemployed in the towns.

JAMES LITCHFIELD

For a young English farmer to successfully meet the challenges of nineteenth-century grazing in New South Wales, adaptability and determination were both required. James Litchfield had these qualities in good measure.

He married at the age of twenty-seven, setting sail almost immediately for Sydney with his bride to try his fortune in a new land. Arriving in 1852 with only a little capital but good references, James Litchfield was able to secure an appointment as overseer at a station at Coolringdon, in the Monaro region in southern New South Wales. The station was one of about twenty sheep runs owned by William Bradley. Young Litchfield adapted well, and three years later Bradley made him manager of his Myalla station.

Bradley encouraged his managers to take up land for themselves, but Litchfield thought the time inopportune to invest his limited capital. But with the passing in 1861 of the government's Land Bills (see pp. 122–4), he made his first investment—a 130-hectare run at Jillamatong in the Monaro. Through selection and purchase, Litchfield gradually extended his holdings by 'dummying'; in Litchfield's case, in the names of his children and employees. Litchfield later gave evidence to a parliamentary committee stating that he disliked this practice, but regarded it as a necessary evil whilst the existing laws governing land acquisition remained.

Litchfield's experience in the Monaro had convinced him of the desirability of producing a strain of sheep suitable to the dry, windy and at times very cold conditions for which the area was renowned. In 1865, at his Hazeldean merino stud (which was to become famous) he began stocking the progeny of Rambouillet ewes; then later he imported selected merinos, mainly of Saxon descent, from Tasmanian studs.

By 1884 Litchfield held more than 8000 hectares in the Monaro on which he ran some 15,000 sheep. By the early 1890s he had established the renowned Wanganella strain at Hazeldean, and in 1891 he retired to Sydney, dividing his properties amongst his four sons.

James Litchfield was a shrewd, hardworking and intelligent pastoralist and sheep-breeder. He had little interest in politics, although he actively associated himself with land organisations in the Cooma district, as well as the Cooma School of Arts and the Church of England. He died in Sydney in 1905, aged eighty.

FREDERICK DALGETY

As we have noted, the rapid expansion of the pastoral industry in Australia during the second half of the nineteenth century was due in part to the intrepid pioneers who harnessed the land for their purposes. The success of their enterprises, however, depended not only upon their skills and hard work but also upon those who were able to provide finance, transport and storage facilities, and marketing expertise.

Britain made available much of the capital and became the principal market for the nineteenth-century Australian pastoral industry. One of the main figures to provide the essential links between the Australian producers and the British market was a young man from Canada, Frederick Dalgety, who made an important contribution to the Australian economy by organising large-scale financial facilities and by developing overseas markets.

Dalgety arrived in Sydney from Canada in 1834 at the age of seventeen. For eight years he worked as a clerk, then moved to Melbourne as manager of a newly established firm. In the course of time he perceived the opportunities presented by 'the settlers' trade', whereby the squatters would be provided with essential merchandise, and in return the business would buy their produce. Within six years he owned the business and had become established as a successful merchant.

Dalgety visited England in 1849 to find market outlets for the squatters' produce and to arrange credit facilities to finance the trade. Returning to Australia in 1851, he capitalised on opportunities that the gold rush offered. He expanded his pastoral business, sold merchandise to the diggers, and reaped a bonanza on gold speculations.

In 1854 Dalgety again travelled to London to establish an office there to handle trading opportunities presented by the Victorian pastoral industry. He now had three partners: Frederick Du Croz, who was Dalgety's most important partner and chief administrator, residing in London; C. Ibbotson, stationed in Geelong and managing the Victorian end of the business; and James Blackwood, who Dalgety had known since the early 1840s, and who forsook a banking career to become managing partner of the Melbourne office. For the next twenty-seven years these four men managed and directed the successful and respected Dalgety & Co. Ltd's businesses in Australia, New Zealand and Britain. It was not until 1884 that another partner, E.T. Doxat, was added to manage the London office.

Dalgety moved permanently to England in 1859, making only one last visit (in 1881) to Australia and New Zealand. By then the firm had offices in London, Melbourne, Geelong, Sydney, Launceston, Dunedin and Christchurch. Branches were later opened in Queensland and Western Australia. The combined capital of the business was £900,000, of which Dalgety held a third. He remained chairman of directors of the joint-stock company until his death in 1894, at the age of seventy-seven.

As the Australian pastoral industry grew, so too did the Dalgety business. Wool was the core of the firm's overseas shipments—by 1880 over 70,000 bales per year were being exported. Marketing, however, was only a part of the business. Just as important were the facilities the firm provided for the graziers and wool-growers: transport services, storage, finance, insurance, wool sales and technical advice.

From the 1860s onwards, pastoralists were required to make increasingly large capital outlays. Dalgety was in a unique position to attract long-term British capital to support the Australian and New Zealand pastoral industries, and in doing so his firm played a significant role in the growth of the rural industries in both countries.

THE NORTHERN TERRITORY

In 1862 the South Australian government in Adelaide assumed administrative control of the Northern Territory. In 1911, Palmerston, the Territory's main centre, was renamed Darwin (after Charles Darwin, the distinguished British scientist, who had visited Australia in 1836 and whose ground-breaking work *The Origin of Species* was first published in 1859). Also in 1911 the administration of the Northern Territory was transferred to the Commonwealth of Australia. The 'Top End', as the Northern Territory is now generally known, became self-governing in 1978 with an Administrator and a unicameral parliament.

LATER GOLD RUSHES

In the 1870s gold was discovered at Charters Towers (inland from Townsville in northern Queensland) and on the Palmer River (in the Cape York Peninsula in Queensland's far north). The latter site was to become Australia's then largest goldfield.

In 1880, at Mount Morgan (near Rockhampton, on Queensland's mid-north coast), a stockman discovered what was to prove to be the country's richest gold mine at that time.

At about the same time, 2000 kilometres to the west, in the Kimberley district in the north of Western Australia, an itinerant bushman from the coastal town of Roebourne, Charles Hall, found gold at Hall's Creek in 1885. The find set in motion the longest overland gold rush Australia had seen.

From the Kimberley district in 1886, the search for gold then spread southwards as finds were made in the Pilbara district (between the De Grey and the Ashburton rivers in north-western Western Australia), and in the Murchison district (about 650 kilometres north of Perth), then at the Yilgarn and Southern Cross reefs (about 370 kilometres east of Perth). The rush continued as thousands of men moved from one prospect to another.

To the east of Southern Cross is an undulating plain covered with millions of eucalypt trees. The miners considered it a desert. The plain was certainly deserted, but it wasn't desert. In 1888 it represented a very real barrier to the gold-seekers who had arrived at Southern Cross and wished to prospect eastwards ...

ARTHUR BAYLEY AND WILLIAM FORD

Amongst the searchers probing east from Southern Cross were Arthur Bayley and William Ford. Bayley, a tall man with a magnificent physique and a liking for gambling, had mined gold in Queensland and on all the Western Australian fields except the Kimberley. He was a tough, gregarious and hard-drinking prospector of whom it was said that he could 'smell' gold. Ford was cautious, wiry and somewhat older than Bayley. He had first seen Bayley fighting in the streets of Croydon in northern Queensland. They met again at Southern Cross, and there decided to team up on the move eastwards.

Bayley, who had found gold on the Murchison (a westwards-flowing river which reaches the Indian Ocean at Kalbarri), had sufficient funds to buy ten horses and enough food for several months. In the winter of 1892, he and Ford rode out towards the rising sun and continued for approximately 250 kilometres before retracing their steps to refill their waterbags. Finding a small rock hole of water, they decided to camp for the night and prospect. First thing next morning, as he was rounding up the horses, Bayley came upon a nugget weighing half an ounce. He hurried back to camp for breakfast, then he and Ford began systematically 'specking' (a mode of prospecting involving close examination of the topsoil for specks and bits) the area. By late afternoon they had gathered 20 ounces. A month later they had gold worth £800. Now short of rations, they returned to Southern Cross, reloaded the packhorses with supplies, then quietly left town.

But they were not unobserved and were followed, although at a slower pace, by a group of miners who were then on strike. They eventually found Bayley and Ford working at a saucer-shaped depression on the plain. Astonished at the sight of gold glittering in the sunlight, the newcomers each collected several ounces for themselves before being warned off by Bayley.

Three months later, after their claim had been registered, the partners had found gold worth £8000—a considerable sum in those days. They then decided to sell the claim—now known as Bayley's Reward—to a Broken Hill syndicate, which happened to be on its way to inspect the Murchison mines. An offer of £6000 was accepted for a five-sixth share of the mine. The syndicate then floated the mine as a public company. One-twelfth of the shares were allocated to George McCulloch, one of the original Broken Hill syndicate (see p. 134). After acquiring one fortune from the rich lodes of silver and lead, McCulloch now had another from gold, for Bayley's Reward proved to be a bonanza.

The mine continued to yield gold for many years, but Arthur Bayley was not to reap the benefits of his success for long. The likeable, hard-driving ruffian became a gentleman and bought a sheep station in Victoria, but died shortly after aged thirty-four. The present town of Coolgardie (557 kilometres east of Perth) is Bayley's memorial.

These men were different from the prospectors who had blazed the gold trail in eastern Australia. No longer did they employ Aboriginal people to tend their horses and to guide them to water and, sometimes, directly to the gold. The new breed of prospectors were men who frequently travelled alone, were less dependent on water and nearby sources of provisions and supplies, and who could more readily endure intense heat, dust and privation. They had mastered the arts of specking and dry-blowing.

PATRICK HANNAN AND SAM PEARCE

Patrick Hannan had arrived in Victoria from Ireland in 1862. He was short and slim, never talkative and with a predilection for keeping his thoughts to himself. These qualities were desirable for a prospector, and that's what Hannan set out to be. Gold held an intense fascination for him.

Hannan learned to find water before searching for gold. He realised the advantages of travelling lightly and away from sources of supply. He adapted himself to working in dry terrain.

Thus it was that, in June 1893, Hannan was following the new rush east from Coolgardie. With him were two other Irishmen, Thomas Flanagan and Dan O'Shea. They were in no hurry, checking on the waterholes and carefully surveying the ground away from the wagon trails.

Their thoroughness paid dividends—big dividends. For, on the side of a low range of hills, Hannan found a slug of gold, then gold in quartz. They dug into the red earth and winnowed the soil. The area was known to the Aboriginal people as Kalgurli. The town-to-be was first named 'Kalcurli', then 'Hannan's Find' or simply 'Hannan's'. It is now Kalgoorlie (596 kilometres east of Perth), and that is where the quartz reefs that Hannan discovered are located. But it was in the greenstone, about 8 kilometres south of the town and extending for about 3 kilometres, that the phenomenally rich lodes were found. They called this area, where the three Irishmen had stood, the Golden Mile.

Within a week, 2000 men went to 'Hannan's Rush' and found hundreds of ounces of gold for the taking. Patrick Hannan hurriedly pegged his 20-acre claim and considered he had the richest mine in Kalgoorlie. He ignored the brown ironstone hills a short distance to the south. So did all the new arrivals—apart from Sam Pearce.

The Pearce family migrated to South Australia in 1849. Sam's parents opened a store at the copper-mining town of Kapunda, where young Sam's interest in minerals was undoubtedly stimulated. But at heart he was an adventurer, and as a youth he ran away to sea. But he returned to Kapunda and there, at the age of nineteen, married a miner's daughter. The pair moved to a newly opened agricultural settlement at Belalie, and there for eight years they struggled to make a living from farming. Sam, believing in the rewards of prospecting, joined in any local rushes, and he discovered traces of various metals on the farm.

Like Hannan, Pearce went prospecting wherever there was a 'smell' of gold. He was in Kalgoorlie in 1893 when Hannan made his famous discovery. It was Pearce who prospected many of the great mines in the area. His first discovery was the Ivanhoe reef. Other famous mines soon followed: the phenomenally rich Great Boulder; then, in association with William Brookman and Charles de Rose, Pearce pegged out the Lake View and a handful of other profitable mines including the rich Golden Horseshoe, Boulder Perseverance, Star and The Australia Mine (Associated).

Development of these and other mines required substantial finance not available to Pearce's syndicate. At the instigation of William Brookman's brother, (Sir) George Brookman, an Adelaide-based company—the Coolgardie Gold Mining & Prospecting Co. Ltd—was formed. This resulted in funds becoming available through the floating of the larger claims in London. Pearce had a share agreement with the Adelaide company, but he received only a fraction of the rewards which were soon to flow to shareholders.

Sam Pearce, tall, strong, gregarious and ever ready to 'shout the bar' whenever he had surplus cash, went on prospecting for the next thirty-five years. He discovered other mines in the Golden Mile—amongst them the Leviathan and the rich Lady Mary (named after his wife). Then he went prospecting elsewhere for diamonds, rubies and silver from the Klondyke to California, across the Mexican sierras, in Africa and in every state in Australia. He took his family on a world tour. In old age he led an expedition to the MacDonnell Ranges, west of Alice Springs, still following the gleam of gold.

It was Hannan whose name is remembered at Kalgoorlie and whose statue in the town's main street is a fitting monument to him. But it was Pearce and William Brookman who held the best claims to the south of the town.

Apart from the lure of gold, Pat Hannan and Sam Pearce, so different in physique and personality, had something else in common: they lived to a ripe old age. Hannan died in Melbourne in 1925 aged eighty-two. Pearce died in Adelaide on the first day of 1932, aged eighty-four.

SILVER

The mining boom, which began with discoveries of copper in South Australia in 1844 and gold in New South Wales and Victoria in 1851, was followed by a boom in another metal—silver. In 1882, rich deposits were found at Silverton in north-west New South Wales, not far north of the present city of Broken Hill. The silver lodes, however, were exhausted by 1885. But by that time a much more important and long-lasting development had occurred about 20 kilometres to the south-east ...

THE BROKEN HILL PROPRIETARY COMPANY

The Mount Gipps station, in north-west New South Wales, was a not-very-remunerative sheep property. It had been acquired in 1866 by a Melbourne firm, McCulloch, Sellars and Co. In the following year, George McCulloch, a nephew of one of the principals, arrived at the station as manager.

At that time fossickers from Ballarat were 'working' the area in quest of gold. They were unsuccessful but nevertheless sunk several unauthorised potholes and were warned off by McCulloch.

In 1871 Charles Rasp arrived at the Mount Gipps station and was hired as a boundary rider (a station hand responsible for repairing fences and preventing stock from straying). He said later that 'my business during shearing time was to go to five different paddocks and find a sufficient number of sheep for shearing. This enabled me to know pretty well the whole of the run.'

Rasp was not quite the normal station hand. He was born in Germany in 1846, where he became a clerk in a chemical firm and later trained as an edible oil technologist with a large chemical manufacturing company. He spoke fluent English and French as well as his native language.

Rasp developed a serious lung weakness and decided to settle in a warmer climate. He arrived in Melbourne in 1869, worked for a short while pruning vines, then went prospecting on the Victorian goldfields. But the days of the big strikes were over, and the harsh conditions prompted him to move north to New South Wales. He found work at Mount Gipps more congenial.

Silver had recently been discovered at the nearby Silverton and Day Dream mines, and station hands throughout the area were constantly on the lookout for traces of the metal.

At one corner of the Mount Gipps run was a long, rectangular hill. Its crest, which somewhat resembled a ragged-toothed saw, had layers of manganiferous ironstone, blocks of which littered the lower slopes. The hill, commonly known as 'The Hog's Back', had undoubtedly been investigated by itinerant prospectors, but they had found no traces of the chlorides of silver which had been discovered not far away.

On 5 September 1883, Rasp decided to have another look at the rocks on the crest of the hill. Picking up some of the black specimens of the ironstone outcrop, he noted that they were heavier and different from rocks at the various small silver mines in the district. From his earlier knowledge of chemistry, Rasp knew that rocks containing valuable minerals usually had a higher specific gravity. He concluded that he had discovered a 'mountain of tin'.

Back at the homestead that evening, Rasp discussed his finding with the two bullock-owners, David James and James Poole, who were then doing contract work for the station. They decided to go into partnership and to peg out a claim at the site of the heaviest outcrop. That site was later known as Block 11.

Such was Rasp's conviction about the find that he decided to give notice to his employers. Discussing this, the station manager, George McCulloch, suggested that Rasp should extend the partnership in order to provide more working capital. McCulloch, with his knowledge of business affairs, offered to join the syndicate. Rasp saw the sense of this, and three more of the station staff agreed to join the venture: George Lind, the bookkeeper and storekeeper; George Urquhart, one of the overseers; and Philip Charley, the jackeroo. The seven partners now put in £50 apiece, each having one share, plus £1 per week each to meet operating expenses.

With the money now available, the syndicate took out three further blocks—Nos. 12, 13 and 14. Later, to keep 'troublesome neighbours' away, they took out additional blocks at each end—No. 10 to the south and Nos. 15 and 16 to the north. Their property, the main part of the ridge, now comprised one 80-acre block and six 40-acre blocks. It was more than 3 kilometres in length.

Conditions were very difficult during the first year's operations. They had no accommodation and little water. Provisions were scarce and the weather was very trying. The first shaft, in Block 15, produced carbonate of lead but only a very small percentage of silver. Further shafts in blocks 14 and 12 also produced large quantities of ore but little silver.

Doubts now arose amongst the syndicate. Some were against continuing, and one, Urquhart, the overseer, withdrew. Rasp, whose faith in the venture never wavered, bought his share for £10.

The main shaft was now deepened, and deepened again. Indications of chloride of silver gradually became more promising, and this prompted the remaining six members of the syndicate to form a non-listed company. It was floated with an initial capital of 16,000 £20 shares—14,000 of the shares going to the syndicate members and 2000 to the public to provide additional working capital. Finds of silver were now sufficient to keep the mine going.

Shares now began to change hands as speculator activity increased their value. Accordingly, the syndicate decided to float a public company, naming it after the hill. The company soon became Australia's largest—the Broken Hill Proprietary Company Limited, sometimes known as 'The Big Australian' or, more usually, 'BHP'.

In the 1880s it was considered that the width of a silver lode would not normally be more than about 5 feet (approximately 1.5 metres). In some places the Broken Hill lode exceeded 500 feet (152 metres). It became the world's largest silver–lead–zinc lode, and by the early 1980s had produced more than 200 million tonnes of ore.

When prospecting first began at Broken Hill in 1886 the 'town' consisted of a handful of tents, humpies (bush huts) and sheds, a few houses, three hotels, two blacksmith's shops and a general store. Two years later the population was over 6000. By 1891 it was 20,000 and still growing. The city of Broken Hill now has a population of about 25,000.

BHP ceased mining at Broken Hill in 1939, and its last treatment plant closed in the following year. By 1992 Pasminco (formed in 1988 by the merger of several of the remaining mining companies) was the only remaining operator at 'the hill'. One of the early mines, Delprat's, now operates as a tourist attraction, providing the public with the experience of descending the main shaft to 610 metres to appreciate something of half-a-century's working conditions in a silver-lead-zinc mine.

As the miners moved into Broken Hill, the original syndicate moved out. The only one of the seven to stay was George Urquhart, who spent his last years near Broken Hill. He died near the ghost town of Silverton in 1915.

James Poole, one of the bullock owners, sold half his interest to Sydney Kidman (see pp. 191–3) in exchange for some poor-quality bullocks, and later the other half for £4500. George Lind, the bookkeeper and storekeeper, sold out for only a modest profit and was not heard of again. David James, the other bullock owner, indulged his passion for horses and won the Melbourne Cup (see pp.158–60) in 1895. He became a member of the South Australian parliament in 1902. Philip Charley, the jackeroo, sold half his interest for £100 but held on to the other half. He was briefly a BHP director (at the age of twenty-one), and finally settled in a palatial house at Richmond, on Sydney's outskirts. George McCulloch, the former Mount Gipps manager, was a director of the young company for eight years and chairman in 1893. He later became a patron of the arts, retired to London and opened several salons for fashionable artists.

Charles Rasp married a German-born waitress in 1886. They bought a house in Adelaide which Rasp named *Willyama* (Broken Hill's official name), where his wife entertained in the grand manner. On such occasions Rasp would usually seek out a quiet corner to smoke his pipe and to yarn with a few friends, or would bury himself in his French or German books and enjoy a glass of two of his favourite German beer.

Charles Rasp became a director of several Kalgoorlie mining companies and held shares in others. He died in Adelaide in 1907, aged sixty-one. His estate was valued at £48,000.

IRRIGATION

Further south, the colonial governments were turning their thoughts to ways of alleviating the drought conditions that were adversely affecting agricultural production. During a visit to California in 1885, the Victorian attorney-general, Alfred Deakin, had been impressed by irrigation schemes developed by William and George Chaffey. Arising from Deakin's recommendation, the Victorian government granted the Chaffey brothers 250,000 acres (101,170 hectares) of land in 1888, as well as rights to use Murray River waters to develop irrigation farms.

Implementation of the scheme fostered the development of farming and the dried fruits and grape-growing industries in Victoria. Shortly afterwards, similar irrigation schemes were developed around Renmark in South Australia and Leeton in New South Wales.

There followed the discovery of vast deposits of artesian water in inland areas, to the immense benefit of agriculture and pastoralism in many hitherto unproductive regions.

Artesian water, however, could not alleviate much of the damage that the periodic severe droughts caused to the pastoral industry. During the prolonged drought from 1895 to 1903, for example, sheep numbers were nearly halved from 100 million to 54 million. However, agriculture developed during this difficult period, largely as the result of improvements in crop yields, soil conservation methods, better farming techniques and the introduction of innovative equipment ...

THE STUMP-JUMP PLOUGH

One of the problems faced by the early settlers, and many who came later, was the tilling of uncleared land. The presence of tree stumps, roots or stones could damage a conventional plough and retard the sowing of crops until the land was cleared.

At Ardrossan in South Australia, Robert Smith and his brother, Clarence, built the prototype of a machine on which the blades (shares) worked independently of one another so that, by means of an ingenious system of weights and balances, if the plough hit a root or rock it automatically moved over the obstacle and then returned to the ploughing position. They successfully demonstrated this 'stump-jump' plough in 1876 at the Moonta Agricultural Show on the Yorke Peninsula in South Australia.

After the Smith brothers had registered their machine in 1877 they were joined by a blacksmith, John Stott, who had produced a similar plough. The three joined forces and in 1881 patented a significantly improved machine. It was soon to revolutionise wheat farming by opening up large areas of light mallee scrub to speedy cultivation.

The Smith brothers' and Stott's invention looked like a normal plough but had its body suspended by a single bolt behind the cross standard instead of being secured to the frame. The body was longer than usual, allowing the coulter (iron blade) to be fixed to the body instead of to the frame. The coulter was adjusted to 13 millimetres below and the same distance forward of the share, so that it glided over obstacles. The coulter was then brought back to its original position by a compound lever and weight.

The three-farrow stump-jump plough was strongly constructed, but no heavier than the normal plough. The machine was to prove important in opening up new land. Various minor modifications have since been made to the original design, but the concept remains unchanged. Eight-farrow stump-jump ploughs are still used, particularly in newly cleared mallee regions.

The grubbing, or digging up of roots, was a tedious and expensive operation frequently encountered during scrub clearance. One solution to the problem, which had sometimes been employed during the 1870s, was mullenising (a rough method named after an Irishman named Mullens). This method involved clearing the undergrowth by dragging across the scrub in every direction a V-shaped log with metal teeth. But many farmers preferred to cut down the scrub and to sell the timber if the land was near to a population centre, or, more usually, to burn it and to roll the ashes evenly over the soil, thereby improving its quality.

In the early days a specially made roller was used, measuring about 115 centimetres in diameter and 290 centimetres long, which was mounted on a strong timber frame and drawn by up to eight bullocks. Such a scrub-roller would roll down even dense scrub, provided the timber did not exceed about 100 millimetres in thickness. The driver would customarily carry an axe to cut down any trees in the way.

Mallee, the principal scrub, which grows rapidly during the summer months, would usually be rolled down between October and February and then burnt.

SHEARING

Another important innovation lessened much of the hard labour in the country's shearing sheds. Traditionally, hand shears were used to remove the fleece from the sheep's back. But in about 1868 Frederick Wolseley concluded that there had to be a less laborious way of shearing.

Wolseley had arrived in Melbourne from Ireland in 1854, and for five years worked for his brother-in-law at a sheep station on the Murray River. Later he acquired an interest in two sheep stations in south-west New South Wales on or adjacent to the Murray River: one at Cobram, south of Tocumwal, the other at Thule, west of Deniliquin.

In 1871 Wolseley procured the Toolong station in the Murrumbidgee district (also in south-west New South Wales), and there continued experiments on a mechanical sheep-shearing machine which he had begun three years earlier. In 1876 Wolseley bought another station. In the following year he and a partner, R. Savage, were granted a patent for a shearing device driven by horse power. Problems with the drive mechanism and other difficulties frustrated development of the machine.

By 1884, in conjunction with R.P. Park, with whom Wolseley had earlier worked in Melbourne, another 'improved shearing apparatus' with a cog-gear universal joint was patented. In the following year Wolseley came into contact with an engineer named John Howard, who had developed a horse-clipper, and bought from him the rights for this machine.

Howard now came to work for Wolseley, and together they made further improvements to the shearing machine. The new machine worked well and prompted Wolseley to form a manufacturing company and to arrange a public demonstration of mechanical shearing compared with the traditional hand-shearing method.

The Wolseley machine was widely demonstrated in eastern Australia and in New Zealand in 1887–88. A shearing shed at Louth in New South Wales was the first to be equipped with the machine, and by the end of 1888 a further eighteen wool sheds were using the new invention.

In the following year the Wolseley Sheep Shearing Machine Co. Pty Ltd was formed in England, whilst in Melbourne production was commenced at the Goldsborough, Mort & Co. Ltd workshops, with Herbert Austin as foreman. Austin, a clever engineer, improved the overhead gear, and in 1893 transferred to England as production manager. Wolseley, now suffering ill health, resigned as head of the English company.

Wolseley, who was a likeable man, lacked practical engineering training and therefore had to rely on the mechanical knowledge of others. But he was an innovator with a sound business sense. He foresaw the need for a better shearing method, and had the determination to bring his ideas to fruition.

Initially, Wolseley's machine did not improve shearing times, but it undoubtedly lessened the fatigue associated with this seasonal occupation. The machine also enabled more wool to be taken off the sheep by shearing closer to the skin. Furthermore, machine shearing did not require the same expertise as was acquired by the hand shearers. (In Queensland in 1892, 'Jack' Howe sheared 321 full-grown merino sheep in eight hours and forty minutes—a record that stood for fifty-eight years.)

Wolseley produced the first workable shearing machine, and with it made a significant contribution to the wool industry in Australia. His name also became well known during the next half-century and beyond through the Wolseley motor car, which Herbert Austin had designed in 1895. The Austin Motor Co. was established in 1905 and produced the famous range of Austin cars. Wolseley cars continued to be made until just after World War II.

Frederick Wolseley died in England in 1899, aged sixty-two.

SAMUEL MCCAUGHEY

It used to be said by some British people that it was a desirable thing to have a rich uncle in Australia. Samuel McCaughey had one, and the uncle persuaded the young Irishman to try his luck in Australia.

And so it was that McCaughey arrived in Melbourne in 1856, at the age of twenty-one. Being thrifty, he decided to walk the 320 kilometres to his uncle Charles Wilson's property near Horsham, north-west of Melbourne, where he became a station hand. He learned quickly, and he learned well. His even temperament and Irish sense of humour enabled him to get on well with the men, and it was not long before he became overseer.

Four years later, with his savings and some cash advanced by his relatives, McCaughey was able to buy a one-third share of Coonong, a 17,010-hectare property north of Urana and west of Wagga Wagga in the New South Wales Riverina. Despite some problems, the venture proved successful. McCaughey was then able to buy two further properties and to become sole owner of Coonong. There he solved the water problem by building dams and deepening the water source, the Yanco Creek.

McCaughey's properties now amounted to 55,485 hectares and were well enough managed to allow him to make a brief return to Ireland to visit his widowed mother. He persuaded his younger brother, David, to return with him to assist in managing the properties.

Perceiving the need to improve the quality of his flocks, McCaughey purchased selected merino ewes as well as some rams from his uncle's property, and then embarked on a period of experimentation with rams procured from well-known studs. He also subdivided and fenced his paddocks, so that by 1883 the Coonong stud was reputed to be one of the best in the Riverina.

McCaughey next purchased some merinos from California, and when the results proved satisfactory he again visited America in 1886 to purchase more selected ewes and rams. A significant increase in the weight of wool resulted.

McCaughey then procured further properties on the Darling River and in Queensland, including 1,012,500 hectares which he took over from another uncle, Samuel Wilson. To ensure that his stock was well watered he put down artesian bores. McCaughey was the first in Australia—at Louth in 1888—to use the Wolseley mechanical shears (see p. 140) for the full clip. He also encouraged the use of heavy machinery for ploughing and soil excavation, and was responsible for design improvements in many farm implements.

McCaughey became increasingly aware of the need for widespread irrigation. In 1900, he constructed over 300 kilometres of channels to bring water to his North Yanco property, using two steam engines to pump water from the Murrumbidgee River. The benefits of this initiative influenced the decision by the New South Wales government to build the Burrinjuck Dam (south-west of Yass), which was completed in 1927.

In 1899 McCaughey was appointed to the Legislative Council. When the Boer War (see p. 224) broke out in the same year he donated £10,000 towards funding a bushmen's contingent. He also gave freely to the Dreadnought Fund, to Dr Barnado's Homes, to the Red Cross and to other charities. He was knighted in 1905, and in 1910 began to dispose of his properties when the federal Land Tax Act was passed.

Sir Samuel McCaughey, who never married, was a renowned philanthropist and one of Australia's most important nineteenth-century pastoralists, at one time owning or sharing in fifteen properties, totalling 1,316,250 hectares. He died in 1919, aged eighty-four.

THE SWAGGIE

Throughout recorded history there have always been nomads: individuals and tribes; itinerant workers; seasonal labourers; wandering minstrels and gipsies; those fleeing from oppression; those seeking a better life; and those in search of work, food or adventure.

In the 1800s, Australia produced its own peculiar version of nomads—the swagmen or 'swaggies'. They provided much of the seasonal labour on pastoral stations, and became enshrined in Australian folklore.

Some of the swagmen moved about alone, but often they travelled in pairs, brought together by mere chance and sometimes staying together for years.

These nomads of the bush were resilient, independent men, as free as the air save for the weight of their swags. They were shearers, drovers, overlanders and timber-getters, usually single men and mostly honest. They became familiar outback figures as they moved from station to station looking for work.

The swaggie was normally a sturdy man carrying in one hand his tin 'billy', black with constant boiling for tea, and his water bag in the other. Across his shoulders, military-style, would be strapped a neat, round, oblong-shaped bundle (or swag), usually covered with white calico. This was his tent. Inside the bundle would be a pair of blankets in which were his worldly goods—perhaps a couple of shirts, two pairs of trousers, a towel, soap and comb, and small bags containing flour, tea, sugar and perhaps a little salt. He wore a broad-rimmed straw hat, a cotton shirt and a loosely knotted handkerchief around his neck.

Some of the swaggies, usually the lazier and less trustworthy men, would contrive to arrive at a homestead at sundown, when they would request rations but be gone in the morning before they could be asked to work. They were known as 'sundowners' and were not usually welcome.

The homestead would invariably provide the genuine swagmen with 'tucker'—dinner at the kitchen door, breakfast in the morning and, if they were moving on, a hunk of damper, a handful of tea and sugar and a refilled water bag.

The Australian poet, Henry Lawson, who had an intimate knowledge of the bush, wrote:

> 'You can only depend on getting tucker once at one place, then you must tramp
>
> on to the next. If you cannot get it at once you must go short, but there is a lot
>
> of energy in an empty stomach. If you can get an extra supply, you must camp
>
> for a day and have a spell. To live you must walk. To cease walking is to die.'

It was said that you could always tell which state a swaggie came from by the way he carried his swag. 'Matilda', as the Victorian swag was known, was between 150 and 180 centimetres long, slim and tapered at the ends which were tied together and worn over the right shoulder and under the left arm. The 'Banana-lander's', or Queenslander's, swag was short and round and was carried perpendicularly between the shoulder blades and held in position by shoulder straps. To newcomers, putting on the Queensland swag was like getting into a tight shirt. It was said that a 'Cornstalk', as a New South Wales swaggie was known, didn't much care how he rolled his swag. It was usually worn on a slant from right shoulder to left hip, with his towel being used as the shoulder strap.

An article on swagmen published on 2 May 1885 by the British magazine *Chamber's Journal* commented:

> *'... You meet him everywhere. He is occasionally to be seen cautiously wending his way through the crowded streets of Melbourne or Sydney. On the decks of coastal steamers, and in second-class compartments of railway carriages, bound, perhaps, to far-off gold 'rushes', but always in close proximity to that same oblong, neatly strapped-up bundle which you saw on his back years ago, when you met him amidst the semi-tropical scenery of the Thompson or the Palmer rivers, the rugged defiles of the Mount Lofty ranges, the scorching plains of Galathera, or the sandy deserts of the western seaboard ...'*

NED KELLY

Apart from the swaggies, there were other, far less reputable characters who roamed the bush in the second half of the nineteenth century: bushrangers. Some became notorious, and one in particular was to make a dubious entry into the pages of Australian folklore.

The Irish Kelly family—a widowed mother, five daughters and three sons—grew up on a small selection (a block of land acquired by free selection) between the north-east Victorian towns of Greta and Glenrowan. The eldest son, Ned, was the wild but shrewd leader of the Kelly Gang, who took to horse and cattle rustling, robbery and other lawless acts, possibly because of their inability to find lawful work in the harsh bush country.

In 1870 Ned Kelly was arrested at Benalla for stealing a horse. Open conflict between the police and the Kellys ensued eight years later when a policeman was shot at when attempting to arrest Ned's younger brother, also for horse-stealing.

This incident prompted the police to mount a calculated campaign to bring to justice the Kelly brothers, Ned and Dan, and two others of their bushranger gang, Joe Byrne and Steve Hart.

In October 1878, Ned shot dead three constables who were leading a pursuing police posse. In June 1880, the gang, hearing that a contingent of police had left Melbourne by train to capture them, tore up part of the track, then took refuge in the hotel at Glenrowan. A school teacher managed to slip out of the hotel and was able to stop the train before it was derailed. The police later surrounded the hotel and set it on fire.

Dan Kelly, Joe Byrne and Steve Hart were burned to death, but at dawn Ned Kelly emerged from the hotel, his head and body clad in armour hammered into shape by some of his bush sympathisers. The police opened fire and a bullet eventually brought him down. He was arrested, taken to Melbourne and there tried and found guilty on a charge of murder. He was hanged for his crimes.

Ned Kelly, despite his lawless and sometimes savage acts, was to become something of a legend in the minds of those who identified him with fearless courage and defiance of authority.

CRICKET

There are records of cricket being played in Sydney as early as 1803, but the first official matches between New South Wales and Victoria were not played until 1856, by which time the popularity of the game was well established.

The first Test Match between Australia and England was played in Melbourne in 1877, with the home side victorious. The first Test in England was played in the following year. But it was ten years earlier that the first Australian side had made a memorable tour of England.

The unofficial Australian team comprised thirteen Aboriginal people and was led by a former Surrey (England) all-rounder, Charles Lawrence. The star was undoubtedly Johnny Mullagh.

Mullagh was born about 1841 in the Victorian town of Harrow, west of the Grampians and not far from Edenhope. He became a reliable stockman, and at the Pine Hills station he and other Aboriginal people learned the rudiments of cricket from the station owner's young son and two squatters, T.G. Hamilton and W.R. Hayman.

In 1864 the fledgling Aboriginal team challenged a European team and won. They then took on a number of Western District clubs, winning on most occasions. The young Mullagh proved the side's most versatile player.

By now one of the squatters, W.R. Hayman, had taken a keen interest in the team and in 1866 arranged for a well-known coach, T.W. Wills, to teach the Aboriginal people of the Lake Wallace district the finer points of the game. In December of that year, Wills, whose services were financed by the Edenhope Club, took the team to Melbourne and, on Boxing Day, led them in a match at the ground of Melbourne Cricket Club (which had been founded in 1838).

By this time the Aboriginal people had come to the notice of Charles Lawrence. Two financial backers came forward, and after further coaching it was decided to send the team to England for the 1868 season. The results were impressive. Captained by Lawrence, the Aboriginal team won fourteen and lost fourteen out of a total of forty-seven matches played on forty grounds over a five-month period. Mullagh played in all but two of the matches. The team was popular wherever it went.

Mullagh confirmed his status as a true all-rounder during the exhausting tour. He always batted in the top order, scoring 1698 runs at an average of 23.65. Although under-arm bowling was permitted at the time, Mullagh had a 'wristy' round-arm action and captured 245 wickets at an average of 10 runs during 1877 overs, of which 831 were maidens.

After a match at Reading, Mullagh was presented with a cup and a monetary reward. But his best performance during the tour was during a game at Burton-upon-Trent, when he scored 42 runs, then had a hand in dismissing all of the opposition's players. He took 4 wickets for 59 runs, caught one man, then stumped the other five after taking over the wicket-keeping duties.

Apart from cricket, the Aboriginal people gave displays of boomerang throwing, dancing, high-jumping and sprinting. Mullagh was usually the star performer.

Mullagh died in 1891 at the Pine Hills station, aged about fifty. He was unmarried.

DAVID GREGORY

One of the best-known of Australia's early cricketers was David Gregory, one of eight sons of Edward William Gregory, twenty of whose descendants were to represent New South Wales at cricket or other sports.

David Gregory was born in 1845 in the city of Wollongong, south of Sydney. He was a keen all-round cricketer, being both a capable batsman and bowler. In 1866 he played in the first intercolonial match against Victoria. In 1877 he captained a combined New South Wales and Victorian side, which defeated James Lilywhite's English touring side by 45 runs in what became known as the first Australia versus England Test Match.

In the following year Gregory captained the first Australian team to visit England, the tour being financed by a contribution of £50 from each player. The tour was highlighted by the victory at the hallowed Lords Cricket Ground against the Marylebone Cricket

Club, captained by the redoubtable Dr W. G. Grace. The win established Australia as a cricketing force, and inspired this *Punch* magazine parody on the first verse of Lord Byron's famous poem 'The Destruction of the Sennacherib':

The Australians came down like a wolf on the fold,

The Marylebone cracks for a trifle were bowled;

Our Grace before dinner was very soon done,

Our Grace after dinner did not get a run.

During the tour, which also included a visit to America, the innovative Gregory introduced a new concept of cricket leadership with skilful bowling changes, field placements and sharp run-getting.

The tour's success placed Australia firmly on the cricketing map. The unifying influence which the team inspired at home was undoubtedly a contributory factor in moulding Australia's forthcoming nationhood.

David Gregory was secretary of the New South Wales Cricket Association from 1883 until 1889. He was married three times and fathered ten children. He died in 1919.

One of David's brothers was Edward James Gregory, born in 1839. He also played against various visiting English teams and in the 1877 Test Match in Melbourne.

One of Edward James's sons, Sidney, played for New South Wales in 1889 and captained every side to tour England from 1890 until 1912. Known as 'Little Tich', Sydney Gregory was a fine batsman and a superb fielder. He represented his country in fifty-two Tests, scoring 201 against England at the Sydney Cricket Ground in 1894. (This record stood until Sir Donald Bradman (see p.302–3) scored 234 at the same ground in 1946.)

FRED SPOFFORTH

Another of Australia's early cricket personalities became known as 'The Demon'.

Fred Spofforth was a 'Balmain boy', born in Sydney in 1853, the son of a bank clerk. Fred also started his working life as a bank clerk, being employed by the Bank of New South Wales.

Like many young men of his time, Fred was attracted to cricket and played as a right-arm bowler for both the Newtown and Albert clubs. In 1874 he played for New South Wales against the English touring side, led by the great Dr W. G. Grace, and in the same year helped New South Wales to their first victory in seven years in the intercolonial match in Melbourne.

Spofforth was a tall, slender but wiry man with an aquiline nose. His height and 'catherine wheel' action enabled him to 'whip' the ball off the pitch. His remarkable control and daunting appearance—he was once described as 'all arms, legs and nose'—made him a formidable opponent. He once rode over 600 kilometres to play in a country game, then twice bowled out each batsman in the home side's two innings, claiming all 20 wickets.

Spofforth quickly attained Test match status, and was a member of the Australian side that toured England in 1878. He soon made his mark, claiming ten wickets for 20 runs at Lord's in a one-day victory over a strong Marylebone Cricket Club team. In the following year, in Melbourne, he became the first Test cricketer to take a hat trick (the feat of taking three wickets with consecutive balls).

Spofforth represented his country in the next four tours of England. In the 1882 'Ashes' Test, England, needing just 85 runs in their second innings, had reached 51 for three wickets. Declaring, 'This thing can be done', Spofforth was at his best and England were dismissed when still 7 runs short of their target. During the

151

match Spofforth had taken 14 wickets—7 in each innings—for 90 runs. That record stood for ninety years.

Following England's defeat in the 1882 Test, London's *Sporting Times* published an obituary of English cricket, giving rise to the 'trophy' known as The Ashes for which Australia and England still compete bienially:

In Affectionate Remembrance of English Cricket

Which Died at The Oval on 29 August 1882

Deeply mourned by a large circle of sorrowing friends and acquaintances.

R.I.P.

N.B. The body will be cremated and the ashes taken to Australia.

In eighteen Test matches, Spofforth took ninety-four wickets at an average of 18.41 runs apiece. In all first-class games he captured 1146 wickets at an average of 13.55 runs.

Spofforth continued playing for New South Wales until 1885, then moved to Melbourne as manager of the Moonee Ponds branch of the National Bank of Australasia. In the following year he married, in England, the daughter of a rich tea merchant. The couple returned briefly to Melbourne, then moved permanently to England, where Spofforth became a representative for the Star Tea Co., and later the firm's managing director. He played occasionally for Derbyshire for two seasons, then for the Hampstead Cricket Club for the next ten years.

Aside from cricket, Spofforth was interested in botany and horticulture, planting many Australian trees in the grounds of his home. He died in 1926, aged seventy-three.

Fred Spofforth was another of cricket's 'immortals'.

AUSSIE RULES FOOTBALL

As with many sports, Australian Rules football was evolved rather than invented.

A type of football was played by Irish soldiers in Sydney in 1829. By the 1850s, the Victorian goldminers had a different version. The Melbourne schools played yet another brand of football, probably modelled on a style of the game as played by the English public schools, especially Rugby.

In 1858 a proposal was put forward by Thomas Wills that a men's football club be formed. Wills, an outstanding cricketer who had been schooled at Rugby, did not relish the six-month idleness between one cricket season and the next, but initially had no success in endeavouring to organise football.

His proposal, however, was later well received, and several football games were played amongst cricketers and others in 1858. In the following year, seven men, all members of the Melbourne Cricket Club, formally codified the game with a set of rules after comparing the rules of the various versions as played by the principal English public schools. The resultant proposed rules were the product of a degree of grafting and some innovation, the main changes postulated being:

• Handling was permitted at any time, but the ball-carrier was not permitted to run more than two or three yards.

• A free kick, without interference, could be taken if a man caught the ball cleanly (a mark) from a kick.

• No offside rule.

• Throwing the ball was banned (this led to the unique Australian method of passing, whereby the ball is held in one hand and propelled with the closed fist of the other).

• Players could be penalised if they continued to hold the ball when tackled.

In 1866 a new rule was introduced that allowed running with the ball, provided the ball-carrier grounded or bounced the ball every five or six yards (5 metres). After 1867 the ball used was the oval-shaped rugby ball. In 1874 it was decreed that to score a goal the ball had to be kicked through the goal posts and not carried through. The goal posts were seven yards (6.5 metres) apart and there was no crossbar.

One notable aspect of the newly evolved game was that it removed the more brutal aspects of rugby, inasmuch as tripping, hacking and 'rabbiting' (up-ending an opponent) were outlawed. (After all, the game was then intended mainly as a winter pastime for 'gentlemen' cricketers who preferred not to be seen in Melbourne's business Collins Street on a Monday morning with a black eye or cracked shins.) Even so, the game as then played still had a close resemblance to rugby, with physical strength being one of the main prerequisites.

It was not until the 1880s and later, when the Saturday half-holiday was more generally accepted and professionalism had intruded into the sport, that Australian Rules football became popular with the general public. Furthermore, the game was now usually played in open parklands on rectangular-shaped pitches, there being no charge for spectators.

The large and rectangular playing areas meant that the game initially was essentially defensive, with scrimmages being commonplace and goals few and far between (until 1869 the match was won by the first team to score two goals). It was only in the 1880s, when the game moved from the parklands to the cricket ovals where there were no trees to restrict long or high kicks, that high marking became a feature of the game.

By now Australian Rules had merited a wide degree of support amongst Melbourne's sporting population. In 1886 a 34,000-strong crowd watched South Melbourne play Geelong. The game was now well established.

In 1877, control of the game had been vested in the Victorian Football Association (VFA). There were then seven established clubs: Melbourne, Carlton, St Kilda (formerly South Yarra), Hotham (later North Melbourne), Albert Park (later South Melbourne), Geelong and Barwon. In the same year the South Australian Football Association came into being, the Victorian rules being adopted. The developments were watched by Sydneysiders, who decided, perhaps more out of parochialism than principle, to stick to conventional rugby. Queensland, with an eye to practicality and interstate competition, also ignored developments in the southern states.

However, in Melbourne there were dissensions amongst the clubs, the smaller and weaker being critical of the professionalism and growing commercialism of the larger clubs. This led to the formation, in 1897, of the Victorian Football League (VFL) by the eight stronger clubs: Melbourne, Essendon, Geelong, Collingwood, South Melbourne, Fitzroy, Carlton and St Kilda. New scoring was introduced: goals were worth six points, whilst the ball passing between a goal post and a 'behind post' (behind posts had been introduced in the 1870s) scored only one point. Also, the number of players was reduced from twenty to eighteen (substitutes were later allowed); and a kick had to travel at least 10 yards (9 metres) to be marked. This led to longer kicking and to high marking, making the game faster, more open and a greater crowd-pleasing spectacle.

In 1906 the Australian National Football Council (ANFC) was created to organise interstate matches and to control the interstate movement of players. The ANFC was superseded by the National Football League, both bodies having been controlled by the VFL. In 1990 that body changed its name to the Australian Football League (AFL).

When Western Australia promoted state games, a national competition became possible. South Melbourne decided to play its home games in Sydney, and later became the Sydney Swans. Some VFL players were drafted northwards to form the Brisbane Bears (now the Brisbane Lions), whilst Western Australia drew mostly on its state players. In 1991 an Adelaide team, the Crows, also joined the competition. They were followed in 1997 by the Port Adelaide club and the Gold Coast Suns in 2011.

In 2003, the Brisbane Lions became only the third club in history to win three consecutive grand finals, and the first to do so in nearly 50 years. The club had high hopes for a fourth as they made it to the grand final in 2004, but lost to Port Adelaide.

The Australian Football 'disease', after nearly a century and a half, has now reached endemic proportions. But no-one is greatly concerned—except perhaps enthusiasts of the other football codes.

'Aussie Rules' is a unique brand of football, developed by Australians to suit Australian conditions. The game is usually a fine spectacle, and with 100 minutes or more of continuous action, it can be said that spectators usually get good value for their money.

AUSTRALIA'S FIRST WORLD TITLE

Australia's first world title was won in London on 27 June 1876. The sport was sculling and the 'champ' was Edward Trickett.

Trickett was born at Greenwich, near Sydney's Lane Cove River, and worked as a quarryman. At the age of 17, and 193 centimetres tall, he won the under-eighteen double skiffs (light rowing or sculling boats) at the Anniversary Day Regatta. In the following year he was first in the under-21 skiffs. In 1874 he won the outrigger race at the Balmain Regatta, and was also in the winning whaleboat crew. Later in the year he was second to Michael Rush in the £200 Clarence River Champion Outrigger Race. In the following year, despite being heavily handicapped, he won the light skiffs race at the Anniversary Day Regatta.

Such was Trickett's prowess that, in 1876, he was taken to England by James Punch, a Sydney innkeeper and former sculler, to challenge for the world championship. An Englishman, James H. Sadler, had defeated all comers and was then the world sculling champion. But Trickett, who had a trump card up his sleeve, triumphed against Sadler in the race on the River Thames. He returned to Sydney to a hero's welcome from a crowd of some 25,000 people.

Trickett successfully defended his world title twice—in June 1877 and again in August 1879—but was defeated on the Thames by a Canadian in 1881.

On 2 July 1877, the *Sydney Morning Herald* published a vivid account of Trickett's first title defence on the Parramatta River against Michael Rush, who had beaten him in 1875 for the Australian championship:

'In appearance Rush had everything in his favour, every muscle developed, and seemingly confident of success. Trickett was also in good form, but apparently less powerful, and looking a trifle nervous.

Their style of pulling also presented a marked difference, Rush's stroke not being cleanly rowed out, while his opponent's was as finished and regular as a machine.

If ever a doubt existed in our minds as to the superiority of a sliding seat over a fixed one, it was dispelled when we saw the ease with which Trickett sent his boat along on Saturday.

Rush went off at 24 strokes per minute; Trickett at 39. For about fifty yards they were level, then Rush went ahead foot by foot, and passing Uhr's point he was a clear length in front. Half a mile from the start he was directly ahead of Trickett, giving him his wash, and not pulling more than forty a minute. The champion seemed to quicken as they neared Blaxland's point, until it became stroke for stroke, and the boats got into dangerous proximity. Rush, responding to his rival's efforts, again left a clear gap between them, and the Clarence man shot the mile mark in 5 minutes 58 seconds, leading by a length and a half.

Coming into the straight pull down the long reach, Trickett was seen to look over his left shoulder as if to gauge his opponent's position. He had, as it were, felt him in the previous spurt, and putting on a little more steam, drew rapidly alongside. There was an effort to keep the other boat ahead, but it was only for a moment, Trickett was not to be shaken off, and ere a mile and a half had been rowed the contest was virtually over as Trickett was a clear length in front, rowing with apparent ease, whilst Rush was already labouring greatly. Before the Hen-and-Chickens were reached the Australian [champion] was at least six lengths ahead. As he passed One-man wharf he was simply paddling, and again *stopped to wave his hands to friends ashore. This was repeated twice before he reached Bedlam Point, where at least 10 000 pairs of lungs gave vent to a perfect tempest of cheers as the champion rowed leisurely by, with Rush some five or six lengths astern pulling a game stern chase.*

In the last few hundred yards Trickett showed the best piece of rowing he did during the match, and, increasing his lead a length or two, finally shot by the flagboat ... Rush, who was very much exhausted at the finish, and had to contend with broken water, came in 22 seconds later. The affair was so completely one-sided for the last two miles that it can hardly be termed a race. Time from start to finish ... 23 minutes 26 seconds.

The stakes will be paid over at Punch's Hotel, this evening.'

The trump card that had won Trickett the world championship in England had been the sliding seat. He had demonstrated the advantages of using the latest technology.

THE MELBOURNE CUP

Many countries have an annual sporting event that virtually brings the nation to a brief standstill. In Australia, it's the Melbourne Cup, more usually known as 'The Cup'. The 3200-metre (until 1972 it was 2 miles) race for thoroughbred horses is the centrepiece of Melbourne's Spring Carnival, and is run on the first Tuesday of November (until 1874 it was run on a Thursday) at the Flemington Racecourse. That day is a public holiday in Victoria, and it is the world's only race for which a holiday is proclaimed by an Act of Parliament.

The American author Mark Twain wrote in *More Tramps Abroad* (1897) that 'The Melbourne Cup is the Australian National Day'.

The first Melbourne Cup was run in 1861 with an attendance of 4000. It is a handicap race, and in that important respect differs from major set-weight overseas races such as the American Kentucky Derby and the English Epsom Derby. Such races usually result in the best-qualified horse winning, with a consequent astronomical rise in the winner's racing and breeding value, and the values of its progeny.

In a handicap race, it is the handicapper's task to attempt to equalise the abilities of the race's entrants so that, in theory, all the horses cross the finishing line together. This, of course, never happens, although there are periodic dead-heats (in the 1987 AJC Epsom Handicap, fourteen horses passed the finishing post with only five lengths between them). Factors that the handicapper cannot possibly take into account will affect the outcome of a race: on a particular day a horse (like a human being) will perform above or below its usual ability; the track may be hard or soft; inclement weather will affect one horse more than another; and so on. The race therefore tends to become a lottery, and huge amounts of money are wagered on each Cup.

History shows that many Melbourne Cups have been won by horses that are good stayers but not, by general consensus, true champions. The majority of Cup winners have not become great sires or dams, and few have been able to repeat their first Cup success. One that did so was Archer, a five-year-old who won the first race in 1861, carrying 60.3 kilograms, and again in 1862 when he won by a massive ten lengths although carrying 64.4 kilograms.

In more recent times, Rain Lover, carrying 51.7 kilograms, triumphed in the 1968 Cup and did it again the following year carrying 60.3 kg. Think Big won in 1974 carrying 53 kilograms and once more in the following year carrying 58.5 kilograms. Galilee carried off the 1968 Cup and continued to race successfully. They were true champions. So, too, according to expert opinion, were Carbine, who won in 1890 carrying 65.8 kilograms; Phar Lap, who won the 1930 Cup carrying 62.6 kilograms; and Peter Pan, who won in 1932 and again in 1934. Few Cups have been won by sons or daughters of previous Cup winners.

History was made in 2005 when a horse won the Cup for the third time in a row. Makybe Diva won in 2003, 2004 and 2005, to the tearful delight of her jockey, Glen Boss.

The main lead-up race to the Melbourne Cup is the Caulfield Cup, which is run on the previous Saturday week. A fancied mare, Grace Darling, won the 1885 Caulfield Cup and was well placed in the finishing stages of the following Melbourne Cup when she was bumped by another horse, Acolyte. Grace Darling, however, recovered and was striding out for the line with two other horses, Trenton and Sheet Anchor, when the former's jockey inadvertently brought his whip down on Grace Darling's nose. The momentary check probably denied Grace Darling the honour of being the first horse to win the double.

There was something of a sensation after the 1866 Cup, won by The Barb by a head from Exile. The judge signalled first and second placings, but declined to place the third horse, Falcon, because that horse's colours were not given in the official list of runners supplied to the judge (in those days saddle numbers were not used). There had been considerable place betting on the race, and eventually the stewards issued a notice declaring that Falcon was placed third. Amidst uproar from punters, many bookmakers refused to pay place bets on Falcon, maintaining that only the judge, and not the stewards, had responsibility making decisions on race places.

Three years later, The Barb carried the heaviest weight ever awarded a Cup winner: 73 kilograms. He had carried 38.5 kilograms when winning the 1866 Cup.

So the Melbourne Cup is a great leveller, giving horses that may not be true champions a theoretically equal chance against good horses who have achieved favouritism and have therefore attracted the attention of the handicapper (and the bookmakers).

The inherent uncertainties of Australia's premier racing event have made it essentially a gambling event as well as a magnificent spectacle. And that seems to fit in well with that bastion of the Australian character, a 'fair go' for all. The *Encyclopaedia Britannica* considers it the 'greatest all-age handicap race in the world'.

Mark Twain also wrote of the Melbourne Cup: 'Cup day is supreme—it has no rival.' A century later he would find no need to alter that opinion.

NEW GUINEA

At various times during the nineteenth century several overseas powers, principally France, Germany and the United States, cast covetous eyes on various Pacific territories.

In the early 1880s, in order to thwart German trading ambitions in New Guinea, Queensland announced the annexation of that territory. The British government declined to ratify the annexation, but in 1884 established a protectorate over south-east New Guinea, allowing Germany control over the north-east portion of the island.

When World War I broke out, an Australian expeditionary force occupied the German-controlled territory. Dutch New Guinea, the eastern half of the island, was annexed by Indonesia in 1969 and became the province of Irian Jaya. In 2002 the province achieved independence and was renamed East Timor. Papua New Guinea became self-governing in 1973 and attained complete independence in 1975.

THE TELEPHONE

The first Australian telephones were operational in Melbourne in 1879. Brisbane had a telephone exchange shortly afterwards, followed by Sydney in 1881, Adelaide and Hobart in 1883, and Perth in 1887. Initially the services were operated by private companies, but by the 1890s telephones had been placed under the control of the various colonial post offices.

LITERATURE AND BOOKS

Long before the advent of radio and television sets, people from all walks of life turned to the written word for relaxation and enlightenment. In addition to the poets (see pp. 168), several Australian novelists produced notable works during the latter part of the nineteenth century, amongst them Adam Lindsay Gordon, Henry Kendall, Marcus Clarke, best known for his novel *For the Term of His Natural Life*, Arthur Hoey Davis, who wrote (under the name of Steele Rudd) the popular *On Our Selection*, Henry Lawson, and Thomas Browne, who managed to pack three separate careers into his eighty-nine years ...

THOMAS BROWNE

Thomas Browne was five years old when he arrived in Sydney from England with his family in 1831. At first the family lived in the heart of Sydney, at Macquarie Place. Later they moved further out to a house built by Thomas's shipmaster father, who named the residence *Enmore*. The area later became the inner-Sydney suburb of the same name. In 1839 the family moved to Melbourne, but Thomas remained at Sydney College for a further two years. Private tuition in Melbourne completed his education.

In 1844 Browne acquired a cattle run near Portland on the Victorian coast west of Melbourne, which he somewhat fancifully named *Squattlesea Mere*. There, after the economic depression had brought ruin to his father, he lived for ten years with his mother and six unmarried sisters. Despite occasional encounters with armed Aboriginal people, Browne lived the life of a squatter. In 1858 he decided to sell the run and to purchase a sheep station on the Murray River near the present city of Swan Hill.

Browne made a brief visit to Britain in 1860. Then, in the following year, he married Margaret Riley at Mulgoa, west of Sydney. (It was at about this time that he added an 'e' to his surname—he had been born Thomas Brown.) The couple were to have four sons and five daughters.

In 1871, after several bad seasons and a severe drought, Browne decided on a career change, perhaps having his growing family responsibilities in mind. He secured an appointment that year as a police magistrate at Gulgong, then one of the largest goldfields in New South Wales. In the following year he became a gold commissioner. In 1881 he moved to Dubbo as magistrate and mining warden, and in 1884 to Armidale. In the following year he made yet another move, this time to Albury as chairman of the Land Licensing Board. He remained a magistrate and warden until 1895, when he retired to Melbourne.

It was in 1870 that the need to supplement his income prompted Browne to commence writing. He had had an article published in London four years earlier, but now turned to fiction. Between 1873 and 1880, seven of his novels had been published as serials in various magazines and newspapers. For these he used the pen-name 'Rolf Boldrewood'.

From 1888 to 1905, Browne published various articles, prefaces to books, sixteen novels—some of which were published as serials—and a few short stories. The novels gave glimpses of pastoral and mining life but have little literary value.

By 1882 Browne had completed *Robbery Under Arms*, which was accepted by the *Sydney Mail* and published as a serial during 1882–83. It became an Australian classic and is still widely read today. The novel received the accolades of such well-known writers as Mark Twain and Rider Haggard. Browne became, in reality, a one-book author.

Thomas Browne was a gentlemanly, friendly and courteous man who was proud of being an Australian whilst retaining a liking for English traditions. He was an affectionate husband and father, and a staunch adherent to the Church of England. He died in Melbourne in 1915.

GEORGE ROBERTSON

A line drawn to portray the career path of George Robertson would be almost straight, for books were central to his life—from his apprenticeship at the age of twelve to a bookseller and publisher in Glasgow until his death at the age of seventy-three. He had few other interests. We might nowadays describe him as a 'workaholic', although 'bookaholic' might be an equally appropriate term.

At nineteen, having completed his apprenticeship articles, there was a slight deviation in the straight line of his career when he emigrated to New Zealand to join his three elder brothers, who were operating a sawmill in the South Island. He enjoyed three years of heavy physical outdoors work, then in 1882 decided to move to Sydney and to return to the trade he had learned in Scotland—bookselling. He found employment with the Sydney branch of a Melbourne bookseller which, coincidentally, carried his own name, but there was no relationship. The business was run by another Scot, George Robertson, and he remained with the firm for four years, becoming manager of the retail department. Shortly after joining the Sydney branch he married a Scottish lady from New Zealand, Elizabeth Bruce.

In Sydney's Market Street at the time there was a small bookstore run by yet another Scot, David Angus. In 1886 Robertson purchased a half-share in the business. Four years later the business had succeeded to the extent that a move to larger premises in Castlereagh Street was made.

Robertson was keen to expand the business into publishing. Angus agreed to this and, suffering from health problems, left the running of the business mainly to Robertson. Angus retired to Scotland in 1900 and died there the following year. Angus's share of the business was taken up by two businessmen, Richard Thomson and Frederick Wymark, but they were content to leave the day-to-day running of the business to Robertson.

Now began the thirty-year phase of Robertson's career which led him to be described as the 'Father of Australian publishing'. Believing that the work of Australian writers could compete with that of overseas authors, he published the first Angus & Robertson title in 1888. With the assistance of J.F. Archibald (see pp. 167–70) he made selections from A.B. 'Banjo' Paterson's poems and published them in 1895 under the title *The Man from Snowy River and other Verses* (see pp. 170–3). The volume was an immediate success. Two works by Henry Lawson appeared during the following year.

Despite the onerous task of running the firm's publishing department almost single-handedly, Robertson found time to talk to and encourage young writers whom he perceived had genuine talent. Although largely self-educated, he had a remarkable talent for selecting appropriate words and phrases, and assisted many of the authors who came to him by editing their work. The business became a public company in 1907, with Robertson as the chairman of directors.

Robertson had a special interest in rare books and literature of historical value. His evidence before the Parliamentary Standing

Committee on Public Works contributed to the decision to construct a library building to house the vast collection of Australiana gathered by David Mitchell and offered by him in 1898 to the Public Library of New South Wales. Priceless books, documents and artefacts forming a significant part of Australia's historical records are now housed in Sydney's Mitchell Library, part of the State Library of New South Wales.

In 1912 Robertson began work on *The Australian Encyclopaedia*, a vast undertaking which took fourteen years to complete. It represented the most authoritative source of information on Australian authors available at the time. *The Official History of Australia in the War of 1914–1918* by C.E.W. Bean (see pp. 248–51) was another of the company's major publications.

One of Robertson's many publishing successes was C.J. Dennis's *The Songs of a Sentimental Bloke*, which the author sent to him in 1915 with the suggestion that the book might sell 300 copies. Within two years nearly 70,000 copies had been sold in Australia and New Zealand. Many more copies were sold in Britain, the United States and in other countries.

Early in the 1920s Robertson enlarged the company's publishing arm by buying a controlling interest in a Sydney printery, which he renamed The Halstead Press (Robertson was born near Halstead in the English county of Essex). It later became Australia's largest book printery.

Apart from Saturday evenings at the theatre and occasional visits to the Sydney Cricket Ground to watch a Test match, Robertson had virtually no hobbies or interests other than his work, and weekends spent with his family at the Blue Mountains home he built in 1892 at Blackheath. In later life he enjoyed bushwalking and fishing. (Robertson's first wife died in 1908 and he remarried two years later.)

George Robertson, or 'The Chief' as he was known to his employees, was a tall man, robust, forthright and single-minded. He died in 1933, aged seventy-three.

The publishing business of Angus & Robertson Ltd has now been incorporated into the HarperCollins publishing group owned by News Ltd, the Australian arm of the international News Corporation. The bookselling department is now Angus & Robertson Bookworld and is owned by a British company.

THE BULLETIN

Traditionally, Sunday in Australia is observed as a day of rest. But from the 1880s and for some time to come, the day of rest for many who lived and worked in the bush was frequently the day on which the *Bulletin*, or 'the Bully' as the weekly publication was commonly known, was read. The paper became known as 'The Bushman's Bible', for it was an important source of news, comment and entertainment amongst bush people.

The *Bulletin* did much to relieve the sense of isolation felt by many country people. The paper quickly won acceptance for its forthright language and attitudes to current affairs, which reflected much of the way of life and outlooks of many of its readers. Sometimes irreverent in its comments, and ever ready to lampoon those who lacked 'the common touch', the paper, at least until World War I, did much to establish the conviction amongst bush people that their way of life, their traditions and their customs, were a true part of the Australian ethos.

The first issue of the *Bulletin* was published on 31 January 1880 by journalists John Feltham Archibald and John Haynes. The paper ran to eight pages and cost four pence. The price of the second issue was reduced to three pence and sold 4000 copies.

Despite early dramas (Archibald and Haynes were gaoled for six weeks for failing to pay legal costs) the *Bulletin*, with William Traill as co-proprietor, soon became the most widely read publication in

Australia. Haynes left the paper to go into politics, leaving Archibald and Traill to set about developing its nationalistic, anti-imperialist, protectionist and republican stance. It became not only a more serious paper but also a more humorous one.

In 1883 Archibald made a brief visit to England, returning with his anti-British outlook all the stronger. While in England he met Rosa Frankenstein, who later journeyed to Australia and married him in 1885. She gradually slipped into alcoholism and died in 1911.

From 1886 onwards, Archibald devoted his entire energy to running the *Bulletin*. When Traill also went into politics, William McLeod, an artist, returned to the paper as business manager with Archibald as editor. His two lieutenants were James Edmond and Alfred Stephens.

Stephens had joined the *Bulletin* in 1894 as a junior subeditor. It was not long before he had transformed the inside front cover of the red-jacketed paper into a vibrant literary column (it had previously been used as advertising space). 'A.G.S.', as the articles were anonymously signed, became the country's most respected and widely read literary critic. Stephens finally left the paper in 1906.

By the mid-1890s, Archibald had gathered as contributors a group of gifted writers, poets and artists, amongst them Henry Lawson, 'Banjo' Paterson, Louis Becke, Steele Rudd and Norman Lindsay.

Archibald was a brilliant journalist and editor, but it was perhaps his patience, encouragement and tireless subediting that resulted in the pages of the *Bulletin* making such a remarkable contribution to the Australian literature of the period. He described his function as a 'souler and healer'. In moulding the talents of those drawn to the paper he not only brought unparalled richness to the *Bulletin*'s growing readership (its circulation in the late 1880s had reached 80,000 copies) but was also instrumental in developing the work of writers and artists whose careers might otherwise have foundered.

Archibald, although impatient of interruption, was invariably kind, open and responsive to any contributor who walked through the door of his small but cluttered office. On one occasion, in 1882, when Henry Lawson was financially impoverished, Archibald gave him £5 (a princely sum in those days) and a single rail ticket to far-off Bourke. Lawson's response to this gesture, and to the outback environment in which he found himself, was a series of his most memorable writings.

The *Bulletin* did more than provide a platform for Australian literature and art. It was to make a significant contribution to the fermentation process of Australian nationalism. In a curious way, its readers, especially those in the bush, felt a bond with one another and a sense of their own equality with city folk. They felt less isolated. The paper's columns served to promote a degree of kinship and nationalism which no other publication had been able to achieve.

In 1902 Archibald handed over the paper's editorship to Edmond. Four years later, Archibald had a nervous breakdown and was admitted to the Callan Park Asylum, from which he was discharged in 1908, readmitted a few months later, then finally discharged in 1910.

Archibald later made a full recovery from his mental illness, and for the next eight years led the life of a quiet, elderly gentleman. In 1914, with some reluctance, he sold his interest in the *Bulletin*. Under Edmond's editorship the paper became more conservative, and it moderated its previous republicanism. The larrikinism of its earlier days was clothed in more respectable attire, this being taken up by other publications during and after World War I.

The *Bulletin* was purchased in 1960 by Consolidated Press Holdings Limited and remained a weekly publication until it closed in 2008.

John Archibald died in 1919, aged sixty-three. There is a worthy memorial to him in the splendid fountain (executed by a French sculptor) in Sydney's Hyde Park. He is also remembered by the country's most prestigious annual prize for portrait painting, The Archibald Prize, which he endowed.

POETRY

From the latter part of the nineteenth century onwards, the writings of a succession of poets made an important contribution to Australian literature. Their work, well laced with humour and drawing upon readily understood themes, provided both a welcome source of pleasure and endearing glimpses of bush life.

One such writer was A.B. 'Banjo' Paterson (see p. 165), who was a lawyer and subsequently a journalist (his pen-name was adopted from the name of a station horse ('Banjo') owned by his family). His various volumes of verse proved very popular, amongst them *The Man from Snowy River and other Verses*, first published in 1895 and in recent times made into a movie. Banjo Paterson's narrative verse provides vivid glimpses of bush life a century and more ago.

THE MAN FROM SNOWY RIVER

There was a movement at the station, for the word had passed around
That the colt from old Regret had got away,
And had joined the wild bush horses—he was worth a thousand pound,
So all the cracks had gathered to the fray.
All the tried and noted riders from the stations near and far
Had mustered at the homestead overnight,
For the bushmen love hard riding where the wild bush horses are,
And the stock horse snuffs the battle with delight.
There was Harrison, who made his pile when Pardon won the cup,
The old man with his hair as white as snow;

But few could ride beside him when his blood was fairly up—
He would go wherever horse and man could go.
And Clancy of the Overflow came down to lend a hand,
No better horseman ever held the reins;
For never horse could throw him while the saddle girths would stand,
He learnt to ride while droving on the plains.
And one was there, a stripling on a small and weedy beast,
He was something like a racehorse undersized,
With a touch of Timor pony—three parts thoroughbred at least—
And such as are by mountain horseman prized.
He was hard and tough and wiry—just the sort that won't say die—
There was courage in his quick impatient tread;
And he bore the badge of gameness in his bright and fiery eye,
And the proud and lofty carriage of his head.
But still so slight and weedy, one would doubt his power to stay,
And the old man said, 'That horse will never do
For a long and tiring gallop—lad, you'd better stop away,
Those hills are far too rough for such as you.'
So he waited sad and wistful—only Clancy stood his friend—
'I think we ought to let him come,' he said;
'I warrant he'll be with us when he's wanted at the end,
For both his horse and he are mountain bred.
He hails from Snowy River, up by Kosciusko's side,
Where the hills are twice as steep and twice as rough,
Where a horse's hoofs strike firelight from the flint stones every stride,
The man that holds his own is good enough.
And the Snowy River riders on the mountains make their home,
Where the river runs those giant hills between;
I have seen full many horsemen since I first commenced to roam,
But nowhere yet such horsemen have I seen.'
So he went—they found the horse by the big mimosa clump—
They raced away towards the mountain's brow,

And the old man gave his orders, 'Boys, go at them from the jump,
No use to try for fancy riding now.
And, Clancy, you must wheel them, try and wheel them to the right.
Ride boldly, lad, and never fear the spills,
For never yet was rider that could keep the mob in sight,
If once they gain the shelter of those hills.'
So Clancy rode to wheel them—he was racing on the wing
Where the best and boldest riders take their place,
And he raced his stockhorse past them, and he made the ranges ring
With the stockwhip, as he met them face to face.
Then they halted for a moment, while he swung the dreaded lash,
But they saw their well-loved mountain full in view,
And they charged beneath the stockwhip with a sharp and sudden dash,
And off into the mountain scrub they flew.
Then fast the horsemen followed, where the gorges deep and black
Resounded to the thunder of their tread,
And the stockwhips woke the echoes, and they fiercely answered back
From cliffs and crags that beetled overhead.
And upward, ever upward, the wild horses held their way,
Where mountain ash and kurrajong grew wide;
And the old man muttered firecely, 'We may bid the mob good day,
No man can hold them down the other side.'
When they reached the mountain's summit, even Clancy took a pull,
It well might make the boldest hold their breath,
The wild hop scrub grey thickly, and the hidden ground was full
Of wombat holes, and any slip was death.
But the man from Snowy River let the pony have his head,
And he swung his stockwhip round and gave a cheer,
And he raced him down the mountain like a torrent down its bed,
While the others stood and watched in very fear.
He sent the flint stones flying, but the pony kept his feet,
He cleared the fallen timber in his stride,

And the man from Snowy River never shifted in his seat—
It was grand to see that mountain horseman ride.
Through the stringybarks and saplings, on the rough and broken ground,
Down the hillside at a racing pace he went;
And he never drew the bridle till he landed safe and sound
At the bottom of that terrible descent.
He was right among the horses as they climbed the farther hill,
And the watchers on the mountain, standing mute,
Saw him ply the stockwhip fiercely; he was right among them still,
As he raced across the clearing in pursuit.
Then they lost him for a moment, where two mountain gullies met
In the ranges, but a final glimpse reveals
On a dim and distant hillside the wild horses racing yet,
With the man from Snowy River at their heels.
And he ran them single-handed till their sides were white with foam.
He followed like a bloodhound on their track,
Till they halted, cowed and beaten, then he turned their heads for home,
And alone and unassisted brought them back.
But his hardy mountain pony he could scarcely raise a trot,
He was blood from hip to shoulder from the spur;
But his pluck was still undaunted, and his courage fiery hot,
For never yet was mountain horse a cur.
And down by Kosciusko, where the pine-clad ridges raise
Their torn and rugged battlements on high,
Where the air is clear as crystal, and the white stars fairly blaze
At midnight in the cold and frosty sky,
And where around the Overflow the reed beds sweep and sway
To the breezes, and the rolling plains are wide,
The man from Snowy River is a household word today,
And the stockmen tell the story of his ride.

THE GOLDEN AGE OF PAINTING

There were artists, too, whose work provides a rich and lasting record of Australian scenes and landscapes. One of a group of young but very talented painters who first came together on the shores of Victoria's Port Philip Bay was Arthur Streeton.

Arguably Australia's foremost native-born landscape painter, Arthur Streeton was the product of the golden age of Australian painting, which flourished from the 1880s onwards.

Streeton's life can be likened to a three-act play with a prologue. Born in Victoria, the fourth of five children, he attended school in Melbourne and showed an aptitude for drawing. At the age of thirteen he went to work in the city as a junior clerk in a firm of importers. Two years later he enrolled in night classes at the National Gallery's School of Design. Although the classes gave him little formal tuition in painting, his sketching skills developed to the extent that he became an apprentice at a lithographic firm in Melbourne's Collins Street.

The prologue began one Sunday morning in 1886 when the nineteen-year-old debonair Streeton was standing on rocks at Mentone, on Victoria's Port Philip Bay, devoting his leisure time to sketching the sea and shore. Absorbed in his work, he was unaware that he was being observed by two young men. They were 29-year-old English-born Tom Roberts and thirty-year-old Victorian Frederick McCubbin, who had set up a painting camp at a farm at nearby Box Hill. Both were to make a major impact on Australian art.

The youthful painters invited Streeton to join them at the weekend cottage they had rented at Mentone, and in the succeeding weekends he began painting in earnest.

Streeton, who had a lifelong habit of letter-writing, recorded of the Mentone days:

'In spite of the heat, the vile hammocks we slept in, the pest of flies and the puce-coloured walls, we had a great time there. On Sundays we took a billy and

chops and tomatoes down to a beautiful little bay which was full of fossils, where we camped for the day. We returned home during the evening through groves of exquisite tea-trees, the sea scene, the cliffs at Sandringham flushed with the afterglow.'

Two of Streeton's big landscapes, *Settler's Camp* and *A Pastoral*, were shown at the Victorian Artists' Society exhibition in 1888. Their sale provided him with sufficient money to begin painting as a full-time occupation.

The first act in Streeton's story began later that year when an estate agent, the brother-in-law of an artist known to Streeton, offered him an eight-room dwelling on a hilltop at Eaglemont. The house overlooked the Yarra River valley near the Melbourne suburb of Heidelberg, then a park-like country district with a few homesteads. Of his first night at Eaglemont Streeton wrote:

'I laboured up the hill with a large swag of canvases and paints, and camped in one of the empty rooms. I lay on the floor in my clothes, my boots for a pillow, and I had no company except a bottle of wine and a candle.'

The group of young artists became known as the Heidelberg School, and their camps at Eaglemont, Box Hill and Mentone were legendary. Their number included Charles Conder, whom Roberts had met in Sydney in 1887. Conder had been greatly interested in Roberts's account of the new Impressionist movement in Europe, and many years later was to remember nostalgically the Heidelberg days when he wrote to Roberts:

'Give me one summer evening again with yourself and Streeton—and the same long evenings—songs—dirty plates—and the last pink skies.'

In 1889 the group held their notorious '9 by 5' (the approximate measurement, in inches, of the cedar cigar box lids on which most of the works were painted) Impression Exhibition in Melbourne, comprising 182 exhibits (of which forty were by Streeton). The exhibition was a statement by the young artists against the conservative tradition of Victorian painting. Their radical impressions disappointed many of the critics, outraged some and amused others. It was, however, a commercial success; each of the artists was to become famous.

The second act of Streeton's career now began. In 1890 he had painted *Still Glides the Stream* and *Shall for Ever Glide*, which gave eloquent expression to the 'plein air' (painting out-of-doors direct from nature) movement which had come into vogue in the 1870s and which became so characteristic of Streeton's style. The work was acquired by the National Art Gallery of New South Wales and prompted Streeton to move to Sydney.

The Eaglemont camp was disbanded at the beginning of 1890. Conder then left for Paris, taking with him Streeton's *Golden Summer, Eaglemont*. This work was exhibited in the following year at the Royal Academy of Arts in London, and in 1892 at the Salon de la Société des Artistes Français in Paris, where it was awarded an honourable mention.

Roberts now joined Streeton in Sydney, where the latter had found accommodation at Little Sirius Cove on Mosman Bay, and there they were joined by other artists. Streeton's Sydney period was highly productive, for the natural beauty of his surroundings inspired many of his best-known works: harbour views, beach scenes, two urban masterpieces and a Hawkesbury River collection. His first large canvas was the dramatic *Fire's On*, which depicted the blasting of a railway cutting in the Blue Mountains west of Sydney. Critics admired his powers of observation, use of colour, texture and tone, and the excellence of his brushwork.

The third act of Streeton's story began in 1890. Although by this time his reputation in Australia was established and his works were represented in public galleries in Melbourne and Sydney, Streeton nevertheless decided that

European experience was essential to the further development of his career. In the previous year he had raised sufficient funds for a European tour resulting from a successful one-man exhibition held in Melbourne. This was attended by one of Streeton's contemporaries, W. Lister-Lister, who wrote:

> *'As a result of our English training, Ashton, Fullwood and myself were painting in low tones, but after seeing Streeton's work we began to observe that the colour and atmosphere of landscapes were brighter than we had previously realised.'*

Apart from three return visits, Streeton was away from Australia for the next twenty-five years. His time in England was difficult, for the English landscape did not inspire him in the same way as did his homeland, and he had only limited success at the main art galleries. He never quite came to terms with the fact that his work overseas did not achieve the same acclaim as had his Australian paintings.

In 1908 Streeton had married a Canadian violinist, Esther Clench. In the years before World War I his paintings began to receive greater recognition not only in England but also in France and the United States.

In 1915 Streeton enlisted in the Australian Army Medical Corps. After being invalided out in 1918 he was appointed official war artist with the Australian Imperial Forces in France.

In London in July 1919, a selection of Streeton's war paintings was shown at the Alpine Club in London. The landscape theme of Streeton's art was again evident in these paintings, most of which depicted the desolation he had witnessed in the battlefields of France.

Streeton returned to Australia for a three-year visit in 1919–22, accompanied by his wife and only son, Oliver. The visit was highlighted by a very successful exhibition of his wartime paintings, together with some of his English and Venetian works. Streeton visited America briefly in 1921, but an exhibition in New York of his Canadian paintings aroused little interest despite generally favourable reviews.

In 1923, Streeton returned again to live permanently in Australia. The family settled in the Melbourne suburb of Toorak and built a cottage at Olinda in the Dandenong Ranges. It was country familiar to Streeton from the happy and productive times he had spent not far away at Eaglemont.

In 1928 Streeton was awarded the Wynne Prize for his landscape *Afternoon Light: the Goulburn Valley*. He was knighted in 1937 for services to Australian art.

When his wife died in 1938, Streeton retired to the cottage at Olinda, where he continued painting and devoted much of his time to gardening. He died there in 1943, survived by his son.

Sir Arthur Streeton was an uncomplicated man, a romantic with a deep feeling for the beauties of his native land and a wonderful talent for interpreting the poetry of the landscapes he loved. He found his own milieu and eschewed artistic modernism.

PAPUNYA TULA ARTISTS

Indigenous Australians used various forms of art, including rock and bark paintings, to record history, environment, daily activities and mythology for at least 40,000 years.

Indigenous art continues to be created today, in contemporary mediums as well as traditional. One collective of artists is generally credited with bringing the form to the world's attention.

Papunya is a small community in the Northern Territory. Members of various local Aboriginal groups were moved there in the late 1960s by the Australian government.

The children at Papunya's small school painted a large wall mural in 1971, at the urging of their teacher, Geoffrey Bardon. The mural used traditional dot painting techniques and depicted sacred symbols. This and another mural painted by community elders was eventually painted over. Their influence, however, was potent: local men began painting their ancestral stories on any available surface. In 1972, they formed an official collective, named Papunya Tula.

Over the years, works produced by the artists' collective have received critical acclaim in the art world, exhibited in galleries, museums and private collections around the world.

THEATRE

By the time a dramatised version of *On Our Selection* (see p. 224) was produced in 1910, the theatre had become firmly established in Australia, thanks to a succession of theatrical entrepreneurs and actor–managers. The first of these was Barnett Levey, who, in 1833, opened the Theatre Royal, constructed as part of a Sydney warehouse. In 1841 an entire theatrical company was brought out from London to perform in Tasmania.

These actor–managers were first and foremost Thespians, but they understood the benefits of staging productions and took an interest in the box office takings. The best-known of these men was an American...

JAMES WILLIAMSON

In the 1860s, James Williamson was endeavouring to establish himself in the theatrical world, willingly accepting any off-stage work available with theatrical companies in the United States and Canada. He found himself in San Francisco in 1871, and there met Maggie Moore, a young comedienne whose Irish parents had migrated first to Sydney and then to California. They married two years later.

Within a few days, James and Maggie were playing the leading roles in a revamped play entitled *Struck Oil*. The production was a success, and when George Coppin (an Australian actor–manager) heard of it he contracted for the Williamsons to perform the play at Melbourne's Theatre Royal. It ran for fifty-seven nights, and was followed by an equally successful season in Sydney. It was estimated that some 93,000 people in Australia saw the play.

The Williamsons, now famous and financially secure, returned to Melbourne, then toured to Adelaide. In 1875 they departed for London, then spent the next four years successfully touring England, Europe and the United States.

In 1879 Gilbert and Sullivan staged the first of their operettas, *HMS Pinafore*, amidst growing enthusiasm in English theatrical circles. The astute Williamsons purchased the Australian rights from W.S. Gilbert, and later that year opened the production in Melbourne under Coppin's management, followed by a season in Sydney. This was the beginning of James Williamson's reign, which was to last nearly thirty years. He was Australia's most successful theatrical entrepreneur.

In 1880 Williamson became sole lessee of the Theatre Royal in Melbourne, and there staged a series of lavish productions. Two years later he entered into partnership with George Musgrove and Arthur Garner. 'The Triumvirate', as they became known, set about transforming the Australian theatrical scene, displacing the old repertory plays with spectacular productions, many featuring well-known overseas artists. These included, in 1886, a production of *The Mikado* at the luxurious new Princess Theatre in Melbourne.

In 1890 Musgrove left 'The Firm', as Williamson's company became known in stage circles. But in the following year Williamson and Garner triumphed again when they brought out from England the most famous actress of the time—Sarah Bernhardt. Garner then also disappeared from the company when Williamson bought him out.

Another disappearance in 1891 was Williamson's wife, Maggie, who left him for another actor. Maggie divorced him in 1899, and shortly afterwards Williamson married a dancer, Mary Weir.

Meanwhile, Musgrove had rejoined Williamson in 1892, and later went to London as the firm's agent. In 1899, another disagreement between the two resulted in the partnership being dissolved for the second time.

Williamson's activities continued unabated into the new century. A Melbourne theatre was refurbished and renamed Her Majesty's, whilst big theatrical 'names' from overseas continued to feature in new productions. In 1902 Her Majesty's Theatre in Sydney was burnt down but rebuilt the following year. In 1904 Williamson took into partnership his Melbourne manager, George Tallis, and his legal adviser, Gustav Ramaciotti. The run of spectacular productions continued. 'The Firm's' permanent staff now numbered over 600.

From 1907, Williamson, now aged sixty-two, took a less active part in the day-to-day running of the company's business. Ramaciotti then departed from the scene, and Williamson sold his half share to Tallis. A new proprietary company, J.C. Williamson Ltd, was then formed with Williamson as governing-director.

James Williamson—JCW to his staff and friends—now devoted much of his time to his family, to a new-found interest in horse-racing and to travel in Europe and the United States. He died in Paris in 1913.

JOSEPH SLAPOFFSKI

In addition to the Thespians, musicians also found their way to Australia from Europe. One was a violinist who looked like a boxer but became a well-known figure in the world of opera.

Joseph Slapoffski, son of a Russian-born musician, was a child prodigy. He grew up in England, attended the Christ Church Cathedral School, Oxford, and studied the violin. His playing impressed Prince Leopold, who arranged for him to be enrolled at the Royal Academy of Music in London. Amongst his fellow students was (Sir) Arthur Sullivan, of Gilbert and Sullivan fame.

'Slap', as he was affectionately known, toured as a violin soloist, played with a London orchestra and was appointed musical director at the Princess Theatre in Manchester. He then joined the famous Carl Rosa Opera Company, eventually becoming chief conductor. In 1881, at the age of nineteen, he had married Charlotte Barrett, by whom he had eight children. She died in 1896. Slapoffski later married again. His partner, Elizabeth Frances, was a singer with whom he performed and toured.

In 1890 Slapoffski was engaged to bring a season of opera to Australia and New Zealand. He returned to Australia in 1892 to conduct a concert at the Exhibition Building in Melbourne to celebrate the opening of the first Federal Parliament. In the following year he was in charge of the orchestral concerts for (Dame) Nellie Melba's Australian tour. Visits to the United States followed, then Slapoffski returned again to Australia to conduct a Wagner season. He remained there to become associated with several Sydney orchestras, and was a foundation councillor of the New South Wales State Conservatorium.

In 1919 Slapoffski was made an associate of the Royal Academy of Music. Then began an association, lasting until 1932, with J.C. Williamson Ltd. (see pp. 179–81) as musical director of its grand opera company and its brilliant Gilbert and Sullivan seasons. In 1925–26 he was the musical director of the Dunedin Exhibition in New Zealand. He continued to support the National Theatre Movement in Australia for many years. A particularly memorable event occurred in Adelaide in 1931 when Slapoffski conducted a Melba memorial concert with 500 players and 3000 singers.

'Slap' was a short, heavily muscled man who had been an amateur boxing champion in his youth. His years as a violinist had caused paralysis in his right arm, so that throughout his conducting career he used his left arm only. He was a good-natured man without cultural frills or social graces. Aspiring singers and players regarded him as a 'holy terror'.

Joseph Slapoffski remained active into old age. He died at Melbourne in 1951 aged eighty-nine.

PETER DAWSON

One of Australia's best-loved singers was Peter Dawson, son of an Adelaide ironworker and plumber, and the youngest of nine.

The young Dawson sang in a church choir as a boy soprano at the age of eight, then took singing lessons on completion of his schooling, when he became apprenticed to his father. By 1900, when he was eighteen, Dawson was singing at concerts with the Adelaide Grand Orchestra, and in that year was a soloist in Handel's *Messiah*.

Two years later, Dawson, with the prompting of his singing teacher and with some financial assistance from his father, went to London, where he was able to support himself with various singing engagements whilst furthering his studies.

In 1905, Dawson, then aged twenty-three, married Annie Noble, a soprano who sang under the name of Annette George. For three years the couple sang together during various international tours until a serious car accident put an end to Annie's singing career.

As a soloist, Dawson continued on the road to success. He sang at London's Covent Garden Opera House and returned briefly to Australia with a touring company. Back in London, Dawson further expanded his repertoire, which included French songs, German lieder, ballads and operatic arias. By 1911 the critics were praising him as the leading baritone of the day.

Dawson returned to Australia during World War I and enlisted in the Australian Imperial Force in 1918.

At the war's end, Dawson's musical career now developed in a number of directions. Initially he concerned himself with becoming an accomplished concert singer, and in this he was undeniably successful. He was prolific as a composer of songs and ballads, many of which he preferred to publish under various pseudonyms. Several of Rudyard Kipling's poems he set to music, amongst which 'Boots' and 'Route Marching' became immensely popular.

Dawson was one of the first artists to realise the potential of the gramophone record. In 1904 he began the third stage of his musical career when he commenced recording for His Master's Voice Records. His recordings were to span fifty years and make him a household name in Australia and many other countries. The recording medium extended from the original two-minute cylinders to the long-playing record. As with his songs, he preferred to record using a variety of pseudonyms. By the end of his gramophone career he had recorded over 3500 titles. Sales of his records exceeded 13 million.

There was something of the genuine theatrical trouper in Dawson's make-up, for he had an outgoing nature and loved the stage. In 1931 he topped the bill at that mecca of British variety, the London Palladium. It was said of him that if he had not become a concert singer he would have made a successful comedian.

Dawson came to live in Sydney in 1939, and during World War II devoted much of his time to singing at troop concerts and appearing at recruitment drives in Australia and New Zealand. In 1950 he returned to the city of his birth to sing the same bass solo part in Handel's *Messiah* that he had sung fifty years earlier. In the following year he published his autobiography: *Fifty Years of Song*. He became president of the Australian Songwriters' and Composers' Association in 1953.

It was also in 1953 that Peter Dawson's wife died. In the following year he married her sister, Constance Noble. His retirement years were spent with her at the Sydney beachside suburb of Dee Why. He died in 1961, aged seventy-nine.

NELLIE MELBA

Born Helen Porter Mitchell at Richmond, Victoria on 19 May 1861 of Scottish parents, she later adopted Nellie Melba as her professional name.

In 1882 she met Charles Armstrong, and married him later that year. Their marriage was a checkered affair and ended in 1900.

Meanwhile, Melba's singing career had blossomed, and having first established herself on the Melbourne concert circuit, she travelled to Europe. She achieved her first success there in 1888, in the title role in Donizetti's opera *Lucia*.

Melba's operatic career then continued for the next thirty years, 'Melba nights' being glittering social events. In 1918 she was appointed Dame Commander of the British Empire for her charity work during World War I. Despite this, she was disliked by many of her peers, although she gained some respect for her assistance in the careers of younger singers. In 1927 she was again honoured, and became Dame Grand Cross of the British Empire.

During her career Melba sang and recorded with many well-known artists including Enrico Caruso, the famous Italian operatic tenor.

In the mid-1920s Melba had begun the first of her famous 'farewell' concerts, which in fact were to continue for three years. The 'final' three 'farewells' took place in 1928 at Sydney, Melbourne and Geelong. But she squeezed in one more concert—a matinee of *La Bohéme* in Adelaide. It really was the last.

Melba died in Sydney in 1931 aged 69. The funeral motorcade was said to be over a kilometre long.

There is a statue of Dame Nellie Melba at Waterfront City, Melbourne Docklands.

DAME JOAN SUTHERLAND

Joan Sutherland was born in Sydney of Scottish parents. Her mother, a mezzo soprano, had taken vocal lessons but did not consider a career as a professional singer. But Joan did, and at the age of 18 began studying voice training. She made her concert debut in Sydney in 1947, and four years later made her stage debut in Eugene Goossens's *Judith*.

She then went to London to further her career and secured an appointment at the Royal Opera House as a utility soprano, making her stage debut there in 1952. Several weeks later she performed in Bellini's *Norma*, with Maria Callas singing the title role.

Sutherland's ability to sing high notes and coloratura now gave direction to her career. From the mid-1950s onwards she sang mostly as a dramatic coloratura soprano. In 1958, at the Royal Opera House, after singing 'Let the Bright Seraphim' (from Handel's oratorio *Samson*), she received a 10-minute-long standing ovation.

In 1954 she married Richard Bonynge, a conductor and pianist. A son was born to them two years later. Bonynge did much to reshape Sutherland's technique, particularly in regard to her diction.

In 1960 she recorded *The Art of the Prima Donna*, comprising mainly coloratura arias. It became one of the most recommended opera albums ever recorded.

Also in 1960, after singing at *La Fenice* in Venice, her performance was such that she was acclaimed as *La Stupenda* ('The Stunning One'). The nickname lasted throughout her career.

Sutherland's voice began to decline in the later 1970s. But she continued singing difficult roles until 1990, when she performed her last full-length dramatic performance at the Sydney Opera House. At the end of that year she made her last public appearance in a gala performance of *Die Fledermaus* at London's Covent Garden. She was accompanied by Luciano Pavarotti (who had once referred to her as 'The Voice of the Century') and mezzo-soprano Marilyn Horne.

Sutherland then retired to her home near Montreux in Switzerland. From then on she had no connection with the world of opera, although she served on the jury of the Cardiff Singer of the World competition.

Sutherland received many honours and awards. In 1961 she was made a Commander of the Order of the British Empire (CBE). In that year she was also named Australian of the Year.

In 1975 she was named as a Companion of the Order of Australia (AC), and in 1979 was elevated within the Order of the British Empire, from Commander to Dame Commander.

In 1991 she was awarded the Order of Merit (OMI), and in 2004 received the Australia Post Australian Legends Award. Various other Australian awards were bestowed upon her during her declining years. In 1991 she opened the Dame Joan Sutherland Music Centre in Queensland.

Dame Joan Sutherland died at her Swiss home on 10 October 2010. She was survived by her husband, her son and daughter-in-law, and by two grandchildren.

Sydney's Opera House is quite magnificent from the outside, and equally wonderful inside when *La Stupenda* was performing.

The Artistic Director of Opera Australia, Lyndon Terracini, said 'We won't see her like again'.

AUSTRALIA'S CENTENARY

By 1888, 100 years had passed since the First Fleet had arrived at Sydney Cove. All but a few of the continent's inhospitable and inaccessible areas, mainly in the north and north-west, had been explored. The descendants of the original European settlers and the immigrants had identified themselves with the vast continent. More than a third of Australia's three million inhabitants now lived in the seven capital cities.

The first hundred years of European civilisation in Australia were marked on 26 January 1888 with appropriate rejoicing and a suitable degree of pomp and ceremony. On a fine and sunny day, some 50,000 loyal citizens gathered in Sydney, not far from the city centre, for the day's celebrations. The setting was the newly created Centennial Park, previously a swamp on the city's southern perimeter. Flags fluttered in the breeze and the nearby streets were gay with coloured bunting. At the park's centre a band played patriotic tunes. Preceded by a troop of Lancers, the Governor of New South Wales, Lord Carrington, arrived in an open carriage and was cheered to the echo by the assembled throng. Appropriate speeches were made and applauded.

The hundred years had thus far been a long and tortuous journey. Much had been achieved, but there were signs then of more difficult times immediately ahead.

However, it would not be very many years before there was to be another gathering of the people to celebrate an even more important community occasion—Federation (see pp. 228–31).

SOCIETY AT THE TURN OF THE CENTURY

During the latter half of the nineteenth century, changes occurred in the make-up of Australian society. As the numbers of native-born increased, there was a corresponding decrease in the proportion of immigrants who occupied positions of influence in all spheres of colonial activity.

The fact that the majority of the population were either British immigrants or, in increasing numbers, locally-born whites of predominantly Anglo-Saxon origin, resulted in a sense of unity throughout the colonies. The people, other than Aboriginal Australians, spoke one official language, had a similar cultural background and generally shared similar dress styles and customs. These commonalities induced a cohesiveness which was to make the process towards Federation remarkably harmonious.

An Act of Parliament in 1902 granted women the right to vote in national elections, although women's political rights had been recognised in most of the colonies several years earlier. Some women were allowed into the professions in the late 1800s, and 1883 saw the first woman graduate with a Bachelor of Arts degree from the University of Melbourne. There were also women students at the University of Sydney in the 1890s.

Men still enjoyed most of the privileges and advantages of citizenship, but the female population was making an increasingly significant contribution to the social structure. The march towards women's liberation in Australia had begun.

Technology, in the form of such innovations as railways, tramways, the telephone and the telegraph, had an impact on social life in much the same way as the Internet did a century later.

SULINA SUTHERLAND

Sulina Sutherland was born in Scotland in 1839 and followed her sister to New Zealand to become a nurse. Strongly influenced by Florence Nightingale, she worked tirelessly for the sick and needy, Maoris and settlers alike, and by 1880 became matron of the Wellington Hospital.

In 1881 Sulina moved to Melbourne, where the plight of destitute children soon aroused her compassion. At her instigation the Scots

Church District Association founded a Neglected Children's Aid Society. Later, in 1883, the Society in Aid of Maternity Hospital Patients was set up in cooperation with all church denominations. Sutherland became a lifelong and active committee member of the Melbourne District Nursing Society, formed in 1885.

In the following year the Presbytery of Melbourne appointed Sutherland as their missionary. Under the Neglected Children's Act of 1887 she was 'specially authorised' to apprehend children in brothels. She now became well-known and respected as, dressed in a firmly fitted coat and skirt, a mannish hat and carrying an umbrella, she fearlessly searched alleyways, gambling houses and brothels for neglected children.

In 1890, giving evidence to a Royal Commission on charitable institutions, Sutherland put forward a plan for a foster home system, arguing that family life, even in a humble home, is far better for a child than confinement in an institution. Her 'Miss Sutherland's Children's Society' became highly regarded, but in 1893 she and fourteen committee members resigned when the society's committee ordered restrictions for financial reasons.

Undeterred, Sutherland now approached the Presbyterian General Assembly in Melbourne. At her instigation the Presbyterian Society for Destitute and Neglected Children was established, with Sutherland as agent. The society flourished, but bitter arguments and press debates developed when the General Assembly's commission directed that preference be given to Presbyterian children, that only children under legal guardianship be received and that only Presbyterian foster homes be used. Sutherland and the entire ladies' committee resigned in 1894, whereupon the Victorian Neglected Children's Aid Society was founded, with Sutherland again as agent. This organisation prospered and grew. The city centre premises were expanded and a home, named the Sutherland Home, was set up in the inner suburb of Parkville.

In the following year, as the need for her work increased, she was assisted by Sister Ellen Sanderson, then by a second assistant whose wages she paid from her own pocket (Sutherland's salary was never more than £100 a year).

Meanwhile, in 1897, Sutherland returned briefly to the United Kingdom, using the opportunity to raise money for her homes. In 1904 she was severely injured in an accident.

In 1908, when thoughts of limiting her involvement in the homes were occupying her mind, a dispute arose over complaints from domestic staff, leading to her dismissal by the Society's committee. Once again, Sutherland had to make a fresh start, and with the assistance of Sister Sanderson and other helpers, The Sutherland Homes for Orphans, Neglected and Destitute Children was constituted with a committee of prominent Melbourne citizens. Sutherland was completely vindicated by a subsequent government enquiry into her dismissal.

The new society became soundly established, helped by generous donations and the gift of a house and property at Diamond Creek. Then, as plans were made to move the home there whilst retaining the city centre premises, news came of Sulina Sutherland's sudden death from pneumonia. She was aged seventy.

Alfred Deakin, three times Prime Minister of Australia, wrote of this sometimes brusque and impatient but always caring and indomitable woman: 'The value of Miss Sutherland's noble work is simply incalculable.'

SYDNEY KIDMAN

One night a youth stole away from his suburban Adelaide home and rode off on his one-eyed horse. In his pocket were his savings—just five shillings. He made his way to a station north of Broken Hill where his brother, George, found him a job with an itinerant bushman, George Raines, who roamed the unfenced runs with his stock, squatting wherever he found good feed.

The youth's first outback 'home' was a dug-out in a dry creek which he shared with an Aboriginal man, from whom he learned tracking and other bush skills. He came to like and admire the Aboriginal people, and for the rest of his life would invariably travel in the outback with an Aboriginal man as guide and companion.

The youth, six feet tall and easygoing, was Sydney Kidman. He was later to become one of Australia's wealthiest and most influential land owners.

When George Raines moved on, the young Kidman worked for a year as a rouseabout (odd-jobs man) at a station about 40 kilometres north of Broken Hill, then as a stockman for a nearby shanty-keeper. With his savings he bought a bullock team and was soon employing others to cart supplies to remote settlements. Kidman also took to droving mobs of cattle and horses, sometimes to markets as far away as Adelaide.

When copper was discovered at Cobar, Kidman opened a butcher's shop there, making enough money from this venture to establish himself as a large squatter. A bequest of £400 from his grandfather provided sufficient additional capital to enable him to establish coaching businesses in western New South Wales and in Western Australia. He supplied his own horses for the coaches, and entered into an agreement to provide remounts to the British Army in India.

As Kidman's entrepreneurial skills improved, so did his wealth increase. He next turned to buying and selling cattle to another brother, Sackville, who had a flourishing butchery at Broken Hill.

In 1886 Kidman bought his first station, Owen Springs, south-west of Alice Springs. He was then twenty-nine. Other properties were later acquired—prime holdings watered by the

Cooper Creek and the Diamantina and Georgina rivers. These properties stretched almost in a straight line from the Gulf of Carpentaria to the Broken Hill area.

Such was Kidman's success that in less than ten years he had acquired a second chain of properties, this time extending from the Fitzroy and Victoria rivers in the 'Top End' southwards to Wilpena in the Flinders Ranges, north of Adelaide.

These strings of properties enabled Kidman, with his astute business acumen and intimate knowledge of the outback, to move stock from one area to another in bad seasons, and to sell in selected markets when prices were at their highest. Tight control of his 'empire' enabled him to withstand the severe depression of the 1890s and the great drought of 1895–1903.

During World War I, Kidman gained national prominence by his gift of fighter planes to the Air Force and other generous gifts to the armed services. In 1920 he donated £1000 and a half-share in one of his properties to the Salvation Army. In the following year his country home was given to the South Australian government for use as a high school.

Sidney Kidman had married a school teacher in 1885. They had three daughters and a son. Kidman's wife brought a broadening dimension to his life, filling a void left by his uncompleted education.

Kidman was knighted in 1921 and retired in 1927, but he and his family retained control of the pastoral empire he had created.

Sir Sidney Kidman was an imposing man with a ready smile and an affable manner. He never touched alcohol or tobacco, nor was he ever heard to use profane language. He had the facility of being able to sleep at any time and in any position. He was strict in his business dealings and could not abide waste.

Kidman, generally known as 'the cattle king', was another of the self-made pastoralists—a dealer rather than a breeder; an exploiter rather than a developer. He was an achiever.

JOHN SHEARSTON

One day in 1872, in Sydney's George Street, a drunken seaman was being taunted and ridiculed by the passing crowd. He was rescued from further abuse by John Shearston, who took the unfortunate man to his home, sobered him up and sent him on his way.

The incident stirred Shearston's compassion for neglected and sometimes homeless itinerant workers. He commenced boarding ships in port and frequently invited seamen to his Double Bay home. He became a hospital visitor, distributing tracts and counselling those in need. In 1878 he was licensed as a Church of England lay reader and began conducting services on board ship. In 1880 he married, and later he and his wife adopted an orphaned naval rating.

In 1881 the Church of England Mission to Seamen was founded. Shearston, who had been employed as a clerk at Sydney's Royal Mint, now resigned his job and worked full-time for the Mission, his new home at Dawes Point becoming its headquarters.

Shearston soon became a familiar sight, being rowed out in a skiff by an Aboriginal boy to visit merchant ships and any naval vessels that were in port. There was an open invitation to seamen to make evening visits to the Shearstons' home, where the men were given refreshments and reading matter and were entertained in a simple and homely manner.

In 1885 the Mission was able to move to larger premises at Trafalgar House, where some residential accommodation was available. In the following year, Shearston responded to a request to act as superintendent of the Goodenough Royal Naval House. By 1889 the number of naval ratings on shore leave had increased to such an extent that larger accommodation was needed. A public subscription was opened, resulting in a new Royal Naval House being established in Grosvenor Street. It could sleep up to 300 men and provided various facilities, including a gymnasium, a billiards room, and reading and dining rooms. The Royal Naval House enjoyed the full support and co-operation of senior naval personnel.

In 1890 Shearston resigned his Goodenough Royal Naval House appointment to become full-time superintendent of the new Royal Naval House. His wife, Mary, acted as housekeeper. Seamen, appreciating the Shearstons' always warm welcome, called the premises 'Johnny's', and that was the name by which it was known until its eventual closure in 1970, when it became affiliated with the worldwide Missions to Seamen.

John Shearston, a compassionate and dedicated man, died in 1916, aged sixty-three. He was buried in the South Head cemetery.

CHEONG CHEOK HONG

Cheong Cheok Hong was the son of a Presbyterian missionary who emigrated from China in the 1850s and initially settled in Ballarat, Victoria. About 1863 he arrived in Melbourne, where he attended Scotch College. Later he matriculated at the University of Melbourne.

For a year or two Cheong was assistant to the minister at the Presbyterian church at Fitzroy, spending much of his time working amongst the Chinese of the district. At this time, in 1869, he married Wong Toy Yen at Ballarat. They were to have five sons and two daughters, all of whom were well educated.

The church's seminary closed in 1877. For several years Cheong, probably for financial reasons, went into business. His Christian faith remained strong.

A significant change occurred in 1885, when Cheong was invited to give an address at the annual meeting of the Anglican Board of Missions. Such was the response to his address that his transfer from the Presbyterian church was requested and approved. He was then appointed as the Board's missionary superintendent, his main task being to organise the work of Chinese catechists throughout Victoria. He also set about raising funds for a mission hall as a training centre for Chinese evangelists. This was duly established in Melbourne's Little Bourke Street in 1897, the property coming under the control of the Church Missionary Association of Victoria, with Cheong as superintendent.

In the following year Cheong resigned, then opened an unofficial Anglican mission at the Temperance Hall in Russell Street. Some 800 people attended the first annual meeting. Once again Cheong set about raising funds, this time for another mission hall, again in Little Bourke Street, but on this occasion under the jurisdiction of the Church Missionary Association Reformed. It was fully recognised by the Church of England in 1904, with Cheong's son, James, being appointed as its ordained chaplain. The mission was later renamed the Church of England Chinese Mission of the Epiphany. Cheong, who was invariably known as 'Mr Cheong', remained its superintendent until his death in 1928.

Cheong was a forthright man who, throughout his ministry, was outspoken against human weakness when confronted with social problems. Opium smoking was one of his main targets and, in 1889, with several friends, he initiated the anti-opium movement in Victoria. He continued his campaign during a visit to England in the same year.

Cheong launched a second anti-opium campaign in 1905, which resulted in the passing of an Act prohibiting the sale and smoking of opium in Victoria.

Cheong unceasingly championed the cause of Victoria's Chinese community, publishing several pamphlets on various issues and making frequent representations to the government to appeal for better treatment of the state's Chinese population. In 1918 he was elected president of the Commonwealth Chinese Community's Representation Committee, but this initiative met with only limited success.

Through his education, intelligence and command of English, Cheong Cheok Hong was able to act as a bridge between Victoria's Chinese people and the Australian churches and business communities, and with the governments of the day. He was a fearless and unremitting campaigner on Chinese social issues, and through his missionary zeal did much to Christianise his own people in Victoria.

ECONOMIC ACTIVITY AND THE UNIONS

The early 1880s were boom years in Australia. As investment money flowed in from Britain, the colonial governments experienced no difficulty in obtaining loans from London, sometimes in excess of their capital needs.

However, doubts gradually arose concerning the economic health of the colonies. The doubts spawned rumours, and there followed a sudden collapse in confidence. Several financial institutions suspended payments; others closed their doors. Bankruptcies increased alarmingly. Borrowings from London diminished markedly, whilst expenditure on public works and on private developments slowed down or ceased. Unemployment and hardship inevitably resulted.

During the 1880s, when wool remained Australia's principal export, prices for the clip in overseas markets steadily declined. The pastoralists responded by increasing production, but with supply outstripping demand, wool prices inevitably continued to fall. Overseas investments in Australia contracted at this time, resulting in reductions in public works programs and an inevitable increase in unemployment. Small investors began withdrawing funds from the banks to meet living expenses. In the early 1890s a number of banks collapsed. A crisis of confidence developed, but legislative measures taken by the colonial governments gradually restored confidence as the end of the century approached.

Seen in perspective, the 1890s collapse was an inevitable pause resulting from a period of excessive spending by both government agencies and private enterprise. It followed the period of steady economic growth which characterised the latter half of the nineteenth century.

The first signs of unionism had appeared in New South Wales in 1831. By 1891 the number of affiliated unions in New South Wales alone totalled seventy-one.

The economic malaise of the 1890s was paralleled by a series of unprecedented strikes, the most damaging of which resulted from the 1890 dispute between the ship owners and the Marine Officers' Association. Every port in Australia was involved. The strike by marine officers and transport workers affected over 50,000 transport and mining workers, lasted for three months, and finally ended when the marine officers accepted the ship owners' terms.

In the following year, the Amalgamated Shearers Union locked horns with the graziers over poor working and living conditions, low wages and other grievances. The graziers responded by employing non-union labour (their action giving rise to the term 'scab', which is a mangy disease particularly affecting sheep), by forming the Pastoralists' Association and by enlisting government support. The strike collapsed in the face of these moves.

There was another three-month shearers' strike in 1894 when declining prices and deteriorating economic conditions caused the pastoralists to reduce wages. Once again, the shearers lost the fight.

The unionists were also unsuccessful in a dispute involving workers at Broken Hill, resulting in several of the strikers being gaoled.

It was not the time for union militancy. The economic crisis and the nation-wide drought during the 1890s, together with the strength of the government-supported employers, combined to defeat the unions.

The response of the defeated workers was to establish their own political party, the Labor Party (see below), which rapidly attracted worker support. By the turn of the century Labor had become a powerful force on the political scene.

Although by 1893 the banks had resumed lending, economic conditions continued to be unfavourable. Some factories had closed and unemployment was high. Many workers in those factories and in retail establishments, which had managed to keep going were forced to work long hours as the purchasing power of their wages declined. The use of 'sweated labour' became commonplace.

By 1896 the circumstances of many workers had given rise to a groundswell of public resentment, which resulted in Factories Acts being passed by both the New South Wales and Victorian governments. Working conditions and wages were regulated, and whilst abuses of the legislation continued, the regulations brought about improvements for those able to find employment.

Lessons had been learned by both capital and labour from the industrial unrest of the 1890s, occurring, as it did, during a period of severe drought and economic crisis.

THE AUSTRALIAN LABOR PARTY

It was against this background that the New South Wales Parliamentary Labor Party was launched in 1891. (The spelling 'Labor' came into use early in the twentieth century to describe the federal and state Labor parties, and to avoid confusion with the industrial 'labour' movement.)

In 1901 at a time of widespread unemployment, Labor parties which had been founded in the various colonies during the 1890s were amalgamated to form the Australian Labor Party (ALP). The ALP, which strongly embraced the union movement, was the first of the national political parties. By the outbreak of World War I, Labor had been in office in the Commonwealth and in all six states.

AUSTRALIAN INDUSTRY

Throughout the nineteenth century and well into the twentieth, Australia was essentially a primary-producing country. But as the populations of the six colonies and the territories grew steadily, so too did imports of consumer goods, machinery, vehicles and heavy equipment.

As a result, there was inevitably a relatively small market for locally manufactured goods—consumers sought better-quality goods, which Australia did not then produce. Unemployment, particularly in the cities and suburban areas, was high, and even skilled men and women frequently found it difficult to get a job.

The slow growth of the manufacturing industry continued until World War I, when Australia found itself far more dependent upon locally-made products.

CHARLES O'CONNOR

Charles O'Connor was an engineer who became an expert in the planning and construction of railways. In 1865, at the age of twenty-two, he migrated to New Zealand and for seventeen years worked in that country on various engineering projects. His interests during that period included the construction and operation of railways and the improvement of harbours.

O'Connor married in 1874 and became the father of eight children. In 1880 he was elected to the Institute of Civil Engineers in London.

In 1890, dissatisfied with an appointment by the New Zealand government, he began to look for employment opportunities elsewhere and made contact with the Western Australia government. The Premier, (Sir) John Forrest, lost no time in offering him an appointment as the state's engineer-in-chief, with responsibility for both railways and harbours. O'Connor accepted.

Forrest first set O'Connor the task of constructing a suitable harbour at Fremantle to accommodate the large British mail-carrying steamers. Forrest's advisers, believing that a harbour at the Swan River entrance was impracticable because of a rock bar at the river's entrance, had put forward a plan, which Forrest had accepted, to construct an outer harbour.

After a detailed examination of the problem, O'Connor concluded that it would be both practical and more economical to remove the obstructing bar, to deepen the river mouth and to keep it clear by dredging; and to protect the harbour by moles constructed from Rose and Arthur Heads.

Forrest now agreed to O'Connor's proposals, and a parliamentary select committee approved the work. Construction of the harbour began in 1892 and the official opening ceremony took place in 1897. The harbour was later extended.

O'Connor, meanwhile, had put forward plans for significant improvements to the colony's railways. The government appropriated funds for the construction of several new lines and the upgrading of existing lines. As both engineer-in-chief and acting general manager of railways, O'Connor had considerable influence and was able to demand improved tracks and better rolling stock. At his insistence the government railways became more efficient and economic, whilst repair and maintenance workshops were well-located and properly run. He continually campaigned for improvements in the conditions of railway staff and was always concerned with their welfare.

One of the railway problems in outback Australia was the scarcity of water for the steam engines. O'Connor, during his frequent tours on the colony's rail system, was well aware of this difficulty and instituted a systematic search for water. Following his surveys, wells and bores were put down, ground tanks installed and condensers built to treat heavily mineralised water wherever it was found.

The lack of water became a serious problem when the rich goldfields were discovered in 1892 at Coolgardie and in the following year at Kalgoorlie. O'Connor immediately began work on a scheme to provide the goldfields with a permanent supply of fresh water. By the end of 1895 he had produced a simple yet bold and imaginative plan: water would be stored in dams on the wet western slope of the

Darling Range, then pumped over the escarpment and across the plateau to a Coolgardie reservoir. From there a series of steel mains would deliver the water to users.

The plan, estimated to cost £2.5 million and to take three years to construct, was agreed to by Sir John Forrest, who now had to persuade parliament to approve a proposal to support the raising of a loan in London to finance the scheme.

The scheme, however, aroused considerable opposition from various quarters. O'Connor, in an attempt to answer the criticisms, suggested that his proposals be examined by an independent commission of experts. He therefore visited London and put his plan before a panel of three British engineers. Their verdict was that the plan was entirely feasible, adding the comment that it would be the finest such water-supply scheme ever undertaken.

But the detractors in Perth remained unconvinced, and criticisms continued. It was not until 1898 that Forrest finally secured parliamentary approval for the Coolgardie Water Supply Scheme. There were then further delays in placing contracts with Melbourne and Sydney companies for the manufacture of steel pipes, and with American and German firms for the supply of steel plate.

Forrest and other visionaries saw O'Connor's scheme in the wider context of a plan to expand the colony's economic development through a series of major projects: the Fremantle harbour project; the expansion of railways and communications; the delivery of water to the railways, to outback settlements and to the goldfields; and the eventual construction of a transcontinental railway to link Western Australia with the eastern colonies.

In 1901 Forrest resigned as Premier of Western Australia to enter the first Federal Parliament (see pp. 231–2), and asked O'Connor to prepare a report on the feasibility of a transcontinental railway linking the terminal at Kalgoorlie with Port Augusta in South Australia. Within a few weeks Forrest had O'Connor's plans and estimates. Construction of the Coolgardie water scheme, although well advanced, was now under threat by the unstable political environment that followed Forrest's departure. Fierce and vocal criticism of O'Connor's plan intensified when he decided to use a new electric caulking machine on the water main. O'Connor patiently prepared a detailed memorandum rebutting the long list of criticisms levelled against his scheme by both houses of parliament. But press attacks continued whilst the responsible government minister remained silent.

The intensity of the attacks depressed O'Connor and resulted in bouts of neuralgia and insomnia.

In March 1902 the success of the Coolgardie water scheme was proved when water was pumped over the most difficult section of the route during a preliminary test.

Two days later O'Connor set out for his early-morning ride along the beach near the family home at Fremantle. His usual companion, his youngest daughter, was unwell that morning and did not accompany him. O'Connor rode alone, past the new harbour he had created and then to Robb Jetty, where he turned his horse into the sea. A single revolver shot ended his life. The distress, overwork and exhaustion had been too much. He was fifty-nine.

HARLEY TARRANT

Harley Tarrant's first job was with a firm of civil engineers. He later worked as a surveyor on the Nullarbor Plain, and subsequently set up his own surveying business in Melbourne.

During the 1890s Tarrant became interested in the development of motor cars, for with Australia's poor country roads and relatively few railways he could see the potential for powered vehicles.

In 1897 Tarrant took out a patent on a kerosene-powered engine. Although it proved unsuitable for a road vehicle, the engine found an outlet on farms for pumping water and was sold interstate.

Tarrant now moved to larger premises and began importing Benz, De Dion and Argyll cars. Business was good, and Tarrant went into partnership with William Lewis. Together they built one of the first Australian-made petrol-driven cars (a steam-powered vehicle had been built in 1896 by Herbert Thomson). It was ready by 1901 and had an imported Benz engine. Within two years the 'Tarrant' car had a 90 per cent local content, including the engine.

In 1905, and again in the following year, Tarrant won the Dunlop reliability trials, for Tarrant cars were built for strength and endurance rather than speed. But the partners found that they could not compete with the increasing numbers of cars being imported, and production of the Tarrant car ceased in 1906.

In 1907 the firm became a proprietary company and acquired the Ford franchise for Victoria. The manufacture of motor bodies continued, and during World War I the firm also made aero-engines and began assembling vehicle chassis. Tarrant Motors also had a thriving spare-parts, accessories and repair business.

Tarrant retired after the war, but in 1932 resumed supervision for several years of an affiliated company, Ruskin Motor Bodies Pty Ltd. He died in Melbourne in 1949 aged eighty-nine. In the following year his company was sold to the Austin Motor Company (see p. 142).

Harley Tarrant, a tall and imposing man with a love of the outdoors, played an important role in establishing the first phase of the Australian motor industry.

THE HOLDEN FAMILY

The Holdens had been in business for a long time—in fact, since 1909, when Henry Holden gained control of the family's leather, saddlery and carriage-building business; and extended the firm's production to include motor-body trimming (Holden's father had founded the business in 1883).

The advent of World War I, when the importing of finished car bodies was prohibited, gave an impetus to the business. A Holden-designed car body affixed to an imported chassis was immediately successful, and enabled Holden to acquire the business of another Adelaide carriage and body-builder. In 1917 the firm became a public company, with Henry Holden's son, Edward, as managing director.

The enlarged business continued to develop after the war, aided by a 100 per cent tariff on imported car bodies. By 1923 the company was employing over 1000 men and making some 240 car bodies per week for various imported vehicles chassis. A new plant at the Adelaide suburb of Woodville resulted in production almost doubling in the following year. Using the latest technology and automated production lines, the plant became the largest of its type outside the United States.

Amongst the manufacturers to which Holden were supplying car bodies was General Motors and Ford. Responding to an approach from General Motors, Holden entered into a reciprocal arrangement whereby the whole of their Woodville plant would be devoted to production exclusively for General Motors, who in return would provide technical and design know-how. The two companies thus became interdependent.

Henry Holden, a self-made manufacturer, always enjoyed good relations with his workforce, due mainly to close consultation and generous social welfare initiatives. He had a passion for quality production and would not tolerate poor work. But he became increasingly out of tune with technological changes, and this led to tensions with his innovative son.

Henry Holden, generous with the time he devoted to civic affairs and with his donations to charitable causes, died at his Norwood home in 1926.

Edward Holden had gone straight into the family business after graduating from the University of Adelaide. In his father's declining years he was responsible for the introduction of automated mass-production methods, and by advocating piece-work achieved a significant improvement in labour productivity at the Woodville plant.

He travelled widely and became strongly influenced by American management methods, cost accounting and production control. Nearly 47,000 car bodies were made in 1927. Two years later the company's workforce had risen to 3400.

But the company now entered a two-year crisis period, with a significant decline in orders from both General Motors and Ford. The lack of orders caused temporary plant closures, and during 1931 only 1630 car bodies were made. Holden's major competitors were similarly affected, but though the company remained solvent, it was still largely dependent upon orders from General Motors.

At this point, General Motors made first an all-cash offer for the business, then a cash-and-share offer. Shareholders were far from satisfied with the latter offer, but when the directors recommended it, the offer was accepted. Holden's increasing dependence on General Motors had resulted in their American customer gaining control of the business.

Edward Holden was appointed chairman and joint managing director of the new company, General Motors–Holden's Ltd. But in 1934 he was replaced as managing director, although he remained as chairman. The company's fortunes recovered and a new plant was opened in Melbourne.

Edward Holden became bitter and disappointed at his displacement, and increasingly turned his attention to other interests. But he was dogged by ill health and resigned as chairman of directors in January 1947. He died later that year.

For twenty years prior to his death, Edward Holden was active in commercial and civic affairs. He was a director of a number of companies and president of the South Australian Chamber of Commerce, the Chamber of Manufactures and of the Associated Chambers of Manufactures of Australia. He served on the Adelaide City Council, on the Council of the University of Adelaide and as a member of the South Australian Legislative Council from 1935–47.

The Holden family made a significant contribution to the development of Australian manufacturing and to the South Australian economy. Despite the relative smallness of the local market, the introduction of large-scale mass-production methods resulted in the development of the first all-Australian car. The Holden 48-215, later known as the FX model, rolled off the production line in 1948 and cost £760. It had a six-cylinder engine developing 60 break-horse-power. The top speed was about 80 miles (130 kilometres) per hour and the fuel consumption approximately 37 miles per gallon (13 kilometres per litre). It had a three-speed gearbox and four-wheel hydraulic brakes. It was immediately popular, with initial production of about 20,000 units a year. Some 8000 people were employed in its production. The Prime Minister, Ben Chifley, placed no restriction on General Motors–Holden's repatriation to the United States of profits on the manufacture of the new car.

AGRICULTURE

In the thirty years from 1861 to 1891, sheep numbers increased from about 21 million to 107 million. During the same period the value of wool exports nearly doubled. Wool was to remain Australia's principal export-earner until after World War II, when the introduction of synthetic fibres resulted in the value of wool exports declining.

Two developments also resulted in a reduction in the number of men employed by graziers. One was the erection of fencing and the use of barbed wire; another was the invention of mechanical shearing (see pp. 140–2) to replace the laborious and time-consuming use of hand shears.

Improvements and innovations were continually made on the land. Aboriginal people comprised a significant proportion of the labour force on the early cattle runs, acting as station hands and boundary riders.

The importance of water conservation was ever in the minds of the graziers. Dams were constructed and windmill pumps installed. Mustering was facilitated by the development of a special breed of the canine species...

THE AUSTRALIAN CATTLE DOG

'Find a cattleman and his dog won't be far away.'

The story of the Australian cattle dog began in 1802 when the parents of one Thomas Hall arrived in Sydney and settled on the Hawkesbury River. They were amongst a small group of Presbyterians who founded a chapel at Ebenezer in 1817. (Still standing, it is the oldest church in mainland Australia.) The Hall family was one of the earliest to settle in the Upper Hunter region, and they soon became substantial farmers.

Thomas Hall managed the family's Dartbrook property (near Muswellbrook), breeding merino sheep, cattle and station horses. In 1840, when the need for good cattle dogs became apparent, Hall imported a pair of blue-mottled smooth Scotch collies known as 'merles'. He is said to have crossed one of the merles with a dingo, producing a silent and intelligent dog. But the breed proved unsuitable for working with horses. Hall then crossed merles with

Dalmatians, which gave the blue speckles; and then with black-and-tan Kelpies for greater intelligence and heading-in instinct.

By 1870 'Hall's Heelers' were famous and much in demand amongst cattlemen. The breed was later improved further by Sydney breeders, and by 1890 the blue cattle dog had bred true. It was the only such cattle dog in the world.

Although cattlemen nowadays sometimes muster with the aid of motorbikes or a helicopter, a good cattle dog remains an important asset.

JAMES TYSON

The dynamic expansion of the Australian pastoral industry was achieved by a breed of pioneers who, in various ways, conquered the frequently discouraging conditions presented by harsh terrain, intolerable climatic conditions and the tyranny of distance in a vast land.

One such pioneer was James Tyson. At the time of his death he held properties in New South Wales and Queensland, with some smaller holdings in Victoria, which totalled well over 2 million hectares. In the nineteenth century he was reputed to be Australia's richest man.

James Tyson was born in 1819. His mother had come to Australia in 1809 as a convict carrying a seven-year sentence for theft in Yorkshire. Her husband, William, arrived in the same transport as a free settler, together with their sons James and William. They later had a third son, John.

By the time James was born, William senior had acquired a 40-acre (16-hectare) land grant at Narellan, south-west of Sydney. At the age of fourteen, James secured work as a farm hand at a nearby property. In 1837 he was appointed to a bootmaker, then returned to the land as a labourer at a property near Yass, south-west of Goulburn in New South Wales. Tyson then managed a property on Victoria's Ovens River (a tributary of the Murray).

The Tyson sons, James, William and John, then took up unsettled land north of Balranald, in the south-west of New South Wales, and succeeded in supplying high-priced meat to the gold diggers at Bendigo, where James and William had set up a slaughter yard and a butcher's shop. They sold the business in 1855 for a reputed £80,000.

James and John next bought three sheep properties in the Deniliquin area in the colony's south-west. James, meanwhile, began lending money to squatters, taking a mortgage on the properties. Later, when hard times came and the squatters were unable to repay the loans, their properties fell into James's hands.

John died at Deniliquin in 1860, leaving his estate to James. Two years later James sold most of the Deniliquin holdings and returned to his Balranald properties.

James Tyson Senior progressively went about acquiring a chain of rich stations in the high rainfall areas of the eastern states, always improving the properties and adding to their stock, balancing losses in one area with gains in another.

Tyson was a physically big man, but he could also 'think big'. An example of this was when he ordered a 13-kilometre channel to be dug from the Lachlan River to connect with a reservoir, thus removing the need for the property's 20,000 sheep and 4000 cattle to go to the river for water.

Although a hard man, James Tyson was also generous and donated to a wide range of charities. On one occasion, to shore up the credit of the Queensland government during the 1892–93 financial crisis, he invested £250,000 in Treasury bills. He was also a member of the Queensland Legislative Council from 1893–98, and for a time served as a magistrate on benches in New South Wales and Queensland.

James Tyson, nicknamed 'Hungry', was a rugged man who neither drank nor smoked and was never known to swear. He was ruthless but strictly honest. He was amongst the first pastoralists to realise that for cattle-raising to be profitable it must be on a large scale. He was a dominant figure on the pastoral scene during the second half of the nineteenth century and a legend in his lifetime. He died in 1898, aged seventy-nine.

THE ROYAL AGRICULTURAL SOCIETY

Easter in Sydney wouldn't be the same without the 'Greatest Show on Earth'. It's the time of year when country folk come to town to show their wares, perhaps to do a little shopping and to catch up with developments in 'the big smoke'. For Sydneysiders it's a chance to recall, perhaps with a touch of nostalgia, that life in the bush is different and to remember that field and farm contribute just as much to the good things of life as do factories and offices.

There's a unique atmosphere about 'the Show', as it is commonly referred to. There's the prize-winning farm animals, the Grand Parade, the creative and picture-like displays of fruit and vegetables in the Exhibition Hall, the sideshows and amusements and, of course, the item which all self-respecting school children must have—the Showbag. There's much more: the woodchopping and various other competitions, the crafts exhibition, the huge range of products on display in and around the various pavilions, the wonderful evening entertainments in the main arena under the stars (if the weather is kind, as it frequently is), and many other attractions.

The Royal Easter Show is promoted and presented by the Royal Agricultural Society of New South Wales (RAS), a non-profit organisation founded in 1822. It all began when one Mr Robertson, a jeweller and watchmaker in Sydney's George Street, resolved to form a society to be named The Agricultural Society of New South Wales. The Society's first president was Sir John Jamison, KGV, a pastoralist and former Royal Navy surgeon who was also one of the founders of the Bank of New South Wales. When the Society was founded there were over 100,000 cattle in New South Wales, approximately 290,000 sheep, and large areas of wheat and maize.

The Society's first agricultural show was held in 1824 at Westmead (near Parramatta). In 1869 the first show in central Sydney was held over four days at the Prince Alfred Park. Ten years later the Society staged the Sydney International Exhibition, which was a tremendous success.

In 1881 the RAS leased an area of land at Sydney's Moore Park. The land was in very poor condition, being largely a swamp interspersed with rocks and depressions several metres deep. Although the Society's finances at the time were in a critical state, the land was drained, the holes were filled in and the rocks removed in time for the first Show at the new site in 1882.

Since then the Royal Easter Show has been held each year, except for 1919, because of the influenza epidemic, and during World War II, when the Army occupied the 29-hectare Moore Park site from 1942–46. The 1997 Royal Easter Show was the last to be held at the Moore Park site. In the following year the Show and the RAS's headquarters were relocated to Homebush Bay, the site of the 2000 Olympic Games.

The Royal Agricultural Society of New South Wales has become one the most influential bodies of its type in the world.

WILLIAM FARRER

The ill health of a young English student was later to result in far-reaching benefits to Australian wheat growers as the end of the nineteenth century approached.

Suffering from tuberculosis, William Farrer, at the age of twenty-five, migrated to Australia's sunny clime in search of improved health. He found good health and a rewarding lifetime career as well. Australia was grateful, too, for his work. A Canberra suburb was named after him, as well as schools, streets and various institutions. He was commemorated on Australian stamps and on the $2 coin introduced in 1988.

Farrer, the son of a tenant farmer, was born in England in 1845. Scholarships enabled him to study mathematics in London and medicine at Cambridge. In Australia he qualified as a surveyor in 1875, and for eleven years worked for the Department of Lands. He married in 1882.

Like his father, Farrer had always been interested in farming, and during his early years in Australia the young man cherished hopes of acquiring a property. In 1873 he had produced a pamphlet entitled 'Grass and sheep farming', but his interest gradually turned to wheat growing. A study of the wheat industry's problems led him to the conclusion that the varieties of wheat being grown at the time were unsuited to Australian conditions. He foresaw the need for blending selected plants with suitable foreign parents through cross-fertilisation. Through correspondence he sought information from overseas on attempts then being made in Europe and America to produce improved wheat.

In 1886 Farrer resigned from his surveyor's job and settled at Lambrigg on the Murrumbidgee River (near present-day Canberra), and there commenced his research in earnest. For twelve years he conducted countless experiments, cross-pollinating, culling and improvising to produce hundreds of crossbred plants. Farrer extended his research to assess the flour yields and baking behaviour of specific varieties, choosing parents and progeny strictly by results.

Farrer pursued his experiments with single-minded dedication, despite the initial lack of interest from the wheat industry. During this period his wife and her father had to support themselves from their own resources. Farrer must have been tempted by the offer from a wealthy uncle to inherit a fortune if he returned to England. He chose to stay in Australia, however. Nor was he deterred by impaired eyesight resulting from a riding accident in 1878.

In 1889 Farrer's first success came with a wheat he named 'Blount's Lambrigg', which, although not widely grown, proved an important breeding parent. From this was derived 'Bobs', his first wheat to be commercially grown. It yielded well and had a good grain quality.

Farrer then addressed the problem of producing disease-resistant varieties and concluded that the answer lay in Indian wheats, which tolerated drought and, because of their early maturity, largely escaped rust.

Farrer now had the help of Frederick Guthrie, an agricultural chemist who had joined the Department of Agriculture in 1892 and was assigned to assist Farrer. Guthrie's earlier studies whilst at the University of Sydney pointed to the advantages of certain Canadian varieties, particularly 'Fife' because of their milling and baking quality. But they were late-maturing wheats. The solution, Farrer decided, was to hybridise the two types. The result, after many tests, was 'Comeback', which had a better grain quality than 'Bobs' and produced a superior flour yield.

In 1898 Farrer was appointed as experimentalist to the Department of Agriculture at a salary of £350 per annum.

Farrer's contacts with flour millers produced evidence of resistance to the improved varieties now available, the millers generally preferring the soft wheats with which they were familiar. However, at a 'Rust in Wheat' conference in Melbourne in 1896 it became evident that there was little opposition amongst growers to the new generation of wheats. A poor harvest that year necessitated the importation of hard wheats from North America, which were similar to the types Farrer and Guthrie were producing. Millers generally accepted the imported wheats, and made adjustments to their machinery, since it became apparent that the new varieties were giving better yields than the older types which the millers had previously used.

Farrer and Guthrie now came to the conclusion that it was desirable to include some of the older wheats as parents in order to produce the maximum grain yield. Experimental crossings were to produce, in 1901, the most widely grown of all Farrer's wheats—'Federation'. It was a cross between the soft and high-yielding wheats extensively sown in the 1880s, a hard Canadian wheat particularly suitable for bread-making, an Indian variety which matured early and was largely rust-free and 'Yandilla', a short straw wheat with upright ears which was especially suitable for stripping harvest. 'Federation' became available in 1903, and by 1920 accounted for some 80 per cent of the Australian wheat harvest. It was ideally suited to Australian conditions.

Farrer-bred wheats were largely responsible for a fourfold increase in wheat growing between 1897 and 1915. Wheat was now grown in some of the drier areas which had previously produced wheat prone to rust and other diseases.

Farrer continued working until his death at Lambrigg in 1906, aged sixty-one. But his work went on, with newer varieties gradually replacing the wheats Farrer had introduced. The Farrer Memorial Fund, commenced in 1911, administers an annual award for outstanding service to agricultural science in research, administration and education; and the Farrer Memorial Research Scholarship is awarded annually for postgraduate research in agriculture.

A granite column was erected by the government in 1939, at the site where William Farrer and his wife were buried at Lambrigg. There is also a bronze bust of him at Queanbeyan, near Canberra.

DROUGHT

Drought was one of the problems that beset the colonies during the 1890s. Of the world's seven continents, Australia is by far the driest, and therefore the most prone to droughts.

The classification of droughts is dependent upon their severity and the area or region affected. It is generally considered that the 1895–1903 drought, which affected almost the whole of the continent, was the worst since European settlement. About half of the country's sheep were lost, whilst cattle losses amounted to over 40 per cent. By 1902, wheat yields had dropped to about one-third.

The 1958–68 drought was also widespread, second only to the 1895–1903 drought in severity.

Other major droughts occurred in 1838, 1864–66, 1880–86, 1888, 1911–16, 1918–20, 1939–45, 1982–83 and 2006–10.

Frequent by-products of severe droughts were an increase in the incidence of dust storms (whereby large quantities of valuable topsoil would be removed from arable land), as well as bush and grass fires.

THE MACDONALD BROTHERS

The MacDonald brothers' father, Donald MacDonald, and mother, Anne, came from Scotland. The couple had married at Goulburn, south-west of Sydney, in 1849. Charles was born in 1851 and his brother, William, nine years later. The family then moved to a property at Laggan, about 50 kilometres north of Goulburn.

The brothers had become inspired by the reported potential pastoral opportunities in the Kimberley region, in the continent's north-west, and decided to make a first-hand investigation. Two cousins and three other men made up their party. In March 1883 they left Laggan with two bullock teams, fifty horses and 500 head of cattle. A further 500 head were added as they slowly drove northwards, where they encountered drought conditions.

Now discouraged by the prospects, the two cousins and three other men decided to abandon the journey and withdraw. Undeterred, the two brothers pushed on slowly, and by the time they reached Cooper Creek, not far from the Queensland–South Australia border, had been able to replace their stock losses.

As the drought continued their stock losses again increased, but despite the extremely difficult conditions they doggedly continued and reached Katherine, in the Northern Territory, in 1885. Here they were beset by a further problem when Charles became ill and had to return home.

Such was William's tenacity that he elected to continue alone with the remaining cattle. Notwithstanding summer heat, harsh terrain, loneliness and menacing bands of Aboriginal people, William succeeded in reaching the Margaret River (in the Kimberley) in June 1886. Here he was rejoined by his brother, and together they took up land near present-day Fitzroy Crossing, which they named Fossil Downs.

The epic crossing from Katherine had taken eleven months, and the entire journey from Laggan more than three years. The 5600-kilometre trek was a feat of great courage and endurance, and went down in history as one of Australia's longest droving journeys.

The two brothers steadily developed and extended the Fossil Downs property. It eventually occupied over 1 million acres (405,000 hectares), and became Australia's largest privately-owned cattle station.

Both brothers later returned to their family at Goulburn, where William married in 1902. He took his bride to Derby, on the northern coast of Western Australia and about 250 kilometres from Fossil Downs.

Charles died at Goulburn in 1903, aged fifty-two. He was unmarried. William, who had one son, died in Perth in 1910, aged fifty.

Charles and William MacDonald were expert bushmen and were noted for their kindness and hospitality. The indefatigable brothers were fine men—worthy representatives of the best traditions of Australian overlanding during the nineteenth century.

EXPANSION IN THE WEST

Development had been slow in Western Australia, but during the latter part of the nineteenth century progress began to accelerate. Large areas of pastoral land, particularly in the north-west, were opened up. Road and railway systems were developed and the telegraph extended. Pearling in the north and timber in the south added to the colony's economic development.

The time had come for Western Australia to manage its own affairs, and so it was that in 1890 the colony became self-governing, the parliament having upper and lower houses.

Eighteen months later, immense deposits of gold were discovered at Kalgoorlie. It was to be the last, and largest, of Australia's gold rushes.

When discussions were held in the 1890s regarding possible federation, Western Australia had been the least enthusiastic of the six colonies. In 1906 a vote was taken in the Legislative Assembly supporting a motion that Western Australia should withdraw from the Commonwealth, but no further action eventuated.

During the 1929–32 depression years, when there was a generally held view (amongst Western Australians) that Western Australia was receiving less than fair treatment at the federal level, there was again talk of secession. A referendum on the issue was held in 1933 and passed by a substantial majority. Representations were accordingly made to Britain (since the Federation Act had been an enactment of the British Parliament), and it was eventually decided that an amendment to the Federation Act could only be made with the agreement of the other states. By 1935, when the next step came up for consideration, Western Australia was experiencing a post-Depression recovery, and the secession issue was accordingly dropped.

DERVISH BEJAH

Towards the end of the nineteenth century in the desert regions of central Western Australia, a specialist from the Indian subcontinent, who had become a good Australian citizen, was demonstrating the advantages of a mode of transport particularly suited to Australia's arid inland regions.

The nineteenth-century Australian explorers had been gradually forced to the conclusion that the horse was not the ideal beast of burden for outback conditions. Camels, the 'ships of the desert', which can carry heavier loads and live longer than horses, and which need little water and usually like eating prickly plants and shrubs, were the answer. This was perceived by various of the explorers and by others who promoted their use—including Sir Thomas Elder, who participated in a number of expeditions.

Dervish Bejah was a camel expert. Born in Baluchistan, a region of Pakistan, he served with the Indian Army, attaining the rank of sergeant. He arrived at Fremantle about 1890.

In 1896 the Calvert Scientific Exploring Expedition, sponsored by the South Australian Survey Department, left Adelaide for Western Australia. The expedition, comprising seven men and twenty camels, was led by Lawrence Wells. Bejah was put in charge of the camels, and was to become a lifelong friend of Wells.

The expedition's objective was the exploration of the central areas of Western Australia—the last major uncharted area in Australia. Starting from Mullewa, inland from the Western Australian coastal city of Geraldton, the intention was to travel north-east towards the Gibson Desert, then northwards through the Great Sandy Desert, across the Fitzroy River, then to the northern town of Derby (on the Kimberley coast). This involved an 850-mile (1386-kilometre) trek through arid, inhospitable desert country with seemingly everlasting sand ridges and scarcely any water.

After eighteen days a depot was established near to Lake Way. From there, Wells made a separate survey of the area, taking with him George Jones, Bejah and seven camels. When they came upon a prominent feature, Wells named it Bejah Hill, such being the respect he had gained for the Pakistani. Later, the knowledgeable camel master came upon an area of poison bush. Realising this would be fatal to his charges, Bejah tethered the camels, then refused breakfast until he had searched for and gathered a scanty supply of feed for the animals.

The expedition continued in a northerly direction, with Charles Wells (Lawrence's cousin) and George Jones travelling on a parallel route to the west. Lawrence Wells now depended heavily on the faithful Bejah. They were in harsh and arid country, scarcely able to find sufficient water to keep themselves and the camels alive. Each rescued the other on occasions when they became separated from the party. When they decided to travel by night on their weakened animals, Wells allowed Bejah to lead the small party, trusting him to be guided by a star whilst he slept in the saddle.

After reaching Separation Well (to the east of Lake George), Charles Wells and George Jones became separated from the main party. Lawrence Wells, accompanied by Bejah, exhaustively searched the area before finally coming upon the bodies of their missing comrades. They had died of thirst.

The tragedy has been graphically and beautifully described by Douglas Stewart in his poem 'Afghan':

Mopping his coppery forehead under his turban
Old Bejah in baggy trousers, bearded, immense;

'Oh ya, oh ya, the young man dead in the sands,
I dig with my hands, I find him, and fifty yards further
The other, both dead, so young; no water, no water.'
The gestures, the voice all larger and wilder than human,
Some whirlwind out of the desert. 'Two days in the sun,
Done when I sight the camp. I shoot off my gun
And Larry Wells he carry me over his shoulder;
Looking for water out there; oh ya, no water.'
Old camel driver, explorer, the giant Afghan
Who steered his life by compass and by Koran,
'Oh ya, believe in God; young man no care;
God save, God help; oh ya, need help out there!'
And fondled his box of brass and kissed his book
So passionately, with such a lover's look,
He whirled in deserts still, too wild for human.

Wells was at first criticised for his handling of the expedition but was later praised for his conduct. He and Bejah eventually returned to Adelaide, where they were accorded a reception at Government House. The expedition's compass was appropriately inscribed and presented to the loyal Bejah.

Dervish Bejah settled at Marree, a small South Australian township to the north of Lake Torrens, at the junction of the Oodnadatta and Birdsville tracks. There, in 1909, he married a widow, Mrs Amelia Shaw. They had one son, Abdul Jubbar, known as Jack.

On Marree's outskirts Bejah and his associates established a large camp containing several thousand camels. Bejah's camels and their loads of wool and stores became well-known throughout the northern areas of South Australia.

Bejah retired in the 1930s and took to growing palms. He was invited by explorer C.T. Madigan to take charge of the camels on an expedition through the Simpson Desert, but declined, sending his son instead.

Dervish Bejah, a tall man with a full white beard, was a devout Muslim who attributed his lifelong health to his faith. Like many bush people before and since, he shared his special skills with the pioneers as they strove to develop the land. He died at Port Augusta in 1957, aged about ninety-five.

ALFRED CANNING

In the Kimberley region of Western Australia, in the early years of last century, a quiet achiever had undertaken a lonely task which would put his name on maps of Australia until the sands of time gradually obliterated his work.

Throughout the fifty years of his working life, Alfred Canning was a surveyor. He was a dedicated man who left his mark.

Born in Victoria and educated in Melbourne, he secured his first job as a cadet with the New South Wales Lands Department. He qualified as a licensed surveyor in 1882 and married two years later.

In 1893 Canning joined the West Australian Lands Department and soon proved himself both as a capable surveyor and a skilled bushman. At the turn of the century he was selected to survey a route for a rabbit-proof fence to counteract the invasion of rabbits from the east.

The job took him three years, and at the time it was said to be the world's longest survey—a distance of about 1900 kilometres from Starvation Harbour (west of Esperance) on Western Australia's south coast, to Cape Keraudren (east of Port Hedland) on the north coast. When a camel died on one section, he had no alternative but to walk nearly 340 kilometres to the nearest community.

In 1906 the state government came up with another scheme—to bring stock from the Kimberley district southwards to the goldfields. The area had been explored in 1897 by David Carnegie, who declared the inhospitable country as 'absolutely impracticable'. Canning thought otherwise.

Accordingly, he set out from Day Dawn (inland from Geraldton) accompanied by eight men, two horses and twenty-three camels, his main objectives being to survey a route and to locate the sites for wells every 24 kilometres. Canning succeeded in his task, reaching Halls Creek (in the Kimberley) in January 1907.

Encouraged by Canning's optimistic report, the government authorised a second expedition to construct wells along the route. Canning therefore set out again, this time with twenty men, two horses, sixty-two camels and, to provide milk and meat, 400 goats. Despite extremes of heat and freezing nights, Canning successfully led the party through the arduous terrain, much of it desert with frequent sand ridges up to 18 metres high. The Canning Stock Route was completed in March 1910 and enabled stock to be brought south from the Kimberley stations. It was a fine achievement.

Canning continued to work as a government surveyor until 1923, when he went into partnership as a contract surveyor.

In 1929, by which time the stock route had been abandoned, the government invited Canning to lead an expedition to reopen his old route. He walked the whole distance twice, pointing out the location of each well; then, whilst it was being cleaned, going ahead alone for another 24 kilometres to the next well.

Alfred Canning died in 1936 in the knowledge that his name was perpetuated by a famous route. It is now used only as a four-wheel-drive track.

OVERSEAS CONFLICTS

Although by 1891 approximately three-quarters of Australia's population was native-born, sentiments of imperial patriotism and support for the 'mother country' remained strong. Accordingly, when the British General Gordon was killed early in 1885 by fanatical tribesmen at the Sudanese capital, Khartoum, Australians felt an obligation to support the British campaign to restore order in the Sudan.

A contingent of over 5000 infantry, together with an artillery battery, 200 horses and an ambulance group, was quickly raised, about half of the soldiers being native-born. They were suitably farewelled on a March day in 1885 (which had been declared a public holiday). During the brief campaign, three were wounded and seven died from illnesses. By the end of June the contingent had returned to Sydney.

In 1899 another opportunity arose for Australians to demonstrate their loyalty, this time in South Africa. Alleged attacks on Britons by the Dutch Boer people resulted in Britain declaring war on the Boers. All the Australian colonies offered to send volunteers to fight alongside the British. Ultimately, a force of over 16,000 volunteers, many of them bushmen, went to the Transvaal.

By the time a peace treaty was signed in May 1902, the Australian casualties amounted to over 500 dead and nearly 900 wounded.

A small group of naval personnel also lent assistance to Britain in suppressing the Boxer Rebellion in China in 1900.

THE FILM INDUSTRY

Australia's first-ever movie, *Soldiers of the Cross*, was shot in 1899 using the imported 'cinematographie' technique. The film was premiered the following year. Other films gradually followed, including *The Story of the Kelly Gang* in 1906, and Steele Rudd's (Arthur Hoey Davis's) masterpiece *On Our Selection* in 1913. The demand for this new form of entertainment was overwhelming, and as local production was very limited, most movies were imported from America, Europe and Britain.

The two world wars and the dominance of the American film industry meant that relatively few films were made by the Australian industry until the

1960s onwards. But the movies remained a popular form of mass entertainment until regular television transmissions (which began in 1956) gradually altered people's entertainment and social patterns.

In the 1970s, Peter Weir was arguably the most prolific Australian film director, and the Australian film industry as a whole benefited greatly from increased funding. Weir's classic films, such as *Picnic at Hanging Rock* (1975) and *Gallipoli* (1981) paved the way for a thriving Australian film industry. Notable Australian directors in the late twentieth and early twenty-first centuries include Rob Sitch (*The Castle*, *The Dish*) and Baz Lurhmann (*Strictly Ballroom*, *Australia*).

Hollywood has also boasted a raft of award-winning Australian stars, including Peter Finch, Geoffrey Rush, Mel Gibson, Nicole Kidman, Cate Blanchett and Heath Ledger, among others.

WILLIAM PENFOLD

William Penfold's father, Edwin, had emigrated to Australia in 1853 and worked on the goldfields before setting up as a tobacconist in Sydney. The business prospered, and in 1874 Edwin sold up and took his family to England for three years. Returning in 1878 the family settled at Burwood and young William completed his education at Sydney Grammar School.

At the age of sixteen, William became indentured to a firm of stationers and booksellers, Turner & Henderson, in Sydney's Hunter Street. In 1886 the enterprising young Penfold persuaded his father to loan him the princely sum of £2000 to purchase the stock and goodwill of William Moffitt's, a Pitt Street firm of printers and stationers which had been established in 1830. He renamed the firm W.C. Penfold & Co., and two years later took his younger brother, Frederick, into partnership.

William Penfold married in 1894. The couple were to have a son and two daughters.

The two brothers set about modernising the business and installed a lithographic printing machine. In doing so the Penfolds established a tradition of continual equipment updating, which was to enable them to compete effectively with their rivals. In 1898 the first linotype machine was imported, enabling the expansion of their printing operations. They broke new ground in 1902 by commencing book production, and were to print many titles for Angus & Robertson (see pp. 164–7).

New and enlarged premises were acquired in nearby Hosking Place in 1912, permitting an expanded printery to be set up. Two years later the company was restructured with a capital of £125,000, with William Penfold becoming chairman and managing director. The firm then made a new departure by expanding into the packaging industry. Further restructuring took place over the years, and in 1937 the name W.C. Penfold & Co. Pty Ltd was adopted.

William Penfold's approach to his company's business was reflected in the motto 'The House of Quality'. His morning walk through the factory ensured that he kept in touch with the company's day-to-day activities and with any production problems. There developed a tradition of long service with the company, and staff at all levels responded to their founder's personal interest in their welfare.

William Penfold was a quiet and courteous man with a conservative outlook. He died in 1945, aged eighty-one.

When petrol rationing during and after World War II restricted the use of motorised vehicles, the company began using a cart drawn by a Clydesdale horse for city deliveries. The attractively decorated cart, still drawn by a Clydesdale, continued to be a familiar site on Sydney streets for many years.

SIR HENRY PARKES

In the 1840s there were occasional discussions amongst thinking men on the merits of the colonies uniting as a means of solving some of the principal common problems: defence; the different railway gauges; inter-colonial customs duties; postal and telegraph services; and quarantine regulations. No decisions were arrived at, however, for at the time there was strong rivalry between the colonies, each being preoccupied with internal affairs and development.

By the 1880s there were leaders in some in the inward-looking and squabbling Australian colonies who were expressing their concerns regarding the influx of Chinese immigrants; and over the territorial activities of the French in the New Hebrides and the Germans in New Guinea. There was also growing realisation that unity is strength, and that there were benefits to a national approach to common economic and trading matters, and to other divisive issues.

The most authoritative voice in the growing debate was that of Sir Henry Parkes. Born in England in 1815, Parkes had arrived in Sydney in 1839 together with his first wife, Clarinda, and their two-day-old child. For a while he dabbled in various unsuccessful commercial activities before turning to writing and journalism. In 1850 he became the founding editor and proprietor of a newspaper—*Empire*. Four years later, Parkes was elected to the Legislative Council. He was in and out of the New South Wales parliament for the next forty-one years.

Parkes, a vain but clever politician, was five times premier of New South Wales and was knighted in 1877. He was an imposing and easily recognisable figure, with his flowing silver hair and bib-like beard.

In 1883, Parkes won the northern New South Wales Legislative Assembly seat of Tenterfield. In 1889, by which time he was firmly committed to the ideal of federation, Parkes travelled to Brisbane to confer with the Queensland government. On the return journey he addressed his Tenterfield electors on the issue of federation, saying: 'The great question ... is whether the time has now arisen for the creation on this Australian continent of an Australian Government. I believe the time has come.'

In March 1891 the National Australasian Convention, presided over by Henry Parkes, was held in Sydney. There were delegates from each of the Australian colonies and from New Zealand, and they debated the draft of a proposed constitution which had been prepared by the Queensland premier, Samuel Griffith. The time, however, was not opportune for further discussion, for the colonies were then in the grip of a depression and had other domestic problems.

Parkes died suddenly in 1896, survived by his third wife, six of the twelve children of his first marriage, and by the five children of his second marriage. He was the father-figure of Australian Federation.

FEDERATION

In 1893, at a private conference held at the south-west New South Wales town of Corowa, it had been decided that there should be a convention, to be attended by delegates chosen by the people, to draft enabling Acts to be put before the colonial parliaments. Queensland declined to participate in the proposal.

It was not until March 1897 that the convention was held, this time in Adelaide. New Zealand was no longer interested in federation with the Australian colonies, and Queensland again decided not to send delegates.

The importance of the Corowa decision was that for the first time the federation issue was to be moved out of the political arena and would in future be debated in the wider public forum—evidence that democracy was well-rooted in Australia.

Despite months of argument at the Adelaide convention, which was attended by two delegates from each of the five colonies, the decision was finally made to hold a referendum in each of the participating colonies (Queensland now being included). But before the referenda could be held, the New South Wales parliament, despite some of its members being by no means convinced of the merits of the federation proposal, passed legislation requiring a majority of at least 80,000 for a 'yes' vote to be carried. It was a classic example of moving the goalposts.

In the event, the constitution proposal was approved, although the 'yes' vote had failed in New South Wales when the required majority was not reached.

A second round of referenda was held in June 1899, and this time majority 'yes' votes were recorded in each of the five colonies. The sixth colony, Western Australia, had not participated, due in part to hostility on the part of the miners at the Coolgardie and Kalgoorlie goldfields towards the Premier, the former explorer Sir John Forrest (see pp. 200–2). The miners were angry over threats to their independence, mainly from overseas mining interests. Forrest, intent on bargaining, wanted concessions, including an undertaking to build a railway to link Kalgoorlie to the eastern colonies.

The five colonies, however, were in no mood to countenance delaying tactics, leaving Forrest no choice but to hold a referendum. In July 1900 the people of Western Australia were asked to vote on the federation issue. A clear majority were in favour, so that the electors in all six colonies had now said 'yes' to the momentous proposal.

The scene now moved to London, where representatives from each of the colonies met with the British Secretary of State for the Colonies, Joseph Chamberlain (father of the future prime minister Neville Chamberlain) to discuss the draft of constitutional legislation necessary to formally secure the consent of the British parliament. Chamberlain had some reservations on minor matters, mainly concerning appeals to the British Privy Council, and it was finally resolved that only the Australian High Court would have authority to allow or withhold permission for appeals to be made to the Privy Council.

The official title of the nation-to-be was queried by Queen Victoria, who indicated a preference for 'Dominion of Australia' instead of the proposed 'Commonwealth of Australia', but she finally agreed to the latter title when the Australians held firm to their view. This was partly in deference to the memory of Sir Henry Parkes, who had first used the term 'commonwealth' when referring to the United States of America during his landmark Tenterfield speech in 1889 (see pp. 227–8).

It had been Parkes's vision that launched the ten-year debate that had finally unified the six Australian colonies. Important though the founding of the new nation was, the equally important fact which emerged from the protracted process was the manner in which the Commonwealth had come into being. There had been no bloodshed, nor had any of the colonies withdrawn as the movement was debated by the people and their leaders. Certainly there had been much argument and disagreement amongst the convention delegates as the federation proposal was subjected to protracted and detailed scrutiny. But, finally, a consensus was reached, and it was the people in each of the colonies who had made the affirmative decision.

The citizens of the colonies had freely decided that they wished to unite as a single, harmonious people sharing a common language, heritage and distinctive way of life, and to share that commonality with the Aboriginal people, the original occupants of the vast land which they now jointly occupied.

The coming into being of the Commonwealth of Australia was a splendid and enduring example of the true meaning of democracy. It had taken only 113 years for the tiny convict settlement to become a respected and freedom-loving member of the world's community of nations.

On 1 January 1901, great throngs of people in the presence of Governor-General elect, Lord Hopetoun, and other notables, gathered at Sydney's Centennial Park, and at other centres throughout Australia, to celebrate the birth of a new nation as Queen Victoria's proclamation was read:

> 'We do hereby declare that on and after the First Day of January, One Thousand Nine Hundred and One, the people of New South Wales, Victoria, South Australia, Queensland, Tasmania and Western Australia shall be united in a Federal Commonwealth of Australia.'

The celebrations were marked by the building of arches in Sydney, and similar decorations in the main centres throughout the new nation. The Sydney arches included the floral Welcome Arch at Government House; the Wool and Wheat arches, both in Bridge Street; the Coal Arch at the entrance to the Domain, made from 135 tons of coal and built by the people of Newcastle; and the Military Colonnade at the junction of College and Oxford streets. There were many others, including those presented by overseas interests: the Commonwealth Citizens' Arch at the corner of Park and Elizabeth streets, the German Arch at the intersection of Park and College streets, and the American and French arches, both in Pitt Street.

THE FIRST FEDERAL GOVERNMENT

Queen Victoria's death, just three weeks after the inauguration of the Commonwealth of Australia, aroused genuine grief in Australia, but did not cause delay in the Federation celebrations, nor in implementing the necessary constitutional proceedings.

In March 1901 the first federal elections were held for the seventy-five seats in the House of Representatives and thirty-six seats in the Senate. Voting was not compulsory (the requirement to vote was introduced in 1925). Barton's cabinet included Alfred Deakin, Sir John Forrest and Charles Kingston, each of whom had played a prominent part in the protracted negotiations that had led to Federation.

On 8 May the Labor members formed themselves into the Federal Parliamentary Labor Party, and generally supported the government.

In the first Commonwealth House of Representatives election, women had the vote only in South Australia and Western Australia. (Two years later all persons over the age of twenty-one were given the right to vote.) Australia's official population at the time was just over 3.5 million, to which figure should be added an estimated half a million Aboriginal Australians.

The first federal government was formed by Edmund Barton, a New South Wales liberal protectionist who had been prominent throughout the federation debate. Barton's cabinet included seven lawyers, whilst the House included ten former colonial premiers and a dozen others with ministerial experience. Amidst much pomp and ceremony, the first federal parliament was opened at Melbourne's Exhibition Building on 9 May 1901 by the Duke of Cornwall and York (later King George V). The Constitution specified that the federal parliament's permanent site should be located in New South Wales but not closer than 100 miles (161 kilometres) to Sydney.

Barton resigned the prime ministership in 1903 to sit in the High Court. He was succeeded by Victoria's Alfred Deakin who, like Barton, was a liberal who had shared Parkes's vision of Federation. Deakin was to be prime minister three times between 1903 and 1910. Barton, Deakin and the Queensland Premier, Sir Samuel Griffiths, who had been responsible for the first draft of the Federation Constitution, had been amongst the dominant political figures during the decade leading to the final referendum decision.

CANBERRA

It was eventually decided that the nation's future capital should be located in high country south-west of Sydney, about 150 kilometres from the coast and approximately midway between the rival cities of Melbourne and Sydney. The Commonwealth formerly took possession of the site, which was then a sheep station, in 1911. The name for the capital, Canberra, came from the Aboriginal word 'kamberra' meaning 'meeting place'.

In the same year, the Commonwealth Government decided to launch an international competition for the design of the new capital. The prize was won by a young American architect, Walter Burley Griffin, who was a product of the Chicago School of Architecture. Also in 1911, Griffin married Marion Mahony, who had worked with the architect Frank Lloyd Wright. Marion was to produce the drawings that embodied Griffin's ideas for the national capital.

Griffin, who had a profound empathy for nature, realised that he had a rare opportunity to blend a city into the natural surroundings of the chosen location. His winning design, which at the time caused deep controversy, was based upon three natural features—the Kurrajong, Ainslie and Yerron hills. Within these dominant positions Griffin designed a series of civic centres brilliantly linked by wide, concentric roads whilst preserving the lines of sight between the area's natural features. Burley Griffin's plan provided for ornamental lakes created by damming the Molonglo River and Ginninderra Creek, which flowed through the floodplain.

The plan created a remarkable harmony between the geometry of the radial avenues within the determining triangle of the three surrounding hills. Canberra's magnificent vistas, its wide, tree-lined avenues and artificial central lake, which was completed in 1964 and named Lake Burley Griffin, bear eloquent testimony to the quality of Burley Griffin's conception.

Construction of the capital was interrupted during World War I, and it was not until 1927 that the first Parliament House was opened by the Duke of York (later King George VI). In 1980 an American firm won another international competition for the design of the present Parliament House, which was built on the site known as Capital Hill. The building was formally opened in 1988 by Queen Elizabeth II.

For seven years, Griffin was the part-time Federal Capital director. During this period, from 1914 onwards, he was also active in private practice, initially through a Chicago partnership, then through his own office in Melbourne. He executed many site-planning commissions in both America and Australia. In 1920 Griffin formed a Sydney company to build residential estates in three Sydney suburbs. The best-preserved of these is at Castlecrag on Sydney's North Shore.

In 1935, Griffin travelled with his wife to India, where he worked on a number of commissions. In Lucknow, in 1937, he fell ill and died, aged sixty-one.

THE COMMONWEALTH BANK

Established in 1911, the Commonwealth Bank was originally intended to compete with the private banks, and to ensure people that they would not lose their savings in the event of private bank collapses—as had happened during the depression in the 1890s.

In 1945 the Commonwealth Bank became the nation's central bank, but was substantially privatised in 1960, although the Commonwealth Government continued to hold a controlling interest. The Reserve Bank of Australia had been established in the previous year as the nation's central bank, its function being to regulate and supervise all banks other than those owned by state governments.

The Commonwealth Bank merged in 2000 with the Colonial Bank to become Australia's largest private bank.

THE ANTARCTIC

The deeds of the great Antarctic explorers—Amundsen, Scott, Shackleton and others—during the early years of the twentieth century were well known to the Australian public. There was, accordingly, widespread interest and enthusiasm in 1908 when news came through that two Australians, Edgeworth David and Douglas Mawson, had reached the south magnetic pole ...

SIR DOUGLAS MAWSON

Douglas Mawson was born in England and was two years old when his family moved to Sydney, where he was educated. He was a graduate of the University of Sydney. In 1905 he was appointed as a lecturer at the University of Adelaide, and there became interested in glacial geology. Three years later he went to Antarctica for the first time as physicist with (Sir) Ernest Shackleton's British Antarctic Expedition. Mawson was able to make important scientific studies during the expedition, and was with the first party to climb Mount Erebus. With two others he was also the first to reach the south magnetic pole, then located approximately 800 kilometres south-east of Commonwealth Bay.

From 1911 to 1914, Mawson led the Australian Antarctic Expedition. Departing from Hobart in December 1911 in the *Aurora*, the expedition first went to Macquarie Island, midway between Australia and the Antarctic continent, where they set up a radio relay station. At Commonwealth Bay they established a base, built a hut (which remains in use) and commenced an extensive scientific program.

Mawson had planned several exploratory journeys, and in November 1912 set out with two companions, Belgrave Ninnis and Xavier Mertz, and a team of dogs on the far eastern expedition.

Crevasses are an ever-present hazard on the Antarctic ice shelf, and after travelling some 500 kilometres Ninnis's sledge broke through a large crevasse. He and his dog team disappeared into the black depth from which there was no escape. Most of the expedition's provisions, including all the dog food, had been on Ninnis's sledge.

Reflecting on this disaster, Mawson decided there was no option but to return, killing the dogs to supplement their meagre food supply. It was not then known that dog's liver is rich in Vitamin A and highly toxic if eaten in quantity. After twenty-five days on the return journey, Mertz died, doubtless due to the combined effects of physical effort, starvation and food poisoning.

Now alone, deeply distressed by the loss of his companions and physically debilitated, Mawson used a pocket saw to cut his sledge in half and began the last desperate 160-kilometre trek towards Commonwealth Bay and safety.

Mawson had no tent, no crampons (metal spikes fitted to boots for walking on ice) and little food. His physical condition was rapidly deteriorating and the sole of one foot was separated from his tender flesh. A blizzard was blowing. It is hardly possible to imagine a more desperate situation.

The fierce winds forced him to seek shelter in a cave for a week. On 17 January, still with 130 kilometres to go, Mawson stumbled into a crevasse. He was saved by the shortened sledge's 5-metre towing rope which had miraculously jammed at the crevasse's opening. Below was the blackness of the chasm.

Mawson would surely have been severely tempted to succumb to his dire situation. He later wrote: 'With the feeling that Providence was helping me, I made one last great effort to haul myself away from the certain death below.' Summoning his last reserves of energy, Mawson somehow managed to climb the rope and to crawl out of the crevasse. He then lapsed into unconsciousness.

For the next thirteen days, over rough ice and in bad weather, his physical condition steadily deteriorating and in great pain, Mawson struggled on. Good fortune had not deserted him, however, for he eventually came upon a cairn erected by a search party. On its top was a bag of food and a note telling him that Aladdin's Cave (the expedition's starting point eleven weeks earlier) was 37 kilometres away. The note also gave the news that the *Aurora* had arrived to take the expedition home.

Mawson reached the cave two days later, but there another blizzard forced him to delay for a further six days. Then a final 8-kilometre dash brought him to the safety of the Commonwealth Bay hut and to a rousing welcome from his five remaining companions—and to the sight of the *Aurora* disappearing over the horizon, for the vessel had been forced to depart because of the danger of encroaching ice.

Mawson and his companions therefore had to spend a second winter in the Antarctic before returning to Adelaide in February 1913.

Mawson continued his scientific work on his return to Australia. He married in 1914 and was knighted in the same year. He was awarded the OBE in 1920. In the following year he was appointed Professor of Geology and Mineralogy at the University of Adelaide.

Mawson returned to the Antarctic during the summers of 1929–30 and 1930–31 as leader of the British, Australian and New Zealand Antarctic Research Expedition, during which the vessel *Discovery* was used instead of land bases. The expedition's work was facilitated by the use of a small aircraft which enabled about half of the Antarctic coast, from the Ross Sea to Enderby Land, to be mapped for the first time. This important data was used in defining the area (the islands and territories between 45° E and 136° E, and 142° E and 160° E) which was claimed as Australian Antarctic Territory (formalised by the Australian Antarctic Territory Acceptance Act, 1933, which was ratified in 1936).

Mawson, who was a tall, strong and exceptionally courageous man, was renowned for his kindness, dignity and friendliness. He carried out extensive fieldwork during his career, always deriving great enjoyment from bush camping in company with a group of students. His interests included farming, conservation and forestry. He was for many years a director of a South Australian timber company.

Australia's presence in Antarctica is due largely to Sir Douglas Mawson's pioneering efforts. He retired at the age of seventy and lived for another six years. Upon his death in 1958 he was accorded a state funeral.

THE FIRST AIR MAIL

In 1913, by which time general aviation was a reality, the Commonwealth Government began thinking about carrying mail by air. A training school was set up in Victoria in 1914, and plans were hatched to carry mail by air on the 800-kilometre Melbourne–Sydney route.

But it was a Frenchman who delivered the first mail to be carried by air. The aviator was Maurice Guillaux, who departed in a Bleriot monoplane from the Melbourne Showgrounds at Flemington on 16 July 1914 carrying 1785 postcards, bundles of greeting letters from various Melbourne officials, a consignment of Lipton's tea and another of lemon squash. It was Australia's first air mail and air freight delivery, and it halved the normal transit time.

On the first day's flying, Guillaux made prearranged stops at Seymour, Wangaratta, Albury, Wagga Wagga and Harden. During the late afternoon he took off from Harden, but strong winds forced him to return and to spend the night there. Next morning he resumed his historic journey, making stops at Goulburn and Moss Vale and an unscheduled landing at Liverpool. He then circled over Parramatta and Manly before landing at Moore Park in southern Sydney. He had flown 934 kilometres.

With Australia's vast distances, the speedy delivery of mail by air was soon going to prove of inestimable advantage as routes expanded. Guillaux was the first to show that it could be done.

The first scheduled internal air mail service in Australia was inaugurated between Geraldton and Derby in Western Australia on 5 December 1921. A regular air mail service linking Sydney, Melbourne and Adelaide commenced on 4 June 1924. The service was extended to Perth in 1929.

SIR NORMAN BROOKES

At about the time when Mawson was performing heroic deeds in the Antarctic wastes, a champion of a very different activity was cementing his sporting reputation on the other side of the world.

One of the earliest of Australia's sporting champions, and certainly one of the most successful, was the well-educated son of a man who, in the early 1920s, became managing director of one of

Australia's major companies, Australian Paper Mills Co. Ltd (now Amcor Limited).

He was Norman Brookes, born in the Melbourne suburb of St Kilda in 1877 and educated at the Melbourne Church of England Grammar School. After matriculating there in 1895, Brookes joined his father's firm as a junior clerk. He became a director in 1904.

Brookes was a natural games player, excelling at cricket, football, golf and lawn tennis. He won the Victorian foursomes golf championship once and the Australian foursomes championship twice. Despite these successes, his sporting passion was for tennis, which he practised assiduously on the court at his family home.

After playing representative tennis for Victoria, Brookes made his first visit to Wimbledon in 1905, where he won the all-comers singles event. In the same year Brookes and a New Zealander, Anthony Wilding, represented Australasia in the Davis Cup but were unsuccessful. In 1907, at the age of twenty-nine, Brookes made his second visit to Wimbledon, winning the singles, doubles (with Wilding) and mixed doubles events. Wimbledon was then regarded as the world championship venue, and Brookes was the first overseas player, and the first left-hander, to win the Wimbledon singles crown. He once more won the singles in 1914 and, again with Wilding, the doubles. He was then aged thirty-six.

Brookes and Wilding repeated their successful Davis Cup partnership in 1908, 1909, 1911 and in 1914. These feats, and Brookes's Wimbledon triumphs, gave an enormous fillip to tennis in Australia.

Brookes spent most of the World War I years as a Red Cross commissioner in the Middle East. He was finally attached to the British Expeditionary Force in Mesopotamia with the rank of lieutenant-colonel. Wilding, his doubles partner, was killed in action in France in 1915.

In 1919, when he was forty-seven, Brookes once more represented Australia in the Davis Cup competition, and again in the following year. He appeared at Wimbledon for the last time in 1924.

As an administrator, Brookes did much to promote tennis in Australia, being mainly responsible for arranging the purchase and development of the Kooyong tennis centre in Adelaide. He was president of the Lawn Tennis Association of Australia for twenty-eight years and president of the Lawn Tennis Association of Victoria for twelve years. He was knighted in 1939 for his services to tennis.

In 1921 Brookes had returned to the board of directors of Australian Paper Mills Co. Ltd, later becoming the company's chairman of directors. He was also chairman of directors of North British and Mercantile Insurance Co. Ltd, a director of several other companies and a partner in William Brookes & Co., the family pastoral business.

In 1911 Brookes had married Mabel Balcombe, who bore him three daughters.

Brookes was a slim and wiry man, an indomitable fighter and shrewd tactician on the tennis court. To his natural skill he added intense concentration. Reserved by nature and unfailingly polite, he could at times be forthright and outspoken. He invariably dressed immaculately, and customarily wore a peaked cap, both on and off the tennis court.

One of Australia's most inspirational sportsmen and a noted businessman, Sir Norman Brookes died at his South Yarra home in 1968, aged ninety.

THE OUTBREAK OF WORLD WAR I

By 1910, Europe's principal nations were aligned into two camps: Germany, the Austro-Hungarian Empire and, later, Turkey on one side; and France,

Great Britain and Russia on the other. In 1913, the possibility of war in Europe was being freely discussed.

In April of that year the Australian Labor government, under Andrew Fisher, was defeated and replaced by a Liberal government led by Joseph Cook.

On 28 June 1914, in the Yugoslavian city of Sarajevo, an eighteen-year-old Serbian nationalist assassinated the popular heir to the Austrian throne, Archduke Franz Ferdinand, and his wife. This fateful act was to precipitate World War I.

Russia was quick to announce its support for Serbia. A domino effect resulted: France indicated it would side with Russia, whilst Britain made it clear that it would come to the aid of France in the event of a conflict. In Australia, patriotic meetings throughout the country affirmed that Australia would stand by Britain should hostilities break out.

Britain declared war on Germany on 4 August 1914. On the following day the Australian Prime Minister, Joseph Cook, announced that as a consequence Australia was at war with Germany and Austria. The nation responded with a spontaneous outpouring of patriotic fervour. Volunteers, including under-age youths, besieged the recruiting centres in an unprecedented rush to 'join up'. It was generally expected that the war would be over by Christmas.

One of the first actions of the Australian government was to place the Australian Navy under British command. The ships included one battle cruiser, three light cruisers (including one under construction), three destroyers and two submarines.

Within a few days, at the request of the British government, Australia and New Zealand sent a small expeditionary force to German-occupied New Guinea. By 21 September the German force there had surrendered and they and their New Guinean sympathisers laid down their arms.

Meanwhile, as volunteers came forward in their thousands, the Cook Government announced the immediate formation of an expeditionary force to serve in Europe. The decision was confirmed by the Labor Party when it won the general election in September. The new Labor Prime Minister was William Morris Hughes.

Thirty-eight transports departed Western Australia on 1 November 1914 with 20,000 Australian and New Zealand troops aboard. The ships were protected by four cruisers—two Australian, one British and one Japanese (Japan was then Australia's ally as the result of a treaty signed in 1902 between Britain and Japan). A week later the German light cruiser *Emden* was detected shadowing the convoy. The Australian cruiser HMAS *Sydney* was ordered to attack the German raider, and in the ensuing engagement the *Emden* was battered and finally beached on the Cocos Islands. It was the first naval engagement of the war.

In June 1915 the Broken Hill Proprietory Company opened a steelworks at Newcastle. This was an indication that Australian industry was gearing up production to meet the necessities of war.

The war also resulted in changes to social patterns in Australia, not least amongst women and children. Women's clothing styles, for example, became much simpler, thereby requiring less cloth. Many women responded to the calls for factory and office workers, their wages permitting a greater sense of independence. Some women, especially the younger ones, moved away from home into accommodation closer to their jobs. Children also made a contribution to the war effort by such activities as knitting garments for the armed forces.

GALLIPOLI

In October 1914, Turkey had entered the war on the side of the Germans, thereby raising the British High Command's concern that the security of the vital Suez Canal could be threatened. It was decided to divert the 'Anzacs' (as the Australian and New Zealand Army Corps became known) to Egypt to counter a possible Turkish move towards Suez.

That the move did not eventuate was due to a plan hatched later by the British High Command, largely at the prompting of the First Lord of the

Admiralty, Winston Churchill. The plan was to relieve Turkish pressure on Russia by driving the Turks out of the Gallipoli Peninsula, to capture Constantinople and thereby to gain control of the Dardanelles.

In March 1915 the British Navy failed in an attempt to penetrate the Dardanelles, their commander, Admiral Roebeck, informing Churchill that land troops would be necessary for the operation to succeed.

On 3 April the Anzacs embarked for the Greek island of Lemnos, some 97 kilometres west of the narrow passage which is the entrance to the Dardanelles. On the northern side of the passage is the Gallipoli Peninsula. On the southern side is the ancient city of Troy, site of the Homeric legends.

The Allied forces for the impending campaign were under the command of Britain's General Ian Hamilton, and comprised British and French troops in addition to the Anzacs. The Anzacs were led by a British major-general, William Birdwood (later to be affectionately known to the Australians and New Zealanders as 'Birdie'). The Australians were commanded by Colonel John Monash.

The revised strategy for the Turkish campaign called for simultaneous landings of British and French troops at sites on the Gallipoli Peninsula. The site selected for landing the Anzac troops was Gaba Tepe. But due to an error on the part of the Royal Navy, possibly as a result of the tides and the darkness, the Anzacs were in fact landed on a beach about 1 kilometre further north. The site was to become known as Anzac Cove (a name that was formally adopted by Turkey in 1985).

The Anzacs' objective was the capture of Gun Ridge, the height dominating Anzac Cove. The ridge could only be reached by surmounting the mass of tangled ravines that confronted the troops. As the Anzacs fought their way ashore, Turkish riflemen from the heights above met the almost defenceless troops on the exposed beach with a murderous fire. Later that day the Turks brought up field guns to intensify the bombardment. Throughout the day, landing craft continued to ferry back the Anzac wounded, then to return with ammunition, stores, equipment and fresh troops, their commander, Colonel Monash, amongst them.

By nightfall on that first terrible and chaotic day, 25 April, some 16,000 Anzacs had been landed. They had secured an area of approximately 6 square kilometres at a cost of 2000 casualties, including 700 dead.

Something of a stalemate then developed. The Allied commander, General Hamilton, told them to 'dig in and fight it out'. (The New Zealanders had used the word 'diggers' to refer to themselves at that time. The Australians adopted the term, and it gradually gained currency in reference to Australian soldiery generally.)

In mid-May the Anzacs climbed out of their network of trenches on the heights above the beach to launch a furious attack on the Turkish lines, costing the enemy some 10,000 dead and wounded. The Australian and New Zealand casualties numbered 500. It was the Turkish army's most serious defeat during the Gallipoli campaign.

On 2 August, five divisions of British troops were landed at Suvla Bay (about 10 kilometres north of Anzac Cove) in an effort to force the Dardanelles passage. Four days later the Anzacs launched an assault against the Turkish army entrenched on the ridges to the north-east, known as Chunuk Bair, Hill Q and Hill 971. Simultaneously, the Australian 1st Brigade launched a diversionary attack on the feature to the south-east known as Lone Pine. Over 2000 men lost their lives during this costly and unsuccessful attack.

The fighting was fierce, the slaughter unrelenting, the heat unbearable and the stench of the dead and dying intolerable. In a month of brutal fighting the Australians were awarded seven Victoria Crosses (VCs), six in one day. Despite the carnage on both sides, the Turks stood firm. A New Zealand force briefly occupied Chunuk Bair, whilst a Gurkha contingent reached the summit of Hill Q. But both positions were soon lost when the Turks counter-attacked in strength.

From the Allied point of view the Gallipoli campaign had been a failure. Recognising this, the British High Command, acting on the advice of General Sir Charles Munro, who had replaced Sir Ian Hamilton as commander of the Allied forces in the eastern Mediterranean, decided on withdrawal from the peninsula. The Anzacs duly began retreating to Lemnos Island at dusk on

18 December. By dawn on 20 December the withdrawal was complete. Within a week the troops had returned to Cairo.

That there were only two casualties during the withdrawal was due in part to ingenious deceptions and devices used by the Australian troops. One such device was the remote-controlled rifle, which was set up atop the trenches. These rifles fired periodically (after the troops had left) when water dripping from an upper container to a lower one would activate a wire attached to the rifle's trigger. Holes of varying sizes ensured that all rounds in the rifle's magazine were fired at irregular intervals.

In addition to some guns, equipment and stores, the Anzacs left behind their dead—8709 Australians and 2431 New Zealanders. The Turkish dead were stated to total 86,692. British casualties at Gallipoli numbered 20,000, and French casualties 27,000.

From a military standpoint, the eight-month Gallipoli campaign had been a disaster, notwithstanding the fact that the Germans had been denied the assistance of the Turkish forces.

Just over sixteen months earlier the Australian public had responded to the outbreak of war with a display of unbridled patriotism. As news of the Gallipoli defeat reached all parts of the Australian vastness, a resolve developed that the heroism of the 'Diggers' at Gallipoli should forever be remembered.

So it was that the first memorial Anzac Day was commemorated on 25 April 1916 with public gatherings and appropriate speeches. A flame of remembrance had been lit, never to be extinguished. The terrible slaughter at Gallipoli was to be the first of a continuing series of military events which became landmarks in the development of the Australian psyche.

It was at Gallipoli that the innate qualities of Australian soldiers (and their New Zealand comrades) became etched on the national consciousness.

Gallipoli gave expression to the Australian ideal of mateship: to be worthy of the trust of mates; not to be found wanting when courage, endurance and leadership are required; and to be every ready to lend a hand when a fellow being needs assistance.

HUGO THROSSELL

George Throssell and his wife, Anne, had fourteen children. George was a storekeeper at Northam in Western Australia, and later became premier of his state.

George's youngest son, Hugo, worked as a jackeroo in South Australia before taking up a property at Cowcowing in Western Australia in partnership with his brother, Ric. Their venture into wheat farming was adversely affected by drought, and with the outbreak of war the brothers decided to enlist in the 10th Light Horse Regiment, which had been formed in October 1914. Hugo was commissioned as a second lieutenant and was sent to Egypt with the regiment for training. On 4 August 1915, the regiment landed at Gallipoli.

Dominating the Anzac beachhead at Gallipoli is a ridge of hills running in a north-easterly direction towards a hill named Baby 700, and beyond to the height named Chunuk Bair, overlooking Monash Valley. Rising towards the crest of Baby 700 is a defile (Monash Gully) which was named the Nek ('nek' is a Dutch/Afrikaans word meaning 'mountain pass'). It is 1.4 kilometres north-east of Anzac Cove, and at its narrowest point is only about 30 metres wide.

The Australian 8th and 10th Light Horse Regiments (now acting as infantry) were ordered to capture the Turkish trenches above the Nek. It was an impossible assignment, for they were exposed to murderous machine-gun and rifle fire from the height above. The Australians were also unaware that a New Zealand regiment, which was due to support them, had fought their way to within a short distance of Chunuk Bair but had been unable to take the important ridge.

It was planned that the assault on the Nek would be made by four lines, each of 150 men, from the two Light Horse Regiments.

The men in the first two lines were decimated. The third line continued the charge before the futility of the action was realised and the men were finally withdrawn, leaving behind their dead, dying and wounded.

Hugo Throssell was one of the few lucky ones to escape injury during the disastrous attack, which resulted in 234 of the 600 Light Horse troops being killed. As he retreated from the Nek, he determined to avenge his fallen and wounded comrades and to prove himself to the regiment.

Five kilometres north-north-east of Anzac Cove is a small knoll, then known as Hill 60. For a week there had been heavy fighting for this feature, with both sides sustaining severe losses.

On 29 August, with the Turks in control of the summit, the reformed 10th Light Horse Regiment was ordered to capture a long trench on the summit.

At 1 a.m., in moonlight and after fierce fighting, the regiment was able to occupy part of the trench and to build a sandbag barricade across its width. Urging his men to greater effort, Throssell stood on guard, killing five Turkish soldiers who attempted to retake the section that the Light Horse Regiment had occupied.

For a time there was a fierce and almost bizarre bomb fight. Holding their grenades to a very short fuse, the Western Australians launched them into the Turkish section of the trench. When the Turks retaliated with their own barrage, Throssell and his men quickly grabbed the grenades and hurled them back. For a time the scene resembled a deadly game of volleyball. Over 3000 bombs were thrown that night by both sides.

When dawn came the Turks made several rushes at the Australians, but were met by a barrage of bombs and rifle-fire. Throssell, who for a time was in sole command, was twice wounded by bomb splinters. But he continued to urge his men to hold their position, and shortly afterwards the Turks were driven from the summit.

Hugo Throssell was evacuated to England and promoted to the rank of captain. For his fearless courage and determination in the close fighting on Hill 60 he was awarded the Victoria Cross. It was the first VC to be awarded to a Western Australian.

Rejoining his regiment and his brother, Ric, in Egypt, Throssell was again wounded in April 1917, this time during the second battle of Gaza. It was in this engagement that Ric went missing. When night fell, Hugo desperately searched the battlefield for his brother, calling with the same whistle that the two had used as children. Ric was later found dead.

Throssell fought in the final offensive in Palestine, and led his regiment's guard of honour at the fall of Jerusalem.

Following demobilisation, Throssell married and settled on a mixed farm at Greenmouth, near Perth, with his wife, the author Katherine Susannah Prichard.

The Throssells gradually fell on hard times, and during the Depression years became heavily in debt. Beset by depression and an attack of meningitis, which he had contracted at Gallipoli, Throssell shot himself on 19 November 1933. He believed that his death would provide a war service pension for his wife and eleven-year-old son.

Hugo Throssell was buried with full military honours at Karrakatta cemetery, Perth. His Victoria Cross was later acquired by the Returned Services League and presented to the Australian War Memorial in Canberra.

CHARLES BEAN

On 6 August 1915, the Australian troops at Gallipoli were preparing for the night assault on the summit of Hill 971, about 11.5 kilometres north-east of Chunuk Bair.

Close by was Charles Bean, Australia's official war correspondent. Suddenly, feeling a sharp pain in his right thigh, Bean realised that he had been hit, probably by a stray Turkish bullet. Limping back to the nearest dressing station, Bean's wound was tended to by the New Zealand staff, then he was told to report to doctors at the Australian casualty station further back.

Late that evening Bean heard of the dreadful ordeals of the 8th and 10th Light Horse Regiments at the Nek (see p. 246).

The injured Bean slowly limped to the nearest divisional headquarters, where his daily despatch reported all that he had observed of the abortive assault on the Nek. He then sought out a medical officer, who told him of the risk to his leg of gangrene infection.

But a few days later an old friend, Surgeon-General Sir Neville House, advised him against having the bullet removed, adding, as Bean later wrote, that 'to have it out would mean leaving Anzac for a while, which I was anxious to avoid.'

So the bullet remained in Bean's thigh for the rest of his life.

Charles Edwin Woodrow Bean was born at Bathurst, in New South Wales, on 18 November 1879, the eldest of three sons of Edwin Bean and his wife, Lucy. Edwin Bean was then headmaster of All Saints' College, Bathurst, where Charles began his schooling.

Due to ill health, in 1889 Edwin Bean left Bathurst with his family for England, where he became headmaster of Brentwood School in Essex. Charles was a pupil there until 1894, when he entered Clifton College in Bristol, a boarding school at which his father had been educated.

In 1898 Charles won a scholarship to Hertford College, Oxford, where he read history and cultivated his prose style. He later studied law, and in 1903 was called to the Bar of the Inner Temple. In 1904 he 'returned home' to Sydney, where he was admitted to the New South Wales Bar.

For the next two years he toured much of New South Wales, writing some articles for the *Evening News*, of which A.B. 'Banjo'

Paterson (see p. 165) was editor. He also wrote a book, articles from which were printed in the *Sydney Morning Herald*. It was at this time that he resolved to abandon the law and to earn a living by writing. He spent four months learning shorthand.

Two more books and various newspaper articles, some being for the *Sydney Mail*, occupied him until 1910, when he returned again to England and there wrote articles for the *Sydney Morning Herald*. By 1913 he was again in Australia as leader-writer for the *Herald*, a position which he grew to dislike.

In October 1914 he sailed for Egypt with an official appointment as war correspondent with the 1st Australian Division. It was Bean's belief that if he was to write about the conflict, he should observe it at first hand and at close quarters, as far as he was able. He reported to General Hamilton's Mediterranean Expeditionary Force Headquarters at Alexandria on 9 April.

Bean was with the Anzacs a few hours after the first troops had stepped ashore on 25 April, his brother, Jack, amongst them. (In 1909 Jack had qualified at Cambridge as a surgeon, and in October 1914 had departed from Australia in the same convey as his brother, bound for Egypt as medical officer to the 3rd Battalion of the 1st Australian Division.) During that first momentous day of the Gallipoli landing, Jack was shot, the bullet lodging near his bladder. Several weeks later he was again hit.

Both brothers remained with the Anzacs throughout the Gallipoli campaign, Charles continually moving by day, and sometimes at night, amongst the Australian front-line positions. He sent back to Australia a continuous stream of despatches, usually writing them or updating his diary by the light of a candle or kerosene lantern.

At times, when the troops were ordered to dig in, Bean would get a spade and join the men in digging for himself a hole in which to snatch an hour or two's sleep, using a waterproof sheet to protect himself from the cold and, sometimes, from the drizzling rain. He shared the troops' experiences and hardships throughout the campaign.

In March 1916, Bean was with the 1st Corps of the Australian 2nd Division when it embarked from Egypt for France. As Australia's official war correspondent, he continued to send detailed reports on the bloody fighting on the Western Front until the Armistice on 11 November 1918.

On his way back to Australia, Bean spent several weeks at the Gallipoli battlefields, observing them from the Turkish side and preparing a report for the Commonwealth government on Australian graves and their maintenance. He arrived back in Australia in May 1919.

Late in 1919, and now Australia's official war historian, Bean settled with his staff at a homestead at Tuggeranong, near Canberra. In 1921 he married Ethel Young, a nursing sister he had met at the nearby Queanbeyan hospital.

Bean's meticulous *The Official History of Australia in the War of 1914–1918* ran to fourteen volumes and nearly four million words. He wrote the first six volumes himself (two on Gallipoli and four on France) and edited the others. Bean had insisted that his monumental work should be uncensored, and that undertaking was given and adhered to. The final volume was published in 1942.

In addition to his wartime despatches and the official history, Bean wrote numerous newspaper articles and eleven books. He was awarded a number of honours in Australia, but declined a knighthood.

Charles Bean died on 30 August 1968, aged eighty-eight, and was cremated following a memorial service at St Andrew's Cathedral in Sydney.

THE WESTERN FRONT

The valour displayed by the Anzacs at Gallipoli was to be more evident, and to be better understood, during the 1917–18 fighting against the Germans in France and Belgium. For it was there that the outstanding fighting qualities of the Australian and New Zealand servicemen played a significant part in the final victory. The Anzac losses on the Western Front amounted to more than seven times the number killed at Gallipoli.

In May 1915, as the Anzacs were consolidating their tenuous position on Gallipoli, a German counter-offensive drove back the Russian Army to regain territory lost during the Russian 1914 offensive.

Europe had always been the main theatre of war, and it was to France that the principal units of the Australian Imperial Force were transferred in 1916. In July, the British launched their offensive on the Somme (the Allied front then extended approximately from the River Somme northwards through the Arras and Ypres areas to the English Channel east of Dunkirk).

The Australians, their indomitable courage at Gallipoli now recognised, were used mainly as front-line shock troops and were heavily engaged in the initial assaults around Fromelles and Pozières (strategic areas in the defensive line north of the River Somme). Amidst appalling conditions—the filth and the stench, the whine and nerve-deadening effect of the almost continuous shell bombardments, the use of poison gas when the wind was favourable to the Germans, and the rain and mud that gave rise to the condition known as 'trench feet'—there were over 22,000 Australian casualties, including 1719 killed in 27 hours of the Battle of Fromelles in 1916. The horror of it all would always be etched deeply on the minds of the men who fought and survived on the Western Front. Notwithstanding the ferocity of the fighting, by the time the Australians had withdrawn the gain in territory had been a mere 2 kilometres.

The slaughter continued into 1917 when the Allied troops won a victory at Ypres (west of Passchendaele and at the northern end of the Allied defensive line extending to the English Channel) and a gain of about 8 kilometres.

48,671 Australians died in France and Belgium.

THE FINAL PHASE OF THE WAR

During 1916–17, Australian, New Zealand and Indian units were deployed in the Middle East to counter the continuing Turkish threat to the Suez Canal.

The Anzac forces, which included the Australian Light Horse and the Imperial Camel Corps Brigade, successfully overcame stiff Turkish and German resistance, pursuing the enemy from Egypt through the Gaza Strip northwards, capturing Jerusalem and Damascus. During the campaign the Allied forces suffered only 139 casualties whilst capturing over 10,000 prisoners.

Meanwhile, several significant events gave rise to a 'cause and effect' situation in Europe. The first Russian thrusts against Germany in 1915 had been parried initially and then repelled. As they were driven back, the Russians sustained enormous losses in men and equipment. This was to result in serious discontent amongst the Russian people and a weakening of morale in the Russian forces. The Bolshevik Revolution in November 1917 followed. Russia signed an armistice with Germany in December and thereafter played no further military part in the war.

As the war of attrition continued on the Western Front, the powerful British and German navies continued the struggle on the high seas. Initially the British were successful in blockading the German ports, thus severely restricting the flow of food and materials to the German nation.

The German counter to this threat was to launch unrestricted submarine attacks against both Allied and neutral shipping bound for British and French ports. Mounting attacks by the U-boats (submarines) on United States vessels, and intelligence that Germany was attempting to persuade Mexico to attack the United States, brought the Americans into the war on the side of the Allies in 1917.

Thus, Russia's withdrawal from the conflict, which released the powerful German forces on its eastern front, was now counterbalanced by the American land and sea forces reinforcing the Allies. The tide was beginning to turn.

In March 1918 the Germans launched a massive assault on the Western Front. But the Allies, now strengthened by over 1 million American troops and with further support from the Commonwealth and British colonies, counter-attacked vigorously. The Australians' final engagement in France was on 28 September. A week earlier the Turkish resistance in Palestine was finally broken. The remnants of the Turkish army and their German commander surrendered to the Australian, New Zealand and British forces.

Britain's losses in what was to be the final assault exceeded 100,000 men. Australia's casualties in the four-month Flanders bloodbath were over 15,000. Their sacrifice is not forgotten, not least by the people of France, who annually commemorate the battlefield losses suffered by the Allied troops.

The German retreat became a rout. The Kaiser abdicated, and when France's Marshal Foch offered an armistice on behalf of the Allies, the Germans accepted. The firing ceased at 11 a.m. on 11 November 1918.

After four years and three months, the conflict was over. Some 331,000 men and women had enlisted in Australia's armed forces. The country had suffered nearly 60,000 dead and there were over 152,000 wounded—some 65 per cent of the young nation's total expeditionary force. It was the highest percentage casualty rate amongst the Allied countries. The total number of deaths worldwide as a result of World War I has been estimated at 8.5 million. 13,249 Australian soldiers deserted in 1917. 2994 of them were court-martialled.

The war had been won by the Allies, albeit at enormous cost. In later years, after the Germans had signed the Treaty of Versailles with its 440 articles in 1919, doubts would be raised as to whether the conquering nations had in fact won the peace. It would be held by some that various of the Treaty's terms led, directly or indirectly, to the outbreak of World War II.

THE POST-WAR PERIOD

Many of the soldiers had left their homeland in a state of euphoria and high expectation, to the cheers and tears of family and friends and just about everyone else. They were doing the right thing: serving their King and Country and the British Empire; fighting the Hun.

Now that it was all over, the reality of the slaughter, the horror and the deprivation had left its mark. Some returned physically unscathed; some wounded in body and in spirit. Some did not return. Those who did return had their memories and a powerful sustaining force—mateship.

They had dreamed of home. But for many the blessed moments of reunion were soon replaced by confusion and disillusionment. There was industrial conflict. There were strikes. The seeds of communism had been sown and had produced industrial disruptions and sporadic outbreaks of civil disorder.

The war had broadened Australia's manufacturing base, but it would take time for industry to adapt to the post-war needs of the population. Unemployment was high, persuading some of the returned servicemen to seek their fortune on the land as small-scale farmers. The state governments provided the land, whilst the Commonwealth provided low-interest loans and other assistance. The scheme was not entirely successful, for in many cases the soldiers had not acquired the skills of land management or animal husbandry.

In the immediate post-war period, Australia's best-known soldier, Lieutenant General Sir John Monash, devoted himself tirelessly to the task of resettling more than 160,000 servicemen who had returned home and needed employment. Within a year of the war's end, more than 120,000 of them had a job, whilst some 20,000 were placed in technical training schemes.

The returned soldiers brought back something in addition to their memories—Spanish influenza. In Australia the disease had reached epidemic proportions by 1919, killing over 12,000 people. It was particularly virulent in New South Wales. People were advised to wear masks and to refrain from kissing.

Inevitably, as disillusionment gradually took over, the men asked themselves whether the sacrifice had been worthwhile. Far-off Germany had been defeated but, otherwise, what had been achieved?

The Commonwealth of Australia remained a solid member of the British community of nations. There was recognition of the fighting quality of Australia's soldiers, of their ability to endure hardship, of their sense of humour, of their independence, and, above all, of their respect for the special quality of comradeship which bonded Australians, particularly in times of adversity. Australia had played a full part in prosecuting the war against Germany. But with the coming of peace, the country was now largely dependent upon its own resources in adjusting to the changed circumstances of the post-war world.

One advantage that emerged was New Guinea. Australia's wartime contribution had been recognised by a seat at the 1919 Peace Conference table, which was given to the Prime Minister, Billy Hughes. The persistent Hughes, who would nowadays be referred to as a 'stirrer', was constantly in opposition to the views of the powerful American President, Woodrow Wilson. Emphasising that Australia's casualty rate in the war was the highest of all the Allied nations, Hughes eventually secured a 'C' class mandate over New Guinea, which was then incorporated into the Australian territory of Papua. The Australian half of the island was renamed Papua New Guinea.

The Returned Soldiers' and Sailors' Imperial League of Australia, which soon became known as the RSL (Returned Services League), had been formed in 1916 as a voluntary organisation, its membership restricted to men who had served in an overseas theatre of war. The RSL became an influential lobby group, especially during the years leading up to the Great Depression and World War II.

'ASPRO' ™

In the years before World War I, the usual answer to a headache, and to other forms of ache, was an 'Aspirin'™, a pain reliever made from acetylsalicylic acid.

The patents and trademarks for aspirin were held by the German company Bayer. At the beginning of World War I, when imports from Germany of acetylsalicylic acid were cut off, the Australian Attorney-General announced that the German patents and trademarks were suspended, and that manufacture of acetylsalicylic acid would be permitted, provided the required standards of purity were reached.

A qualified pharmacist, Victorian-born George Nicholas, with a pharmacy at the Melbourne suburb of Windsor, now entered the scene. Using kerosene tins and his wife's kitchen utensils, he attempted to produce acetylsalicylic acid, or aspirin, by reacting salicylic acid, a white powder, with acetic anhydride, an acrid-smelling liquid.

Nicholas had no knowledge of the process necessary to produce the reaction, but after much perseverance eventually succeeded in making acetylsalicylic acid—but it was impure.

Nicholas now enlisted the help of a freelance entrepreneur, Henry Shmith, and after many weeks of experiments the pair succeeded in making a batch of pure aspirin.

The partners now registered a company, Shmith, Nicholas & Co., and in June 1915 applied under wartime legislation to take over Bayer's Aspirin trade name. At first the application was ignored, but Nicholas and Shmith persisted and eventually arranged for the government analyst to test their product. In September the Attorney-General announced that their product was pure, that it contained no free salicylic acid and that in all respects it complied with the requirements of the British *Pharmacopoeia*. Shmith, Nicholas & Co. were duly granted a licence to make and sell Aspirin in Australia.

Various technical problems now had to be tackled, but after many months the partners were able to produce sealed tablets punched out on a hand-operated machine.

George Nicholas now became alert to the likelihood that when the war ended, Bayer would reclaim the Aspirin trade name. A substitute was necessary, and in April 1917 the two men registered the trade name Aspro (devised by using the last two letters of 'NicholAS' and the first three of 'PROduct').

By the end of the year, with the business heavily in debt, Shmith pulled out. George, who was physically frail, now called upon his elder brother, Alfred, for assistance. Alfred was a grocer and later a merchant and importer, but his business had been adversely affected by the war.

In 1921 the two brothers changed the name of the business to Nicholas Pty Ltd and moved to larger and better-equipped premises at South Melbourne. Production of Aspro increased, and by 1923 the business was on a sound footing. Manufacture then commenced in New Zealand, and in the following year the first sales were made in England, where a separate manufacturing company, Aspro Ltd, was established. Sales were made to South Africa in 1928, to Belgium in 1929 and to France and Egypt in 1935. Business was also developed with countries in South-East Asia and Africa.

George and Alfred had succeeded far beyond their original expectations. Their affluence now enabled them to make substantial charitable gifts.

By 1934, Alfred Nicholas, who had been fully responsible for the management of the expanding business, found that the strain was affecting his health, and thereafter devoted himself mainly to more leisurely horticultural and agricultural pursuits. He died in 1937.

George now assumed a more active role in running the business, adding to its product range vitamin supplements, veterinary products and pharmaceuticals. His last official action was to open new and larger Aspro headquarters at the Melbourne suburb of Chadstone. He died in 1960. One of his three daughters, Nola, became the first wife of the internationally famous violinist Yehudi Menuhin, whilst one of his three sons, Lindsay, became the first husband of Yehudi's sister, Haphzibah Menuhin.

In 1969 Nicholas Australia Ltd purchased the English company Aspro-Nicholas Ltd, and in the following year the conglomerate became Nicholas International Ltd, selling its products in over

100 countries. In 1981 the company was merged with Kiwi International Ltd.

The Nicholas brothers and Henry Shmith undoubtedly had a few headaches in the initial production of aspirin, but their resolute efforts were to bring pain relief to millions the world over.

JOHN FURPHY

Occasionally someone's surname passes into the English language ...

John Furphy was born at Kangaroo Ground, Victoria, in 1842 and served an apprenticeship as a blacksmith. He became a specialist in farm machinery, producing an amazing variety of implements to suit local conditions. Other of Furphy's grain-stripping machines won prizes, some he patented.

One of Furphy's products was a 180-gallon (819-litre) cylindrical iron tank mounted horizontally on a horse-drawn wooden frame with cast-iron wheels. Furphy did not attempt to patent the water cart, but had his name painted in large letters on both sides of the tank. The cart soon became known as a 'Furphy'. Hundreds were made annually over a period of about forty years.

Furphys proved very popular on farms, and many were later used during World War I to carry water to the troops. The drivers of the water carts, moving from one unit to another, became noted for the spread of gossip and idle rumour. A 'furphy', according to *The Macquarie Dictionary*, is 'a rumour; a false story'.

John Furphy was a devoutly religious man and became a pillar of the Methodist Church at Shepperton. He was a forthright lay preacher, and had cast on the rear end of his water carts the homily 'Good, better, best; never let it rest, till your good is better, and your better best.'

John Furphy died in Melbourne in 1920, aged seventy-eight, but his name lives on in the English language.

ELECTRICITY

The important benefits of cheap electrification became more apparent in Australia in the early 1920s when fossil fuels and hydro-electric energy were used to drive the power-station turbines. Electricity came to city railways, trams, homes, factories and to street lighting, and was gradually extended to country areas.

Electricity brought noticeable increases in industrial productivity, and removed much of the drudgery in the home as housewives acquired various electrical appliances.

AVIATION

Australia's national and international airline, Qantas, was first formed in Winton, Queensland, as the Queensland and Northern Territory Aerial Services Limited (Qantas). It commenced passenger and postal services in 1920.

In 1928 Australia's best-known aviator, Sir Charles Kingsford-Smith was the first to cross the Pacific by air in his famous Fokker tri-motor aircraft *Southern Cross*. He was accompanied by Charles Ulm and two Americans. Soon afterwards, Kingsford-Smith and Ulm made the first trans-Tasman Sea crossing, again in *Southern Cross*.

(In 1915, Kingsford-Smith, at the age of eighteen, had enlisted in the Australian Imperial Force. He served at Gallipoli as a sapper and, later, as a dispatch rider in Egypt and France. In 1916 he transferred to the Australian Flying Corps, and after training in England, was commissioned as a second lieutenant in the Royal Flying Corps. In 1917 he was shot down and wounded in France. He was awarded the Military Cross, and in the following year served as an RFC flying instructor.)

Kingsford-Smith's feat in crossing the Tasman had been preceded in 1928 by Bert Hinkler's flight from London to Darwin in a single-engined aircraft. At the time it was the longest solo flight in aviation's short history.

In 1934 Melbourne celebrated the city's centenary. As part of the festivities an air race was held from England to Melbourne. It was won by two British airmen, C.W.A. Scott and Campbell Black, in a twin-engined Comet aircraft.

In the early 1800s the journey from England to Melbourne had taken about 170 days by ship. Travelling by air, Scott and Black made the trip in three.

Another entry in the aviation record book was made by Amy Johnson, a British aviatrix who was the first woman to fly (in a Tiger Moth biplane) solo from England to Australia.

Australia's interstate 'two airlines' policy was initiated in 1946 when the overseas-owned Australian National Airways (ANA) was allowed to enter into direct competition with the government's own carrier, Trans-Australian Airlines (TAA).

JOHN FLYNN

It was in 1928 that another pioneer, but not himself an aviator, wrote the first chapter in an inspiring and continuing story which is an important part of Australia's aviation history.

As a young man, John Flynn knew the direction of his life's work. He began studying for the ministry at twenty-three. In 1911, having been ordained into the Presbyterian church, he volunteered for missionary work. In the following year, after Flynn had submitted detailed reports on the needs of Northern Territory Aboriginal people and white settlers, the Presbyterian General Assembly appointed him as superintendent of its Australian Inland Mission (AIM). He was to continue to direct the AIM for the next thirty-nine years, developing a network of hospitals and hostels, each linked by a patrol padre.

In 1928, after ten years work on the part of Flynn and his helpers, the Aerial Medical Service came into operation—the central need in Flynn's vision of a 'mantle of safety', harnessing the benefits of aircraft, radios and medicines to provide medical and dental services to the widespread outback communities. The service commenced operating from the inland Queensland town of Cloncurry. The first flying doctor was Dr St Vincent Welch.

In the initial twelve months of operation the Mission's first doctor flew 32,000 kilometres and attended 255 patients. The service steadily expanded, and Flynn now devoted much of his time and energy towards securing the support of state and Commonwealth governments. This he had achieved by 1933, the year in which he was awarded an OBE. In 1942 the organisation's name was changed to The Flying Doctor Service of Australia. 'Royal' was added in 1954. By then it was using some thirty aircraft and attending to over 1 million patients annually.

The Royal Flying Doctor Service (RFDS) does much more than bring doctors to patients and, when necessary, fly emergency cases to hospital. It also provides regular clinics in remote areas, and assists in dropping food and supplies in times of flood and bushfire. In emergency situations the RFDS has been used in search-and-rescue operations.

The RFDS has radio networks in all states and territories except Victoria and the Northern Territory. They are also used for School of the Air transmissions, which began in 1951.

Not only was radio vital to the development of the AIM operations, it was also, as Flynn realised, the key to linking the many remote and widespread outback communities.

It was in 1926, two years before the Aerial Medical Service was launched, that Flynn recruited the services of Alfred Traeger to conduct radio experiments and to develop a transceiver for two-way radio communication with the outback. It had to be simple, durable, small, easy to operate and cheap to produce.

Traeger, who had studied electrical and mechanical engineering at Adelaide and had already experimented with a pedal transmitter-receiver, now produced his famous pedal-operated generator and transceiver, operated by a small generator and fitted with bicycle pedals.

The sets were first introduced in Queensland in 1929 and were hugely successful. Traeger later invented a typewriter-like Morse keyboard, and in 1935 produced a transceiver which could be voice-operated.

Traeger's pedal-powered transceivers were widely used throughout the outback, permitting emergency communication with hospitals. They were operated by doctors, ambulance services, inland padres, drovers, transport drivers, councils, taxis, airlines and ships.

By 1939 Traeger had modified the sets to operate from a vibrator unit instead of pedals.

Alfred Hermann Traeger (he had German grandparents) was awarded an OBE in 1944. His manufacturing company sold pedal radios to African countries in 1962, and in 1970 the company installed an educational radio network in Canada. He later designed a turbo-driven car and a solar-power converter to make salt water drinkable. He died in 1980, aged eighty-five.

John Flynn was elected in 1939 to the position of Moderator-General of the Presbyterian Church of Australia. Several overseas academic degrees were conferred upon him in recognition of his work. During World War II he established a home for elderly people in Alice Springs and a children's holiday and health scheme in Adelaide.

In 1932, then aged fifty-one, Flynn married his devoted secretary, Jean Blanch Baird, who remained his companion until his death in 1951.

The John Flynn Memorial Church was opened in Alice Springs in 1956. There, a simple tribute to him reads: 'His monument is in the hearts of the people'.

RURAL RESEARCH

In the post-war period there was awareness on the part of pastoralists and graziers, as well as by the federal and state governments and academic institutions, of the significant benefits to be derived by ongoing agricultural research programs. In time, research and development programs would be extended to improve productivity in other areas.

In 1920 the University of Sydney established a Faculty of Agriculture. The University of Melbourne did likewise shortly afterwards. A Research Institute was founded in South Australia in 1924. Both the federal and state governments readily provided funds for rural research. Pastoral organisations set up private facilities that proved beneficial, particularly in the areas of chemicals, fertilisers and food processing.

The Council for Scientific and Industrial Research was established in 1924 by the Commonwealth Government. It was renamed in 1949 as the Commonwealth Scientific and Industrial Research Organisation (CSIRO).

RABBITS

The early nineteenth-century immigrants brought with them many of the things they were used to. One such was a popular source of food—rabbits.

In 1859, rabbits were intentionally released in Victoria, and by the 1890s had reached plague proportions. With few predators, the rabbits spread rapidly, particularly in rural South Australia and in southern Western Australia, destroying pasture lands, consuming grain and vegetable crops, ringbarking trees, transforming paddocks into dust bowls and causing costly soil erosion. By the 1930s it was estimated that Australia's rabbit population had reached 750 million.

To combat the menace, unaffected farmers had little choice but to take the expensive option of erecting rabbit-proof fencing. Eventually, by the early 1950s, a more effective answer to the problem was found with the introduction of the myxoma virus, which killed off many millions of rabbits. Forty years later, by which time the reduced rabbit population had built up a degree of resistance to myxomatosis, an alternative method of control, the calici virus, was successfully introduced.

COMMUNISM

In 1920 the more extreme elements of the workers' movement, inspired by the 1917 Russian Revolution and the teachings of Marx and Lenin, formed the Communist Party of Australia.

The issue of communism played an increasing part in political affairs during the 1920s and 1930s, successive Australian governments generally maintaining an anti-communist stance. In the post-World War II period there was concern that Asian countries to Australia's north would be successively dominated by anti-democratic forces. As a result, the conservative parties in Australia had no compunction about making capital of the 'menace of communism' to achieve their electoral ends.

The prime example of this occurred during the 1954 election campaign, when a Russian diplomat and self-confessed spy, Vladimir Petrov, defected to Australia and made allegations of a spy ring within the country. At a time when the Australian economy was experiencing a severe downturn, this development was seized upon by the Liberal and Country Party Coalition, led by Robert Menzies, to again raise the bogy of anti-communism. The Coalition duly won the election.

Thereafter, the Communist Party gradually faded from the political spectrum as worker support declined.

POLITICAL PARTIES

A political organisation that emerged during the immediate post-war period was the Country Party. Founded in 1919 and initially led by Dr Earle Page, the party represented some of the more conservative farming associations which considered their interests were not being adequately represented by the Nationalist Party and its leader, Billy Hughes.

Page had become Deputy Prime Minister following the 1922 general election. In 1932 the United Australia Party (UAP) formed a government in coalition with the Country Party. Thereafter, the latter retained its identity until amalgamation in the 1970s with the National Party. The alliance between the current Liberal Party and the National Party, now known as the Coalition, operates on a state-by-state basis.

The UAP had been formed in 1931 under the leadership of the respected and popular Joe Lyons. When Lyons died in April 1939 he was succeeded by the Attorney-General, Robert Menzies, a brilliant barrister and constitutional lawyer who had entered politics in 1928. Menzies had acquired the nickname 'Pig-iron Bob' following a dispute with wharf labourers over the loading of a cargo of pig-iron.

Menzies resigned as Prime Minister and leader of the UAP in August 1941.

In October 1944, Menzies was instrumental in forming the broad-based Liberal Party, which represented various conservative elements including the then-named Country Party. Menzies remained as the Liberal Party leader until his retirement from politics in 1966. By then he had been prime minister for a total of eighteen years, including a record sixteen years continually in office.

The most recent Liberal-National Coalition Prime Minister was John Howard, who took up the position after the 1996 federal election. He was re-elected in 1998, 2001 and 2004 before being defeated in 2007 by the Labor Party, headed by Kevin Rudd.

John Howard remains the second-longest serving Prime Minister of Australia, after Robert Menzies.

THE COUNTRY WOMEN'S ASSOCIATION

Life in the bush was always hard, especially for women. With their menfolk away for most of the day, and sometimes for days and weeks on end, there was the loneliness to contend with, and much more besides.

During the nineteenth century, and for part of the twentieth, there was no refrigeration, no insecticides to combat the hordes of flies and mosquitoes and no air conditioning. There was no electricity and no telephone service. Housework was enervating when summer heat danced outside, whilst if the home had an iron roof the sun's rays added to the heat of the kitchen stove. Roads and tracks were often hazardous, especially after rain. And in dry spells there was the ever-present threat of a water shortage. These and other factors caused both mental and physical strain.

A hundred years ago there were no free hospital maternity wards. Therefore, if private hospital fees could not be afforded, it was a case of make the best of it when it came to giving birth. When there was an accident or illness, someone had to make a journey if assistance was necessary. When a telephone service eventually became available (from the 1890s in the cities), it was not always reliable. The Bush Nursing Association provided help whenever possible, but the organisation lacked finance and could not provide adequate facilities in the country.

Transport was always difficult and expensive, so bush families, especially those who lived in the more remote areas, probably went for years without a holiday and rarely, if ever, saw the sea.

There were other difficulties as well. When women accompanied their menfolk to stock sales in distant country towns, there was nowhere to rest, to attend to their babies or small children, and nowhere to make a cup of tea. When the sales were over, the men customarily gathered at a hotel to 'talk shop' and slake their thirst, but where were the women and children to go? Usually they had little choice but to spend hours sitting idly in a buggy, sulky or cart, sometimes under the sparse shade of a gum tree, sometimes not.

When railway transport first arrived, and for a long time afterwards, there were usually no station refreshment rooms or rest rooms for women. On long, hot journeys on crowded trains, milk for children was unavailable, and if there was a carafe of water in the compartment it was usually emptied quickly.

In the early 1900s attempts were made to remedy the situation, but World War I put an end to various schemes. In 1921, following a campaign in *The Stock and Station Journal* (now *Country Life*), a bushwomen's conference was mooted, to be held during the forthcoming Agricultural Show in Sydney. A large room was reserved at the Country Club in Sydney's Castlereagh Street and the conference duly took place under the patronage of the wife of the New South Wales Governor, Lady Davidson. The room was full to overflowing.

One of the attendees at the conference was Mrs Hugh Munro from the Keera Station at Bingara (near Inverell in the state's north). Mrs Munro was a woman of immense energy and outstanding organisational ability. She presided over the meeting, and it was resolved to establish a women's movement to be organised and run entirely by country women themselves, to be known as the Counry Women's Association (CWA).

Mrs Munro put forward a list of aims for the movement. These have remained largely unaltered to this day, and are summarised briefly as follows:

- To improve the welfare and conditions of women and children in country areas;
- To draw together all women, girls and children;
- For meetings of women in towns and rural districts to share friendships and experiences and to air their views on family matters;

- To voice rural women's opinions to federal, state and local governments;
- To share ideas, skills and resources; and to improve rural women's communication and leadership skills;
- To support schemes for providing medical research, scholarships, relief during emergencies, international projects, units for the aged, a residential club in Sydney providing accommodation at a reasonable cost, holiday homes, hospitals and other local organisations, hospital visiting committees, and, later, the Royal Flying Doctor Service and the School of the Air;
- To promote international goodwill, friendship and understanding between women everywhere; and to encourage development in regional areas.

Mrs Munro threw herself immediately into the new organisation's work. The first branch meeting was held at Crookwell, south-west of Sydney, on 26 April 1922. Within six months some sixty-eight branches had been formed—an indication of the enthusiasm that the ideal of the CWA had generated.

Steadily, the desired facilities came into existence: baby health centres; seaside holiday homes; home nursing services; accommodation in towns for expectant mothers; hostels for students attending regional schools; support schemes providing skilled medical treatment; rest homes; and sleeping berths on long-distance trains.

During World War II, CWA members manned factories and produced large quantities of knitted woollen garments and food to support the war effort.

The CWA's membership presently numbers about 14,000 in New South Wales and approximately 50,000 throughout Australia. It is affiliated to the Associated Country Women of the World, an organisation with headquarters in London.

The determination and indomitable spirit of Mrs H. Munro, MBE, and the many leaders who followed her, lives on as the essential work of the CWA continues and grows. They remain true to their original motto: 'Service to the country, through country women, for country women, by country women.'

SISTER KENNY

There's nothing unusual about being criticised, reprimanded, pilloried, blamed, censured, reproved or otherwise admonished—if you've done something wrong. But it's rather sad if you're the target of such adverse opinions when you've done something right.

In 1910, Elizabeth Kenny, born at Warialda in northern New South Wales, was working as a self-trained nurse from her family home on the Darling Downs, riding on horseback to treat patients, and without charge for her services. In the following year, after a Queensland surgeon had diagnosed by *telegram* cases of poliomyelitis (infantile paralysis), Nurse Kenny treated the patients with hot fomentations. They recovered.

In 1915 Nurse Kenny enlisted for war service, using a recommendation from the same surgeon to establish her nursing experience. She was appointed to the Australian Army Nursing Service, and was wounded in France. For a brief period she was matron at an English military hospital, then served on troopships bringing the wounded back to Australia. In 1917 she was promoted to the rank of Sister, and two years later, after her army service was terminated, she returned to home-nursing in Queensland and became the first president of the Nobby chapter of the Country Women's Association (see pp. 267–9).

In 1927, she designed and patented an ambulance stretcher, known as the 'Sylvia', which enabled patients in shock to be treated whilst being transported.

In 1932, at Townsville, she set up a clinic for the treatment of long-term poliomyelitis sufferers. At a time when there was no vaccination for poliomyelitis, Sister Kenny's methods of treatment, which included the use of hot baths, the discarding of braces and calipers and the substitution of therapy through the use of movement and specific exercises, aroused strong controversy and hostility amongst the conservative medical profession. But although political pressure mounted, the Queensland government was not swayed by the majority adverse opinion of the doctors. After approval had been given for Kenny clinics to be opened in Townsville, Brisbane and other Queensland centres, interest in her work for long-term poliomyelitis patients was aroused both interstate and overseas.

In 1937, after publishing a paper on infantile paralysis, with a foreword by the professor of anatomy at the University of Queensland, Herbert Wilkinson, Sister Kenny went to England where she was allocated two hospital wards for her work. But English doctors were shocked to hear of her condemnation of orthodox treatment of poliomyelitis and to find that she did not use splints to prevent deformities.

She encountered a similar reaction on her return to Australia, where some leading Queensland doctors again condemned her methods. Notwithstanding, she was given a ward at the Brisbane General Hospital for the treatment of early cases of the disease. The hospital's medical superintendent noted that the limbs of Sister Kenny's patients were more supple than those treated by orthodox splinting, and that the patients had a higher recovery rate. But her methods continued to be opposed by the medical profession generally.

In 1940 Sister Kenny travelled to the United States, where doctors initially rejected her theories. However, she was allocated beds in the Minneapolis General Hospital, and there her methods soon merited widespread approval. She began running courses for doctors and physiotherapists from around the world, and was able to arrange for the construction, in 1942, of the Sister Kenny Institute in Minneapolis. Kenny clinics were later established in other centres.

Sister Kenny was awarded many honours and honorary degrees in America and became something of a hero. Her autobiography *And They Shall Walk* was published in 1943, and she was eulogised in a film. In 1950, Congress accorded her the rare honour of free access to the United States without entry formalities.

In Australia, bitter controversy still centred around Sister Kenny's work, despite a recommendation in 1947 by the Queensland director-general of health that the Kenny method be used for treatment in the early stages of poliomyelitis. She returned several times to Australia, where her intolerance of opposition may have contributed to the general medical profession's continued rejection of her theories, despite the acceptance that her methods had gained elsewhere.

Elizabeth Kenny retired to Toowoomba in 1951, where she died the following year. She had never married, but was survived by an adopted daughter. Her book, *My Battle and Victory*, was published posthumously in London in 1955.

RADIO

A weekly radio program began broadcasting from Sydney in 1921. In 1923 a concert in Sydney was broadcast from Station 2SB, later to become the ABC's 2BL. In the following year the federal government issued four broadcasting licences: two in Sydney and one each in Melbourne and Perth.

The national broadcaster, the Australian Broadcasting Corporation (ABC), was formed in 1933. The Special Broadcasting Service (SBS) was established in 1978, operating a television station as well as two radio services. By 1990 there were over 150 commercial radio services operating throughout Australia; by 2010 this had increased again to around 260.

In 1998, a new era of radio was ushered in with the first program to be streamed on the internet: The Vinyl Lounge on NetFM. Most commercial radio stations are now online at near-CD quality.

VEGEMITE™ AND KRAFT™ CHEESE

Cyril Callister took full advantage of a good education and upbringing. Born in the Victorian town of Beaufort, west of Ballarat, he went first to state schools, then to Grenville College at Ballarat and the Ballarat School of Mines, and finally attended the University of Melbourne.

In 1915 Callister worked briefly for a manufacturer of food and household products, then enlisted in the Australian Imperial Force. After only three months he was withdrawn to join the Munitions Branch and was sent to Britain to work on explosives.

In 1919 Callister married in Scotland, then returned to Australia to rejoin his previous employer. When that company was taken over he secured an appointment with a small food company, Fred Walker, to develop a yeast extract for retail sale. Now an established food technologist, Callister began research on the yeast process, using brewer's yeast for his experiments.

The product Callister created was placed on the market in 1924. Gradually it became an accepted item. The product's trade name was Vegemite™.

Fred Walker was also interested in a method of preserving cheese. This led Callister to the study of microbiology and to experiments in preserving cheese. Using a process patented by an American, James L. Kraft, Callister developed an acceptable form of processed cheese. Walker now persuaded Kraft to license the manufacture in Australia of Kraft™ cheese. The Kraft Walker Cheese Co. was established in 1926 with Callister as chief chemist and production superintendent.

Meanwhile, in 1925, Callister had sent samples of Vegemite™ to London to test them for vitamin B activity (at that time very little research had been done on vitamins). The test results confirmed that Vegemite™ had a high vitamin B content and was very suitable for children and nursing mothers.

In 1926 Callister began a detailed study of the cheese-making process with the assistance of a bacteriologist who had been added to the staff. This led to an improvement in Vegemite™ and to increased knowledge of cheese manufacture, food dehydration and vitamins. Considerable quantities of service rations were produced during World War II by the Kraft Walker Cheese Co. for the Australian and American forces.

Cyril Callister died in 1949, having made a significant contribution to Australian food science and technology. He was noted for his professional excellence and great personal integrity.

LIFESAVING

For a long time, drowning has been one of the main causes of accidental death in many countries.

In England in 1774, concern for lifesaving and the 'restoration of life' resulted in the formation of the Royal Humane Society. One hundred years later a branch of the Society was formed in Melbourne. Within a few years, lifesaving instruction was being given in Victorian schools.

In London, in 1891, the Royal Life Saving Society (RLSS) was founded by William Henry. Three years later, by which time the Society had gained its Royal Charter, a branch was formed in New South Wales. By 1912 there were branches in each of the eastern states. Additional branches were established in Western Australia in 1924, in the Northern Territory in 1965, and in the Australian Capital Territory in 1975. The RLSS's national headquarters was set up in Sydney in 1981.

In 1908–1909, the Surf Bathers' Association had been formed in Sydney, its activities (in addition to some sporting contests) being concentrated on lifesaving on ocean beaches.

The Queensland Surf Bath Association was founded in 1920, by which time various clubs had been formed in populous coastal districts.

Thus, by 1924 there were two main organisations in Australia concerned with lifesaving: the RLSS and the Surf Life Saving Association of Australia, now named Surf Life Saving Australia (SLSA). The latter's interest is in lifesaving and related activities on ocean beaches, whilst the 'Royal', as it is known, is responsible for all other waterways—rivers and their estuaries, lakes, dams, reservoirs, tanks and pools.

Australia's thousands of glorious, golden beaches present wonderful opportunities for healthy recreation, fun in the surf and board riding. But there are also dangers.

This was dramatically and tragically exemplified on Sunday 6 February 1938 at Australia's most famous beach, Sydney's Bondi, where in mid-afternoon a series of large waves rolled up the beach in quick succession, building up a huge volume of water which was prevented from receding by the waves which followed. There was suddenly a powerful back-surge which swept some 300 bathers, who had been standing in a metre or so of water on what they thought was a sandbank, into a deep channel.

To their aid rushed members of the Bondi Club patrol, together with about seventy other club members who had recently arrived to take part in training. Sixty of the rescued bathers needed medical treatment from doctors, nurses, police and ambulance officers who quickly gathered on the scene. About forty of the patients were in a serious condition. Four of them later died. One swimmer was reported missing, his body being recovered several days later. The day of the tragedy came to be known as 'Black Sunday'.

These were the first fatalities since the Bondi Club had been formed on 1 February 1906, with twenty-three members. One of the club's first tasks on being formed was to perfect the newly-acquired reel, line and belt equipment. The technique for using the equipment was to remain for many years as an essential part of surf lifesaving. In the following year the equipment was used to rescue two young lads at Bondi Beach. One of them, Charlie Smith, was later to become Australia's most famous aviator, Sir Charles Kingsford-Smith (see p. 260).

THE GREAT DEPRESSION

In the late 1920s Australians enjoyed a higher standard of living than did people in most other countries. Exports of wool and wheat continued to account for the greater part of the country's overseas earnings, but when prices for these commodities and other exports fell sharply in 1928 and onwards, the economy rapidly moved into a state of depression. Most other countries among the world's developed nations were similarly affected.

Australia's inability at that time to raise new overseas loans prolonged the economy's malaise. Unemployment steadily increased during the Depression years, rising to 30 per cent in 1932. The federal government faced considerable difficulty in making interest repayments on the high level of overseas loans, thus impacting on its ability to alleviate the distress and suffering of the many people affected by the Depression, especially the unemployed. Strikes, protests and demonstrations beset the Labor government, which was led by James Scullin. In the December 1931 federal election, the ALP met with a crushing defeat, and was replaced by the newly-founded United Australia Party (UAP), led by Joe Lyons (see p. 266).

Recovery from the Depression did not come until 1932–33, by which time wool prices had improved considerably, unemployment had begun to decline steadily and confidence had returned as evidence of a healthier economy encouraged a higher level of local and overseas investment.

In 1932, as signs of the recovery were confirmed, two headline-catching events occurred in Sydney ...

THE SYDNEY HARBOUR BRIDGE

On 20 March 1932, approximately three-quarters of a million people gathered in the vicinity of the northern harbourside suburb of Milson's Point to witness the grand opening of the Sydney

Harbour Bridge. It had been fabricated in Britain by Dorman Long & Co. Ltd, who had designed and successfully tendered for the single-arch bridge.

A harbour bridge had first been proposed in 1857, but the present bridge resulted largely from the initiative of a senior engineer in the New South Wales government's Department of Public Works, J.C. Bradfield. The necessary Act permitting construction of a bridge was passed by the New South Wales parliament in 1922, and tenders were called for in the following year.

Each half of the bridge's arch was built from opposite sides of the harbour as a cantilever, the cantilevers successfully meeting at the centre of the span in August 1930, thanks mainly to the skill and courage of the Australian workers who were fully responsible for the bridge's erection. The main arch is made of silicon steel and weighs just over 39,000 tonnes. The total weight of steel in the bridge is nearly 53,000 tonnes. The original capital cost of the bridge was £9,577,507.

At the opening ceremony, the Premier, Jack Lang, in the presence of the New South Wales Governor, Sir Philip Game, Lady Game and a distinguished gathering, made an appropriate speech and formally declared the great bridge open for traffic. As Lang was preparing to cut the customary ribbon with a pair a scissors, there was commotion as a horseman, dressed in a Hussar's uniform, suddenly rode forward and at the second attempt cut the ceremonial ribbon with his sword. He was dragged away by police and later identified as Francis E. de Groot, a member of the 'New Guard', a quasi-military anti-communist organisation opposed to the activities of Jack Lang and the State Labor government. De Groot was later charged with offensive behaviour and fined £5 with £4 costs.

BODYLINE CRICKET

In the summer of 1932–33 there erupted a furore which at least temporarily diverted the minds of the sporting public (which in Australia means a large proportion of the population) away from the after-effects of the Depression. Such was the crisis that there were suggestions, even at the highest level, that Australia should consider withdrawing from the Commonwealth forthwith.

The Test Match series against the visiting English cricket side inevitably aroused widespread interest, the more so as at that time the quadrennial home Test matches against England were the only official international contests played on Australian soil.

There was no indication that the 1932–33 series would arouse anything but the usual high expectations of interest. No-one was prepared for the outbreaks of what amounted to sporting warfare which erupted on and off the cricket pitches. And 'sporting' was very much the operative word, for the Australian players, public and officials regarded the proceedings as decidedly *unsporting*.

The trouble first exploded in a pre-Test Match in Melbourne, when the English captain, Douglas Jardine, instructed his two fast bowlers, the great Harold Larwood and Bill Voce, to bowl at the bodies of the Australian batsmen to a packed leg-side field. It was an entirely new cricketing gambit which the Australian cricket public generally regarded as 'not cricket'. (Sir) Don Bradman (p.303–4), by then recognised as perhaps one of the greatest of all Australian batsmen, made 36 runs before being trapped l.b.w. by Larwood.

The match was followed by the First Test in Sydney, where the hapless Australian batsmen, unaccustomed to the lightning-fast head-high deliveries, were battered by the barrages from Larwood and Voce. The crowd and the newspapers were incensed, despite a rousing century from another great Australian batsman, Stan McCabe, who went on to make 187 not out and became an instant hero.

The Englishmen were unrepentant and repeated the 'leg theory' in the Australian second innings, this time using four fast bowlers. The game progressed without further incident or serious injury, Bradman making 103 not out in the Australian second 'dig'.

It was in the Third Test at Adelaide that the fireworks reached a crescendo. One of the Australian opening batsmen, Bill Woodfull, was struck over the heart by a ball from Larwood, collapsed and had to be helped from the field. Other members of the Australian team were struck and bruised. The Australian cricket authorities made their feelings known by cable to the Marylebone Cricket Club (English cricket's ruling body) in London. At home, the Australians and the English continued thundering at each other, the Australians pressing for 'bodyline' bowling to be banned. Some in high places began talking darkly about Australia's place in the British Empire, and of the need for action to restore the great and unifying game of cricket to its former glory.

After some exchanges between the two governments, it was decided that the Test series should continue. Tempers and temperature during the remaining two Tests gradually cooled, despite the Englishmen continuing with their leg theory.

Towards the end of the final Test, Harold Larwood, after making 98, was cheered as he returned to the pavilion. He was later to bring his family to Australia and to make his home in Sydney. It was a gesture widely appreciated by the Australian public, who had recognised the skill and athleticism of a great cricketer. They also came to understand that Larwood and the other English fast bowlers were only doing what their captain had ordered.

The irony was that half a century later the 'bouncer', or fast ball aimed at a batsman's head or upper body, had become an accepted tactic of modern cricket. By then, of course, batsmen wore helmets and otherwise protected themselves with padding. The fact remains, however, that Jardine's 'leg theory' was really no more intimidating than the present-day 'bouncers'.

THE OUTBREAK OF WORLD WAR II

The early 1930s saw the emergence in Germany of the Nazi Party, led by Adolf Hitler. Still smarting from their defeat at the hands of the Allies in World War I, Germans were generally receptive to the doctrines that Hitler so forcibly propounded, especially the younger generation. As the Nazi Party rose in power, fed on Hitler's creed of asserting the superiority of the German race, the expansionist intentions of the Germans became apparent to those international observers—Winston Churchill amongst them—who foresaw the threat of another major conflict in Europe.

The rise in Germany of Hitler and the Nazi Party was mirrored to some extent in Italy, where Benito Mussolini and his Fascist Party came to power in the early 1930s.

Germany began to rearm in 1934. Two years later, Hitler ordered the German Army to reoccupy the demilitarised zone of the Rhineland. On 15 March 1939, German troops invaded Czechoslovakia. A fortnight later Neville Chamberlain, the British Prime Minister, responded by reversing his previous policy of appeasement towards Germany, sending Poland an offer of support in the event of any action that threatened Poland's independence.

Hitler countered the British move by concluding a secret pact with Soviet Russia, which provided for the partitioning of Poland between Russia and Germany.

The British government, whilst having no liking for the Russian regime, had been slowly working towards a defensive agreement with Russia in the belief that an Anglo-Russian alliance would be a deterrent to Hitler's territorial ambitions. Germany also had no liking for the Russians, but despite Hitler's deep-seated antipathy towards communism, it was held that a Soviet-German agreement would neutralise any threat to Germany's eastern frontier. The Germans also hoped that the pact with Russia would discourage British intervention in support of Poland.

On 1 September 1939, Germany attacked Poland with powerful armoured columns supported by the Luftwaffe air arm, resulting in a new form of warfare (which in fact had been devised in Britain and given the name 'lightning'). The Germans called the theory *blitzkrieg*, or lightning war, and adopted the concept enthusiastically. The term '*blitz*' would later pass into the English language.

On 3 September, Britain declared war on Germany in response to its treaty obligations with Poland.

A fortnight later, on 17 September, the Russians invaded Poland. Within three weeks all organised Polish resistance had ceased, although guerilla activity continued during the winter. More than 80,000 Polish troops managed to escape through neighbouring neutral countries, and were later to make an important contribution in the ensuing struggle against Germany.

During the following eight months nothing very much appeared to happen. The Americans called the phase the 'phoney war'. In fact, there was intense activity on both sides during the winter months, as forces were mobilised and preparations made for the impending conflict.

In Australia, the Prime Minister, Robert Menzies, had formally announced on 3 September 1939 that the country was at war with Germany. Compulsory military training for home service was introduced in November. In the following month the 6th Division, under the command of Lieutenant-General Sir Thomas Blamey, was despatched to Palestine for training preparatory to the Division's intended service alongside the British Expeditionary Force (BEF) in France.

By April 1940, the 7th Division had also been equipped and despatched to the Middle East for training.

THE WAR IN EUROPE AND NORTH AFRICA

On 10 May 1940, the German armies launched their attack in the west, through Belgium, on a narrow front which was quickly widened into a huge gap.

Also on 10 May, Winston Churchill replaced Neville Chamberlain as Britain's Prime Minister.

By 20 May the German *panzer* (armoured) divisions had moved swiftly through the Belgian Ardennes forest (a move thought unlikely by the Allied strategists) and had reached Abbeville at the mouth of the River Somme. They then swung northwards, effectively cutting off the BEF from the French. By 26 May, following the surrender of the Belgian Army, the BEF had been driven back to Dunkirk and the English Channel, and were isolated.

At this point, Hitler, for reasons that were never fully explained, ordered his armoured forces to halt for three days. The British took full advantage of this unexpected respite to mobilise every available naval and civilian craft, even the smallest, to make repeated crossings of the 40-kilometre width of the English Channel to rescue the exhausted British troops. It was expected that the 'small ships armada' would be able to ferry back no more than about 45,000 troops. In the event, some 800 craft, the smallest no more than 9 metres in length, snatched from the jaws of the Germans an astonishing 338,000 men. The troops lost most of their equipment, but lived to continue the fight.

With the collapse of France, Britain effectively was now alone in the struggle against Nazi Germany. Whilst most of the sixteen divisions that had been brought back from Dunkirk were safely in England, they were exhausted and almost totally lacking in equipment. Britain's land forces then comprised just a single fully-equipped division. Had the Germans decided to cross the English Channel during the weeks following the Dunkirk escape, they would have met with little effective resistance.

Having driven the BEF into the sea, the German panzer divisions swept south-west towards Paris, having had little difficulty in turning the French Maginot Line and thereby cutting off a significant proportion of the French army. The French had little option but to capitulate and seek an armistice. The German terms were accepted on 22 June, the armistice becoming effective three days later. The French government resigned and was replaced by a 'puppet' government under the ageing Marshal Pétain. The seat of the government was at Vichy in the south of France.

Following the French capitulation, the German High Command set about planning an invasion of Britain to be launched by mid-August. As a preliminary, the German Luftwaffe was ordered to launch a day-and-night air assault on London and southern England, designed to disrupt Britain's defensive preparations and to weaken public morale. They succeeded in neither, although the almost non-stop bombing caused heavy civilian casualties and extensive property damage, especially in the London area.

The Battle of Britain, as it was called, lasted from July 1940 until the end of October. The Germans lost 1733 aircraft and the Royal Air Force 915. The Blitz, which continued with heavy and mainly night air attacks, lasted until 16 May 1941, when the German air strength was switched eastwards for the coming invasion of Russia. However, sporadic air attacks continued on London and other targets until 1944, when the V1 'Flying Bomb' attacks on south-east England began.

The indiscriminate German bombing of Britain in 1940–41, and particularly of London, met with a response from Britain in 1942 when the RAF's Bomber Command launched the first of a protracted series of air attacks on German cities and strategic targets. It was to be a long and devastating campaign. During 1942–43, the Allied aircraft and aircrew losses reached such proportions that the attacks had to be temporarily curtailed. But by early 1944 the main problem had been overcome with the introduction of protective fighter aircraft which were more than a match for the Luftwaffe's fighters, and which also had the range to enable them to fly to any part of the German Reich and return.

A number of Australian airmen fought during the Battle of Britain, having been trained in Canada under the Commonwealth Air Training Scheme. As the air war with Germany progressed, increasing numbers of Commonwealth aircrews trained under the scheme became available to meet the need for fighter and bomber air crews.

In April 1941 the Germans invaded Greece and succeeded in cutting off the main part of the Greek Army. British and Allied forces stationed in

Greece were hastily evacuated to Crete. A month later some 3000 German parachutists dropped out of the sky to the astonishment of over 28,000 British, Australian and New Zealand troops then stationed on the island. The parachutists were quickly reinforced by air and sea, so that within a few days some 22,000 German troops had landed, although some of the airborne troops had been killed or wounded on landing.

To meet this threat, the Australian 6th Division was deployed in Crete in a vain attempt to halt the German advance through Greece. Following the evacuation from Crete, the Australian 7th Division fought a successful campaign in Syria against local forces controlled by the French puppet government, known as the Vichy Government.

In northern Africa, the Allied forces protecting Egypt and the Sudan were now faced with the threat posed by numerically superior Italian troops in Libya and, on the southern front, in Eritrea and Abyssinia.

The Allied troops, which included about 36,000 Indian, Australian, New Zealand and South African men under the command of General Sir Archibald Wavell, wasted no time in attacking the Italians, and by the beginning of February 1941 had captured the port of Benghazi at the western end of Cyrenaica.

Disturbed by the ineffectiveness of the Italian effort, Hitler despatched German troops (the Africa Korps) to northern Africa. They were under the command of the young, decisive and forthright General Erwin Rommel, who had been outstandingly successful in *panzer* operations during the German drive into France. Rommel quickly transformed the situation, and by the middle of April had swept the Allied forces out of Cyrenaica.

Rommel continued to drive eastwards towards Cairo, cutting off the important port of Tobruk, which was garrisoned by the Australian 9th Division (the 'Desert Rats', as the Germans disparagingly described them) and which bore the brunt of the siege (they were later reinforced by the 18th Brigade of the 7th Australian Division and by units of the Royal Tank Regiment). Despite setbacks, the Africa Korps's thrust continued as far as El Alamein. The first—and most decisive—of the three battles of El Alamein was then fought, causing the Afrika Korps and the Italians to retreat. This important July 1941 battle at Alamein had been won by the 8th Army, but at the cost of more than 13,000 casualties.

By the end of April 1943, the Anglo-American First Army had moved eastwards from Algeria into Tunisia and was threatening Tunis.

On 9 May 1943, the 5th Panzer Army, caught between the British and American spearheads, surrendered, and Tunis was occupied. Within a few days the remaining Axis (German–Italian alliance) forces to the south had been mopped up.

Once the Germans and Italians had been driven out of northern Africa, the Allies lost no time in implementing their plan to attack what Churchill called 'the soft under-belly of the Axis'—Italy. The first step, the clearance of Axis forces from Sicily, took a month, due partly to the hilly nature of Sicily's terrain.

The Allied forces made slow progress in their advance northwards, due mainly to the stiff resistance put up by the German and Italian armies and to the mountainous terrain of central Italy. Salerno was occupied on 9 September 1943. Following the announcement of Italy's capitulation, the US 5th Army finally entered Rome on 4 June 1944.

During 1942, as the Russian and German armies remained locked in combat deep within Russia, the Soviets made insistent demands to the Allies that a Second Front should be opened as a diversionary tactic to draw off German forces assaulting their homeland. Planning went ahead for a massive Allied attack through France which would answer the repeated Russian demand. By the end of 1942, the German advance eastwards had been halted by the Russian armies and the severe winter weather. At the end of January 1943 the German 6th Army had been encircled and had surrendered at the approaches to Stalingrad. In March the Germans began their withdrawal from the front facing Moscow. Throughout 1943 and 1944, despite bitter fighting as they retreated, the German armies were steadily rolled back by the resilient Russians.

The Second Front, against a still-powerful enemy, was finally launched on 6 June 1944, when Allied troops landed on a number of beaches on the heavily fortified Normandy coast in northern France.

Despite stiff German resistance, the main beachhead, to the north of the strategic town of Caen, was quickly secured, due largely to the combined Allied air force's 'thirty to one' superiority in aircraft numbers. The Allied air power, supported by intensive naval gunfire, was used to destroy bridges over the Seine and Loire rivers, thereby delaying German efforts to bring up *panzer* reserves to support their troops at the sites of the main British landings and the positions further west where the Americans had landed.

Despite fierce fighting, the Allied bridgeheads had been secured by mid-July, allowing the massive build-up of troops and equipment necessary for the ground assault against Germany.

Germany was now committed to a land war on three fronts.

By July 1944 the Allies were able to move out of the Normandy beachheads and to advance westwards towards the Brittany submarine bases at Brest, Lorient and St Nazaire; and eastwards towards Paris, which was re-occupied on 25 August. Brussels also was re-occupied on 3 September 1944—exactly five years after the declaration of war against Germany.

By the beginning of September the Germans had been pushed close to their frontiers with occupied France, Belgium and Holland. The pursuit from Normandy had been relatively easy—in fact, too easy. As Christmas approached, a relaxed atmosphere pervaded the Allied Command headquarters, for it was considered that the Germans did not have the forces to defend both its eastern and western frontiers against the advancing enemies, not to mention the rapidly deteriorating situation in Italy.

It therefore came as a major shock to the Allies when, on 16 December, the Germans launched a powerful thrust against the British and American positions.

Spearheaded by *panzer* divisions, the Germans attacked through occupied Belgium and Luxembourg against the thinly-held Allied line bordering the Ardennes woodlands.

The 130-kilometre Ardennes sector of the Allied front was held by only four divisions, which were quickly swept aside by twenty-four German divisions comprising nearly 1000 tanks and armoured assault guns. Within a week, however, the powerful thrust had lost momentum, and by 26 December the Germans had begun falling back. The strength of the Allied ground forces, supported by several thousand aircraft, was sufficient to ensure that there would be no second 'Dunkirk'.

Despite determined fighting by most of the German troops, particularly the *panzer* units, the Allies steadily regained the lost ground. On 7 March 1945 the US 3rd Army reached the Rhine River. A fortnight later the Allied assault on the Rhine defences began.

By the spring of 1945, well over 1 million Axis and Allied troops faced one another in northern Italy, although the Allies had more and better-trained men and were supported by some 60,000 partisans.

It was the partisans who, on 28 April, captured and shot the Italian dictator, Mussolini, and his mistress.

A fortnight earlier, the US 5th and the British 8th armies, supported by some 1800 bombers and 1500 guns, had launched an assault on the remaining German forces in Italy. Steadily driven back, the German commanders sought permission from Berlin to retire behind the River Po. Permission was denied. On 25 April there was a general uprising of the Italian partisans, who attacked the Germans at every opportunity. Within three days all the Alpine passes had been blocked.

On 29 April, recognising the futility of continued fighting, the Germans agreed to the Allied demand for unconditional surrender.

As German resistance collapsed in the west, the Russians continued to drive towards the German frontier. In mid-April they entered Vienna. The Allies, meanwhile, had crossed the Rhine, and by 11 April were within 100 kilometres of Berlin, where they halted. The Russians, however, continued to drive towards the German capital.

By 25 April Berlin was surrounded. Four days later, Hitler married his devoted mistress, Eva Braun. On the following day, in the ruins of Berlin's Chancellery, they committed suicide together.

The war in Europe officially ended at midnight on 8 May 1945.

HUGHIE EDWARDS

In 1941, with Britain under almost continuous air attack, and with the ever-present threat of invasion, Britain's Bomber Command launched a long succession of bombing raids aimed at causing maximum damage to the German war machine.

At a time when the Allied fortunes were at a low ebb, these 'hitting-back' attacks served to provide a significant boost to the morale on the home front.

The attacks, small at first, steadily built up to the '1000-bomber' raids. They were made against heavily defended targets, causing severe aircraft losses and crew casualties.

In command of the Royal Air Force's No. 105 Squadron was Wing Commander Hughie Edwards, son of a struggling Western Australian migrant family. On 6 July 1941, Edwards led a small force of sixteen aircraft on a daring daylight raid against the heavily defended city of Bremen, the main target being the city's docks. Nine of the Blenheim bombers were from Edwards' own squadron, and six from No. 107 Squadron.

The bombers flew at almost ground level over northern Germany and in line abreast formation to provide the smallest target for the anti-aircraft defences. Each of the aircraft was hit by the intense enemy fire, four of the bombers being shot down. Undeterred, Edwards continued to lead the battered force towards their target, withdrawing only when their bombs had been released.

For his outstanding courage in planning and executing the raid, Edwards was awarded the Victoria Cross.

Some weeks before, Edwards had been awarded the Distinguished Flying Cross (DFC) for another daring bomber attack against shipping; and he was later to add the Distinguished Service Order (DSO) for his part in leading a 93-aircraft raid against the Philips radio works at Eindhoven. Edwards was the first Australian to win all three decorations.

Hughie Edwards remained with the RAF until 1960, when he returned to Western Australia and became closely involved with his state's mining industry. In 1974 he was appointed Governor of Western Australia.

THE WAR IN THE PACIFIC

The American entry into the war had been precipitated by the unexpected Japanese air attack on 7 December 1941 on the American naval base at Pearl Harbor in the Hawaiian Islands. Three hundred and sixty aircraft were launched from six Japanese aircraft carriers and, undetected, bombed and decimated the American West Coast Fleet. Of the eight American battleships in port at the time, four were sunk (although one was later refloated), one was beached and three were severely damaged.

By crippling the US Pacific Fleet, the Japanese were able to invade the Allied positions in the Philippines, Burma, Malaya (now Malaysia) and the Dutch East Indies (now Indonesia), and to threaten Australia and New Zealand.

In August 1941 the Menzies government had fallen, and the Labor Party, under John Curtin, had taken office. Curtin had viewed with grave concern the Japanese advance through Malaya and the fall of Singapore. With the full backing of his Cabinet, Curtin cabled Churchill, suggesting that Australia's three battle-hardened divisions be returned immediately to stiffen Australia's defences. Churchill responded by suggesting that the 7th Division be sent immediately to Burma, and in fact sent an order to that effect to the commander of the fleet which was returning the Australian troops.

Curtin, to his eternal credit, would have none of this, and insisted that all the Australians be returned. A clash of wills quickly developed, with Churchill seeking the American President Roosevelt's intervention in applying pressure on Curtin to change his mind. But the Australian Prime Minister stood firm, and Churchill reluctantly acquiesced to his request and ordered the ships to continue the voyage to Australia with the three divisions.

On 10 February 1942, two British capital ships—the battleship *Prince of Wales* and the battlecruiser *Repulse*—lacking air cover as they sailed northwards up the Malay coast, were easy targets for Japanese aircraft and were duly sunk. The Philippines were invaded on the same day. Singapore was occupied on 15 February. The island's great guns, mounted to point seawards, were useless against the Japanese infantry pouring in from the north after they had quickly replaced the Johore Bahru causeway which had been blown up by the British in a final act of defiance.

The mateship of the Australian servicemen was again demonstrated in full measure when Singapore fell to the Japanese. Over 3000 were killed or wounded during the futile defence of the great British naval base. More than 15,000, mostly from the 8th Division, and 2300 civilians were taken prisoner of war. Nearly half died before the war ended. Many were incarcerated in the notorious Changi Prison, where they suffered great hardship. Others were forced to work on the infamous Burma Railway, nearly half of them dying before the Allies regained Burma.

On 11 January, Japanese troops landed in Borneo and Celebes. A week later they launched their attack on Burma from Thailand. Rangoon, the Burmese capital, fell on 8 March 1942. What was left of the defending British forces were driven northwards towards India.

By taking Rangoon, which was the entry point for Anglo-American equipment delivered along the Burma Road to China, the Japanese had achieved a major objective. They could now turn their attention to the next and vital phase in their tide of conquest—the capture of the numerous island territories in the South Pacific, which extended to approximately the 180° meridian (the International Date Line). This huge sweep eastwards was made possible by Japan's powerful naval and air forces.

Four months later the Japanese had virtually attained their objective. Their ultimate intention in the South Pacific was to isolate Australia, thereby cutting the Allied sea line of communication with America, a development that would seriously disrupt the Allied campaign in the war against Japan.

By May 1942 the Japanese had overrun the Philippines, and had built an air base at Rabaul in New Britain. They planned to build a seaplane base at Tulagi (one of the Solomon Islands' territories), then to capture Port Moresby. Guadalcanal, the larger and strategically important island south of Tulagi, had been taken on 7 February 1942.

On 19 February the Japanese made two air raids on Darwin, using fifty-four land-based bombers and about 188 attack fighters launched from four of their aircraft carriers. The city's casualties numbered at least 243 killed and over 300 wounded. Twenty military aircraft were destroyed and eight ships sunk in the harbour. A number of military and civil facilities were destroyed.

The air attacks continued until November 1943, by which time Darwin had been bombed sixty-four times. Other northern Australian towns bombed by the Japanese were Broome, Derby, Port Hedland, Wyndham, Katherine and Townsville.

The Japanese also pushed southwards by sea, and in the ensuing Battle of the Java Sea the cruiser HMAS *Perth* was sunk.

As the threat of invasion increased, Australia looked to the United States for assistance. In March 1943 General Douglas MacArthur was appointed supreme commander of the Allied forces in the Pacific. He made his headquarters in Melbourne.

At the end of May 1942, Japanese midget submarines penetrated Sydney Harbour and shelled harbourside suburbs (see p. 294–5). Newcastle was similarly attacked a few days later.

Between 1942 and 1945, some twenty-nine merchant ships were sunk in Australian waters. The Battle of the Coral Sea took place from 4 to 8 May 1942, when American naval forces decisively repelled a Japanese convoy that had been sailing towards Port Moresby.

In June 1942 the Americans inflicted a crushing defeat on the Japanese in the Battle of Midway, north-west of Pearl Harbor and close to the International Date Line. It was a major turning point in the Pacific War, for although the

Japanese tide of conquest had not quite reached its full momentum, their losses in the battle—four fleet carriers, a heavy cruiser and about 330 aircraft, along with their well-trained crews—were to seriously weaken the Japanese ability to resist the growing strength of the Allies.

Nevertheless, in March 1942 the Japanese had landed troops at Lae, on the north New Guinea coast. The Japanese invading force, which initially comprised 300 combat troops was quickly built up to over 13,000 men. They were opposed by two brigades of barely-trained Australian militiamen.

The Japanese intention was to capture Port Moresby by advancing along the Kokoda Track, which crosses the Owen Stanley Range at heights of up to 2591 metres.

On 28 July, with the Japanese occupying Kokoda, the small plateau on the eastern slopes of the Range, the Australians then fought a series of desperate delaying actions, suffering heavy casualties. During September, the Australians, with Allied air support, conducted a fighting withdrawal along the Track, both sides being tormented on the rough and dark rainforest track by mud, mosquitoes and tropical heat, some suffering from malaria and dysentery.

By mid-September the Japanese were within 50 kilometres of Port Moresby. There, at Imita Ridge, the Australians made a stand, supported by 25-pounder guns that had been brought from Port Moresby. On 25 September, following fierce hand-to-hand fighting and bayonet charges by the Australians, the Japanese forces were ordered to retreat from positions constructed near Templeton's Crossing. They had been defeated by the determined resistance of the gallant Australian troops, and by the problems caused by a long and difficult supply line. Kokoda was retaken on 2 November and the airfield reopened despite fierce resistance by the Japanese. Had the battle been lost, the entire strategic situation in the south-west Pacific would have been altered.

Another serious enemy defeat was inflicted by the Americans in February 1943 when they forced the Japanese to evacuate Guadalcanal, the strategically important island south-east of the Solomon Islands. After a prolonged sea and land struggle the Americans were able to build up their strength on the island to over 50,000 men and to drive out the enemy forces. Once again, the Japanese losses were to be severe—over 25,000 men and at least 600 aircraft and their trained crews.

The net was gradually closing on the Japanese. In Burma, by early 1944, their drive northwards had been stopped at Imphal, the Indian city close to the Burmese border. By October, with the cessation of the monsoon rains, Allied forces, under the command of Admiral Lord Louis Mountbatten, began an advance southwards. By mid-January, the Burma Road (the strategic link with China) had been re-opened. The Japanese, denied reinforcements because of the American pressure in the Pacific, continued to retreat until their resistance was overcome. Imphal was recaptured in March 1945. Rangoon was reoccupied on 2 May, and four days later Mountbatten was able to announce that the liberation of Burma was complete. The remaining 60,000 Japanese troops in Burma attempted to escape into Thailand, but prompt action by the Allied forces prevented all but about 17,000 from getting away.

In November 1944 the Americans, using an airstrip in the Marianas Islands, began a bombing offensive against Japan. One hundred and eleven B-29 Superfortress bombers were used in the first attack against a Tokyo aircraft factory. High-altitude day attacks continued for the next three months but did not achieve the hoped-for results.

On 9 March 1945, a force of 279 B-29s, carrying incendiary instead of high-explosive bombs, made a low-level night attack which devastated a large area of Tokyo. There were approximately 185,000 civilian casualties, whilst over 267,000 buildings were said to have been destroyed. Over the next nine days similar damaging raids were made against the cities of Osaka, Nagoya and Kobe.

After a pause, the raids were resumed in July with much greater intensity. Thousands of sea mines were dropped to block Japanese coastal routes. More than 1.5 million tons of shipping was sunk. Japanese opposition to these continuous attacks was negligible.

More significant than the huge losses was the effect the raids had on the Japanese Emperor, the military high command and the people. They now realised what had been clear to the Allies for many months, namely, that Japan no longer had the power to defend itself against enemy attacks.

Japanese resistance was finally broken on 17 June at a cost of some 49,000 American casualties. It had been the most costly American campaign in the Pacific. Japanese losses were put at about 110,000 men, including more than 1500 kamikazi pilots whose self-sacrifice had caused the Americans considerable losses.

Wewak, on the northern New Guinea coast, was recaptured by Australian troops in May 1945. In July, the oil centre at Balikpapan, on the south-east Borneo coast, was also recaptured by troops of the Australian 1st Corps.

The war against Japan was brought to an end by the use of atomic bombs—the first being dropped on Hiroshima on 6 August, and the second three days later on Nagasaki.

SYDNEY UNDER ATTACK

In the early hours of 30 May 1942, a seaplane, its navigation lights switched on, twice circled Sydney Harbour. It was initially thought to be an American plane, but from events which soon followed it became clear that in fact it was a Japanese reconnaissance aircraft.

The following evening, several midget submarines were launched from Japanese 'mother' submarines positioned off Sydney. Probably as a distraction, these supporting submarines shelled Sydney's eastern suburbs, but with minimum damage.

An hour or so later one of the midget submarines entered Sydney Harbour, but it became entangled in an anti-submarine net. Its two-man crew blew up the craft and themselves.

Two hours later, another midget submarine was detected by an American warship, the USS *Chicago*, which was moored in the

Harbour. The *Chicago* opened fire on the midget, but could not prevent the Japanese craft from firing two torpedoes at the ship. Both missed, but one hit an old Sydney ferry, the *Kuttabul*, which was being used as a dormitory for sailors awaiting sea duty. Nineteen of the sleeping sailors were killed, and another ten were wounded.

Meanwhile, a third midget submarine was detected entering the harbour and was attacked with depth charges. It was later located on the harbour floor, its motor still running. The midget's crew were found to have shot themselves.

Several Sydney suburbs were damaged by shells from the offshore submarines, which later fired at Newcastle. The damage in both cities was minimal.

THE COAST WATCHERS

A significant contribution to the defeat of the Japanese was made by a specialist group of unpaid volunteers, mostly Australians, known as the Coast Watchers. Admiral William F. Halsey, the American Commander-in-Chief, South Pacific, said, after the final defeat of the Japanese on Guadalcanal, that the Coast Watchers had 'saved Guadalcanal, and Guadalcanal saved the South Pacific.'

The Coast Watching Organisation, administered by the Australian Navy, had first come into being in 1919. Comprising planters and others who lived and worked in the Pacific Island territories, and supported by resident missionaries and the mostly friendly native population, by 1942 the Coast Watchers numbered over 800 dedicated men who transmitted coded messages through their tele-radio sets, providing valuable information regarding Japanese air, naval and troop movements.

As the Japanese advanced southwards through the Pacific territories, the Coast Watchers, usually hunted by Japanese land forces when their island was captured, would remain hidden at their vantage point, but would move their equipment and themselves into the jungle if information from the native population indicated that they were being hunted.

From 1942 onwards there were many instances of heavy losses being inflicted on Japanese aircraft and naval vessels as a result of warnings transmitted by the Coast Watchers. Being alerted of an impending attack, the Allied forces were usually in a state of readiness when the Japanese launched their attacks.

The Coast Watchers were frequently in danger of discovery and execution by the Japanese. They were brave men who made a significant contribution to the Allied cause.

THE POST-WAR PERIOD

At war's end, nearly three-quarters of a million Australian men and women had enlisted for service in the armed forces, 557,799 of them having served overseas. The casualties amounted to some 39,366 dead and more than 66,553 wounded or injured.

Whilst the country had suffered little physical damage, Australia's dominant post-war economic and social problem was employment. More than 600,000 returned service personnel had to be found work. And there were other problems: the severe housing shortage had to be addressed; the nation's industry, expanded by war-time production, had to be readjusted; the domestic transportation systems were in need of expansion; much work needed to be done to restore the land's fertility; the rabbit plague had to be eradicated; there was need to extend the supply of electricity to rural areas; and it was necessary to increase the nation's population.

That these objectives were progressively tackled without causing economic instability was largely the result of realistic planning by successive post-war governments: first by Labor, led by the respected Ben Chifley until 1949, then by the Liberal-Country Party Coalition dominated by Bob Menzies, who was to remain in office continually for the next thirteen years. After 1949, Labor was to be in the political wilderness until 1972.

By 1954 unemployment had fallen to below 3 per cent, and was to remain at around that level for the next twenty years. Although foreign trade was initially sluggish, the Australian economy was in step with the worldwide boom, which followed the ending of the Korean War (see p. 308–9) in 1953.

THE SYDNEY TO HOBART YACHT RACE

In 1945, with the World War II just over and with units of the British Fleet temporarily based on Sydney Harbour, a tall, slightly diffident and softly spoken Royal Navy engineer, Captain John Illingworth, was enjoying some leisure time sailing his newly acquired 34-footer yacht *Rani*.

With the approach of Christmas, the Cruising Yacht Club of Australia proposed that its members should participate in a cruise. Illingworth suggested that instead they should have a race, with boats to be handicapped according to the British Royal Ocean Racing Club's formula. This was agreed to, and it was decided to make Hobart their destination.

On Boxing Day, nine yachts, including *Rani*, sailed out of Sydney Heads in a sparkling nor'-easter and turned south. After about 80 miles (129 kilometres) there was a change in the weather, the seas built up and untested gear started to fail. Several of the yachts began to resemble colanders, whilst below deck the complexions of some of the poorly trained hands changed, they declined all food, made gurgling noises and profoundly wished they were dead. The weather deteriorated further into a southerly gale directly from the Antarctic. Two of the boats retired and sought shelter.

The conditions, however, were much to Captain Illingworth's liking. After seeing him don his oilskins, the *Rani*'s crew began to realise that their intrepid skipper was in fact a tough, hardened salt determined to drive his boat for all it was worth. He sailed *Rani* away from the coast into the southerly-setting current and trimmed sails for a close-reaching run into the tempestuous seas.

When water rose above the floor boards, Illingworth informed the crew that baling was much more efficient and reliable than pumping. When the freshwater tanks began to run salty he handed around drinking rations in bottles. And when the youngsters complained about their saturated sleeping bags, Illingworth said that with an improvement in the weather they would have the chance to dry them out.

When the southerly eased, worried race officials organised aircraft to search for the small fleet. They located six of the yachts, but *Rani*, the smallest boat in the race, was by then so far south that they missed her.

After six days at sea, Illingworth and his crew made a much-publicised appearance at the entrance to Tasmania's Storm Bay. *Rani* was first across the finishing line in a time of six days, fourteen hours and twenty-two minutes, seventeen hours ahead of the next yacht. *Rani* won on corrected time by some thirty hours.

The innovative race was given widespread press coverage and caught the imagination of the general public as well as the yachting fraternity. Illingworth modestly attributed success to the efforts of the crew and to a degree of luck. But the opinion of many blue-water yachtsmen was that being in the right place at the right time had something to do with it.

The annual Sydney to Hobart Yacht Race soon became established as one of the world's great blue-water sailing events.

POST-WAR IMMIGRATION

Australia's population in 1939 was just over 7 million. The post-war Labor government, led by Ben Chifley, decided it wasn't enough. The government therefore established a new Department of Immigration, and appointed Arthur Calwell as its first minister.

In 1947 Calwell announced an ambitious scheme to increase the nation's population by 1 per cent annually through migration.

In the immediate post-war period, the country's demobilised men and women had gradually been absorbed into the labour force, but there remained a shortfall of skilled workers. Hence there was bipartisan support for the government's realistic immigration program, whereby assistance with passage costs, jobs and accommodation was available.

Initially the scheme applied only to British immigrants, but as economic conditions slowly improved in Britain and the flow of immigrants declined, the scheme was extended to settlers from other countries, including Displaced Persons (DPs) from Germany, Austria, Italy, Malta and Holland.

In the period 1947 to 1951, 310,000 assisted settlers arrived, nearly two-thirds being DPs. Another 160,000, mainly British, Dutch, Greek, Italian and Cypriot migrants, paid their own passages. Only a small proportion (about 1 per cent) of the immigrants elected not to stay.

The intake of migrants fluctuated during the 1960s. A credit squeeze at the start of the decade reduced the flow of settlers, but when the Liberal Party returned to power in 1961 the immigrant target was steadily increased to 175,000 in 1970.

By that time, almost 1 million post-war British migrants had arrived, of whom 86 per cent were government-assisted.

There was a significant intake of Italian, Greek, Dutch and German migrants during the 1960s, most of them coming at their own expense.

By the end of the 1960s, by which time nearly 10,000 non-European settlers were being admitted annually, it became apparent that the country's rigid 'White Australia' policy was slowly crumbling.

By 1970 the number of post-war immigrants who had stayed totalled approximately 2.5 million.

Natural increase added to the post-war population during the 'baby-boom' years, but whilst this meant more families, it was noteworthy that the number of children per family decreased.

Aboriginal Australians had not been counted and therefore had not been included in the census population figures. But in a referendum in 1967 the nation voted to count and identify Aboriginal Australians in all future national censuses. By the 1980s, over 150,000 people had claimed to be recognised as Aboriginal Australians.

The 1972 Labor government put a break on the immigrant intake, considering it more important to find jobs for the unemployed rather than to develop economic resources.

The incoming Fraser Liberal government was the first to add multiculturalism to its official immigration policy, in 1978. It was at this time that the refugee problem first appeared on the Australian political horizon. Impetus to the notion of Australia as a haven for asylum seekers gained momentum as 'boat people' sought entry into the country from war-torn Vietnam and, later, from Iraq, Iran, Lebanon and other Middle East countries.

SOCIAL SERVICES

Full employment, rising wages and the rapidly increasing population brought a demand for a wider range of social services. Various schemes were introduced: child endowments, medical insurance, subsidised pharmaceutical benefits and a significant increase in funds for education at all levels.

In the late 1940s the government launched one of the most successful housing schemes in Australia's development. Over 200,000 new houses had been built by 1950, thus fulfilling one of the essential needs of the returning servicemen and the newly arrived immigrants.

CHAMPIONS

Australia's climate lends itself to sport. So it is not surprising that Australia has produced its share of sporting champions. Several have already been referred to these pages. In 1876 Edward Trickett won the world sculling (rowing) championship (see pp. 156–8). In 1882 an Australian cricket team won the first 'Ashes' Test Match against England (see pp. 151–2). In 1907 Norman Brookes became the first world tennis champion (see pp. 238–40). And in 1983, at Australia's sixth attempt, Alan Bond's *Australia II* won the America's Cup yacht race—the first time the coveted trophy had been wrested from the Americans since they had won the trophy from the British in 1851 (see pp. 331–2).

Thoroughbred horse racing had become part of the Australian culture by the middle of the nineteenth century. The Melbourne Cup, now held annually on the first Tuesday in November (a public holiday for Victorians), has produced some great thoroughbred champions, including Phar Lap, Tulloch, Bernborough, Carbine, Kingston Town and Makybe Diva.

Australia, at present, has nearly four hundred race courses, and the sport attracts more spectators than any other in Australia except Australian rules (AFL) and rugby league (NRL).

Basketball has become a popular sport through two competitions: the National Basketball League (NBL) men's competition (the 'Boomers'); and the Women's National Basketball League (the 'Opals'). Some of the more talented players leave to play professionally in the United States.

National Rugby League (NRL) is strongly established in New South Wales and Queensland, and is gaining support in Victoria. But attendance numbers are fewer than for the Australian rules (AFL) code, which is based in Victoria and also has professional teams in many other states.

Golf was first played in Australia in 1839 at the Bothwell course in Tasmania. Victoria's Royal Melbourne Golf Club course is the oldest to be in continuous use (since 1891). Four Australian professional golfers have been inducted into the World Golf Hall of Fame. They are Peter Thompson, Greg Norman, Karrie Webb and Kel Nagle.

It is generally accepted that cricket is Australia's most popular sport. Club cricket first developed during the second half of the nineteenth century, and became established at the inter-state level in 1856. In 1878 the first Test Match was staged in England.

DON BRADMAN

From 1927 until 1949, one playing figure—Sir Donald Bradman, sometimes known as The Don—dominated Australian cricket. He was born at Cootamundra, New South Wales, and brought up at Bowral, the Southern Highlands town in New South Wales (where he is reputed to have practised with a cricket stump and a golf ball).

Bradman made his cricket debut at the age of 18, playing for St George, the Sydney grade cricket club, where in his first innings he made 110 before being run out.

The statistics of Bradman's first-class career are amazing. He played his last match in 1948 at London's Oval ground, needing just four runs to bring his career average to an all-time high of exactly 100. Perhaps it was the emotion of the occasion, for he was bowled second ball by Eric Hollies to close his illustrious career.

During his Test career, Bradman made 29 centuries, including 10 double hundreds, and two triple hundreds. He suffered from fibrositis during his long career. Overall, Bradman scored 28,067 runs at an average of 95.14. He played 338 innings, including 117 centuries, 30 double centuries, five triple centuries and one quadruple century.

Bradman met his wife-to-be, Jessie Menzies, in 1920. They were married in 1932 and shared a 65-year marriage. Bradman frequently paid tribute to Jessie's support throughout his playing career. But their married life was beset with tragedy. Their first-born son died in infancy in 1936. Their second son, John, contracted polio, and their daughter, Shirley, was born in 1941 suffering cerebral palsy. Burdened by the family name, John changed his surname by deed poll to Bradsen in 1972. Jessie died from cancer in 1997. The loss of his wife deeply affected Bradman, but improved the relationship with his son to the extent that John changed his name back to Bradman.

Sir Donald Bradman was by nature a very private man. He died of pneumonia on 25 February 2001, aged 92.

We will never see his like again.

HARNESSING WATER RESOURCES

The problem could be simply stated, but solving it would require immense courage, an enormous financial investment and dedicated work by many hundreds of skilled people, some from overseas, in a remote area where the difficult terrain and frequently forbidding weather combined to discourage all but the most determined and courageous.

It was the Snowy Mountains Hydro-Electric Scheme.

Stretching northwards from southern Victoria to the north of Queensland lies the Great Dividing Range, the mountain range separating the coastal fringe from the dry inland plains. Precipitation occurs as the winds cross the mountains, resulting in hundreds of small rivers and streams which carry water to the coastal strip and into the Tasman Sea. The Snowy River waters flow into the sea near Orbost in eastern Victoria. The rivers which flow westwards from the mountain range meander on their long passage through the dry plains until they reach the Southern Ocean.

Near the New South Wales–Victorian border, and forming part of the Great Dividing Range, are the Snowy Mountains which rise to a height of 2228 metres (Mount Kosciusko). The area is snow-covered during the winter months and usually receives significant summer rains.

Three main rivers rise in the Snowy Mountains: the Snowy River, which flows eastwards, and the Murray and Murrumbidgee rivers, which flow westwards. It is these westerly-flowing rivers which provide irrigation to the extensive farming lands in the dry plains.

Since the 1880s there had been various proposals for diverting the waters of the Snowy and other rivers westwards to supplement water flows to the inland areas. Such proposals were not adopted because of the technical problems and the high expenditure involved on schemes where the benefits were limited to improved irrigation and better water resource control.

Then another factor entered the equation—electricity. Greater industrial and domestic usage of power gave fresh impetus to proposals to harness the waters of the Snowy River for hydro-electric and as well as irrigation development.

The key decision was whether to divert the Snowy River waters from Jindabyne northwards to the Murrumbidgee River (the proposition favoured by New South Wales) or to take the Jindabyne waters westwards through the mountain bedrock to the Murray River catchment (the Victorian scheme). Both proposals would provide hydro-electric power to supplement the existing thermal power developed in each state.

Such, then, was the problem.

In 1947 a joint Commonwealth-States Technical Committee was set up to thoroughly evaluate the proposals. The committee's principal recommendation, which was promptly adopted, was to divert water on the Tumut River to activate the Jindabyne–Murray scheme.

In 1949 the Snowy Mountains Hydro-Electric Power Act was passed by the Commonwealth Parliament, and the Snowy Mountains Hydro-Electric Authority came into being. It was a bold and decisive step.

Briefly, the scheme involved diverting the waters of the Snowy River and its tributary, the Eucumbene, through two tunnel systems bored westwards through the mountain bedrock to feed the Murray and Murrumbidgee rivers, thereby allowing for irrigation expansion in the valleys. The scheme would involve the construction of some 80 kilometres of aqueducts, 140 kilometres of tunnels, sixteen large dams, a pumping station, seven power stations and hundreds of kilometres of transmission lines to interconnect with existing electricity supply systems in New South Wales and Victoria. It was a mammoth undertaking. The estimated cost was $180 million.

The Snowy Mountains Hydro-Electric Authority, headed by Sir William Hudson, set up headquarters in Cooma, New South Wales, and lost no time in getting to work. All the major construction works were contracted out. The acceptance of tenders from overseas groups meant that skilled teams were brought to Australia with experience in every important facet of the work.

Construction commenced in 1949. Thirty nationalities were represented in the workforce which totalled 100,000, including many refugee migrants and skilled tradesmen from Germany and other European countries. Some stayed on after the job was done and were later welcomed as Australian citizens. In all, overseas nationals made up about a half of the construction workforce. The Authority's own staff supervised the establishment of large camps, many kilometres of roads and maintenance facilities for the large construction crews.

The essential part of the scheme was the construction of two main tunnel systems: the Snowy–Tumut Development, which diverted the waters northwards; and the Snowy–Murray Development, which diverted the waters southwards.

The Snowy–Tumut Development was to take the headwaters of the Murrumbidgee River by tunnel to the man-made Lake Eucumbene, created on the Eucumbene River by the Eucumbene Dam. From Lake Eucumbene the combined Murrumbidgee and Eucumbene waters would be diverted inland through a trans-mountain tunnel to the Tumut Pond Reservoir. Here they would join waters diverted by tunnel from the Tooma River and waters from the Tumut River, which rises to the west of the Great Dividing Range. From Tumut Pond Dam the combined waters of the four rivers would pass in succession through four power stations in the Tumut Gorge, eventually to be released to flow down the Tumut River to the Murrumbidgee, thereby augmenting the flow of irrigation water from that river.

The Snowy–Murray Development was to capture the Snowy River waters at Island Bend, where they would be diverted either by tunnel for storage at Lake

Eucumbene, or directly westwards through the second trans-mountain tunnel to the Geehi Reservoir on the western face of the mountains. From there, together with the Geehi River waters, they would pass through two power stations before being released into the headwaters of the Murray River, whence they would flow downstream for use in the Murray Valley irrigation areas.

Downstream from the main diversion at Island Bend, additional water was to be taken from the Snowy River by a pumping station at Jindabyne. This water would be lifted through a tunnel to join the main east–west diversion of the Snowy–Murray Development.

The day-and-night work of the construction crews merited the highest praise. The American contractors who constructed the Eucumbene Dam had the work completed in half the estimated time. The Australian teams, which bored the gigantic tunnels through the Great Dividing Range to bring the Lake Eucumbene waters to the Tumut River, broke world records for drilling through hard rock. All concerned with the construction work laboured under climatic conditions that were sometimes extreme: the heat of summer, periodic winter blizzards; snowstorms, icy winds and sub-zero temperatures. Steel tools cannot be handled in freezing conditions, so there was no alternative but to wait for hot steam to be sprayed on them. Tragically, 121 lives were lost during the construction work.

In her book *The Thirsty Land*, Eve Powell has given graphic descriptions of some of the conditions which the Snowy men encountered:

'There were no roads and few tracks where the men had to go to begin their investigations. In places bulldozers blazed a trail through the rugged bush for the men to follow. But in other areas they made their own trails as they went. Men rode into the hills on horses hired from mountain farms, leading packhorses loaded with gear. They splashed across rivers and mountain streams. They felled trees and cleared away scrub to make a bridle path for the horses. In flat areas they set up camp and lived in tents. They knocked together pieces of rough timber to make tables and chairs.

The men were their own cooks. Food and supplies came in by packhorse, or by four-wheel vehicles which could negotiate the steep grades of the hills, the snow and mud. When rivers ran fiercely with water from the melting snow, bulldozers sometimes battled their way through the racing torrents with supplies for the camps. In early winters of the Scheme dog teams dragged sleds to some snowbound stations and camps.

They had to find their way through deep gorges, and scramble over slippery rocks and boulders. Dangerous river eddies sucked at their feet as they crossed the streams. They stumbled along uneven ground beside rivers, or picked their way among thorny scrub. On sharp rises they learnt to avoid razor-leafed plants that cut their hands, and others that gave way under a climber's foot.

As they covered the ridges, sun blazed on their heads and backs. A quarter hour later the temperature might have dropped so sharply that the men could be shivering and reaching for extra pullovers.

Linesmen for the wires that carry electricity to regional towns and to the main networks have worked in some of the most rugged country in Australia. In places it has taken weeks to clear a way for the line to be surveyed.

The men trudged over the ranges, strung wires across raging rivers, and brought poles into position on ridges and gullies. In bad weather and in very rough country, bulldozers have hauled the poles in, lashed together in a great bundle.

Driving on ice-covered roads is bad enough today, but some of the first access roads to the work sites had hairpin bends so tight that a vehicle only got round the worst of them by running forward, then back, then forward again. Drivers were accustomed in certain stretches to leave the vehicle door open and be ready *to jump if the machine got out of control. Repairs and maintenance have to be carried out on dams and tunnels in all weathers.'*

The Snowy Mountains Hydro-Electric Scheme took twenty-five years to complete. The final cost was $820 million. In 1997 two major overhauls were completed. Long-term updating and asset management plans are in operation.

The project ranks as one of the world's major engineering achievements. It has brought inestimable benefits to the Australian people and the country's economy. It was 'a vision splendid', and it was splendidly executed.

THE KOREAN WAR

On 25 June 1950, the North Koreans unleashed an attack on the South Korean army. Four ill-equipped American divisions were rushed into the ensuing battle, but they and the South Koreans were soon overwhelmed and driven southwards across the 38th parallel.

The United Nations Security Council summoned member countries to come to the aid of the South Koreans, the call being answered mainly by the United States. In Australia, the Menzies government also undertook to provide military support.

In mid-September, American forces under General Douglas MacArthur launched a daring raid behind the North Korean invaders. Attacked from north and south, the North Koreans were heavily defeated, with more than 125,000 prisoners being taken.

Advancing northwards, the Allied forces, which now included units from Australia and several other countries, were met by large numbers of Chinese 'volunteers'. Heavy fighting resulted in the Allied troops being driven back to the 38th parallel, where the front lines were finally stabilised.

After a veiled threat by the Americans that they were prepared to use nuclear weapons, an armistice was finally concluded on 27 July 1953.

The cost of the war, in terms of human lives, had been the loss of an estimated 1,300,000 South Koreans (many of whom were civilians), 1 million Chinese, 500,000 North Koreans and approximately 54,000 Americans. Australian casualties included over 1500 soldiers and forty-two airmen either killed, wounded or missing. There were also losses amongst the British and Turkish forces, which were included in the United Nations contingents.

NATIONAL SECURITY

The Korean conflict served to heighten the importance that the Australian post-war defence planners placed on United States assistance in the event of a threat to the country's security.

Australia's position was formalised in 1951 with the signing of the ANZUS Treaty, a somewhat vaguely defined agreement between Australia, New Zealand and the United States.

In 1954 the South-East Asia Treaty Organisation was formed, the initial signatories being the USA, France, Britain, Australia, New Zealand, the Philippines, Thailand and Pakistan.

TELEVISION

Australia's first television service (TCN Sydney) was introduced in 1956, which was the year of the Olympic Games in Melbourne (see p. 341). By the turn of the century there were some forty-five television stations, including the Australian Broadcasting Corporation (ABC), transmitting throughout the country.

THE MINERALS BOOM

The gold rushes in the 1850s and later years had had a positive effect on Australia's economy. Similarly, the minerals boom, which began in the 1960s, had a significant and lasting effect on the nation's exports. Valuable deposits of copper, zinc, lead, nickel, alumina, gold, manganese and iron ore were discovered. In 1966 the first shipments of iron ore from Mount Newman and the Hamersley Range were made through the newly constructed port at Dampier. Major oil and gas fields were found, principally in Bass Strait, on the North-West Shelf (off the Western Australian coast) and in South Australia. New and important coal seams were also discovered, mainly in New South Wales and Queensland. Bauxite was rediscovered in northern Queensland in 1955, and along Western Australia's Darling Ranges in the early 1960s.

The minerals discoveries were also important for Australia's strategic needs. By the 1990s nearly 100,000 people were employed in the mining industry. By then, exports of crude oil, coal, non-ferrous metals, metal ores and scrap amounted to nearly one-third of the total value of Australia's exports (wool and cereals accounted for approximately one-sixth).

By the early twenty-first century, the value of the Australian dollar began to be linked more closely with minerals than wool, as had been the case previously.

LAND TRANSPORT

It took a century to rectify the blunder of Australia's multiplicity of railway gauges (see pp. 112–4), but by 1970 all states had standardised on the 143 centimetres track width for the major trunk routes, and it was then possible to cross the continent from east to west without a change of gauge. The Indian Pacific train provided a popular passenger rail service linking Sydney (and later Brisbane) directly with Perth. That part of the Trans-Australia Railway that crosses the Nullarbor Plain has the world's longest straight section of track—475 kilometres in length.

The post-war era saw a significant increase in the country's road systems. The greater proportion of freight movements was by road transport, articulated vehicles being extensively used for long-distance haulage.

In outback areas, 'road trains' became a common sight as sealed road systems were constructed, providing pastoralists with the welcome benefit of fast long-distance transportation for sheep, cattle and produce.

LEN BEADELL

Like Alfred Canning (see pp. 222–4) before him, Len Beadell was a survivor. And, like Canning, he had a particular interest in roads.

Beadell surveyed the site for the Woomera Rocket Range in 1947, and in 1953 for the Maralinga Atomic Test site, both in the northern regions of South Australia.

Beadell's next assignment was to gather a team of six men and begin construction of the Gunbarrel Highway in Western Australia— 1450 kilometres of road from Wiluna (949 kilometres north-east of Perth) eastwards through the Simpson Desert to the Docker River (near the South Australian border). The team became known as the Gunbarrel Road Construction Party. Over eight years they constructed some 6500 kilometres of roads, which included the Great Central Road from Laverton to Warburton, in the barren emptiness of Western Australia. In doing so, they opened up 2.5 million square kilometres of country virtually unexplored by white settlers and inhabited only by isolated Aboriginal communities.

(It is no longer possible to drive the full length of the Gunbarrel Highway, for several of its sections have been abandoned, whilst other sections pass through restricted areas.)

Beadell's roads were constructed in lonely and inhospitable country—seemingly unending sand ridges interspersed with spinifex, mulga scrub and mountain ranges. The road team's many problems included flat tyres and broken gearboxes, scorching daytime heat and bitingly cold nights, periodic and violent sandstorms and devastating floods. For long periods there was no other human company apart from occasional meetings with Aboriginal groups.

Len Beadell wrote of his remarkable outback experiences in seven books. He died in 1996 aged seventy-three, and ranks alongside Australia's true pioneers.

MANUFACTURING

By the late 1950s Australian industry had geared up to meet the demands of an expanding population. Significant quantities were produced of motor vehicles and car bodies, radio and televisions sets, electric and gas cooking stoves and ovens, refrigerators, petrol-driven lawn mowers, vacuum cleaners, and other essential items including furniture and clothing. The spur to expanded production was in part due to the high tariffs with which the government protected the manufacturing industry.

By the late 1950s General Motors–Holden's (see pp. 205–7) production accounted for approximately half of car sales on the domestic market. In the 1960s, four competitors established production plants in Australia, providing employment for over 80,000 workers, many of them migrants.

THE HILLS HOIST™ AND THE VICTA™ MOWER

Necessity, it is said, is the mother of invention.

Mrs Hill had a problem. The Hill family's washing had to be dried, but in her Adelaide garden the overhanging trees had gradually reduced the space available for a line, limiting the amount of drying sunshine and breeze.

So, Mrs Hill adopted the time-honoured course and complained to her husband about the problem. And Lance Hill, for the sake of a quiet life, set about doing something about it.

He gathered some old pieces of gas piping, some steel tubing, some rods and scraps of metal, and then bent, hammered, welded and screwed the bits into what he thought might be the answer to the problem. It didn't look like a conventional clothes line, but it was very compact and it went round and round whenever there was any breeze. It worked well. It was, in fact, a rotary clothes hoist.

Mrs Hill was delighted. And, as is usually the case when there is something to talk about (or even if there isn't), she had a yarn with her friends and neighbours. Very soon there were requests being made for the new-fangled clothes line.

Lance Hill was by trade a motor mechanic, and it didn't take him very long to decide to manufacture the hoist. His father advanced most of the necessary capital and, early in 1946, the two went into partnership. Metal and other materials in the immediate post-war years were in short supply, but Lance was able to obtain a supply of galvanised piping and other materials, so production commenced. Demand for the Hills rotary clothes hoist grew steadily, and remains popular to this day.

In 1948 the business moved to a blacksmith's shop at the Adelaide suburb of Glen Osmond, then in 1955 became a public company. By 1970 a number of modifications and design changes had been made to the original model, and new products had been added to the firm's range. Hills Industries Ltd had now become a multinational company, exporting to many countries.

Lance Hill retired in the mid-1950s and died in 1986.

Mervyn Richardson's invention is best described as a flash of inspiration rather than the answer to a specific problem.

Richardson had a son, Garry, who was a university student. To supplement his income, young Garry ran a small lawnmowing business using the family's reel-type mower. When he sold the business to return to his studies, his father set about designing a 35-centimetre self-propelled mower using a two-stroke engine.

Rotary mowers powered by electricity had been around for some years but were not powerful enough for Australian conditions. Why not, thought Richardson senior, fit the petrol engine to a rotating blade mower?

So, in 1952, he pottered around with scraps of angle iron, some billy-cart wheels of different sizes, an empty jam tin and other bits and pieces. The resultant little machine looked odd and frail, but when he pulled the handle, it worked! The Victa (adapted from Richardson's second name, Victor) rotary mower was born.

Richardson now arranged for subcontractors to make selected components, then assembled in the family garage an initial batch of thirty of the new mowers. They sold quickly.

Richardson, putting his faith in the invention, now decided on a bold move—he ordered from Britain 100 two-stroke engines. He also resolved to leave his salesman's job and to devote himself full-time to production.

Thus, in 1953, the Victa mower became a business. One hundred of the machines were sold in the first year's operations, and demand remained strong. Four years later, some 60,000 machines were being made and sold annually. The mowing habits of the nation were changed, and Victa became a household name.

Over 6 million Victa mowers have now been manufactured and sold to thirty-five countries. The original model, of course, has been modified and improved many times, but the basic concept remains the same.

In the realm of manufacturing, the Hills rotary clothes hoist and the Victa rotary mower are two of Australia's most successful products. Each had its origin in the family garage.

GORDON EDGELL

From the 1930s and for another sixty years, Edgell's canned vegetables, fruits and soups were a household name.

In the 1880s, Gordon Edgell, after serving an apprenticeship as a draughtsman, designed a number of bridges and then became a roads superintendent. He married in 1896. Ten years later, at the age of forty, he retired from the public service and bought a property near Bathurst, west of Sydney. It was to be a turning point in his career.

Edgell initially planted 100 acres (40 hectares) with apples, pears and asparagus. He also made a study of the latest farming techniques and innovations, including soil analysis, irrigation and mechanical cultivation.

In 1925 Edgell sent his eldest son, Maxwell, to the United States to investigate canning techniques. Later that year, in partnership with Maxwell and another son, Hampden, he set up a cannery in one of the property's sheds. Employing a small staff, they made their own cans, sealing them with hand-held soldering irons. Their output in the following year was some 8000 cans, and they all sold well.

In 1930, Gordon Edgell & Sons Ltd was registered as a public company. Edgell was to remain as chairman of directors until his death in 1948.

During the 1930s the company expanded both its range of production and its factory and administrative block. Canned green peas were added to the range and proved very popular. During World War II the company supplied not only the domestic market but also the Australian and American armed forces. Carrots, sliced apples, Brussels sprouts, potatoes, tomatoes and silverbeet were added to the range. Several varieties of soups were also introduced. In 1943 land was purchased at Cowra, west of Bathurst, and another cannery was started there.

In 1961 Gordon Edgell & Sons Ltd merged with Petersville Sleigh Ltd. There were subsequent further mergers and takeovers. Edgell's trademark, an 'E' enclosed in a triangle (and familiar to two generations of housewives), was gradually displaced as other brands came on the market. The company was re-formed in 1998 by a group of local investors and is again producing many of the traditional Edgell products for sale.

Gordon Edgell launched an old-style family partnership which placed a range of canned foods on grocery shelves for half a century. The partnership worked well.

THE TIED TEST

Close finishes add spice to all sporting contests, and have frequently occurred in cricket ever since the modern game was first played in the 1770s.

But never in the history of Test Match cricket had there been a finish so breathtakingly dramatic as happened in the first Test Match between Australia and the powerful West Indies side at Brisbane in December 1960.

In their first innings, the West Indies amassed 453 runs, thanks largely to a superb innings of 132 by Garfield Sobers (who was later knighted for services to cricket). Australia replied with 505 runs, the largest contribution being a majestic 181 by Norman O'Neill.

In their second 'dig', the West Indies scored 284 runs, Alan Davidson being mainly responsible for their modest total, with 6 wickets for 87 runs.

On the fifth and final day, with only five hours and twelve minutes left for the Australians to score 233 runs for victory, a draw seemed the most likely result.

The match had been followed thus far with intense national interest. But as the run chase gathered momentum, excitement at the ground reached fever pitch, whilst throughout the country (and overseas) countless supporters gathered around radio sets as the final drama unfolded.

With playing time ending at six o'clock, and the Gabba (an abbreviation of Wooloongabba, the suburb where the Brisbane Cricket Ground is located) clock approached 5.30, Australia needed just 31 runs to bring off an improbable victory.

Richie Benaud, the Australian skipper, and Alan Davidson, who had bowled and batted so well, were together at the wicket. A mix-up between the two resulted in Davidson almost being run out. With 19 minutes remaining, Australia still needed 16 runs to win.

Attempting a quick single, Davidson was finally run out for a gallant 80—his highest Test cricket score. His match contribution had been 11 wickets and 124 runs.

Wally Grout, the Australian wicket-keeper, now walked in to face the seventh ball of the penultimate over (at that time, eight-ball overs were played in Test cricket), with 7 runs now needed and just six minutes remaining.

Tactically, the plan should have been to leave Benaud to face the last over from the fast and hostile Wesley Hall. But Grout had other ideas, taking a single off the first ball he faced and giving Benaud the strike. Six runs required!

As Sobers bowled the last ball of his over, Benaud was determined that, come what may, he was going to get down to the other end to play the final over from Hall. But Sobers bowled him a straight delivery of perfect length, and with six West Indians crouched around him, Benaud was unable to score the single. Grout now had to face Hall's last over, which few thought he could survive.

Spectators who had crammed into the ground, and the millions glued to their radio receivers, were by now in a state of frenzy.

Hall's first ball was of terrifying pace and hit Grout on the thigh. Grout would normally have collapsed in pain, but he saw Benaud charging towards him, intent on making an improbable run. So Grout set off for the other end like a scalded cat, and made his ground before the close-in West Indian fieldsmen realised what was happening.

So Benaud now faced Hall with seven balls to go and needing five runs to win.

Although Hall was under orders from his captain not to bowl any more bouncers, his next delivery was nevertheless a short, rearing head-high ball, which Benaud swung at but succeeded only in snicking to Alexander, the wicket keeper. The umpire raised his finger in response to the vociferous appeal from the entire West Indies team.

Benaud was out, having batted for over two hours for a gallant 52 runs. He was replaced by fast bowler Ian Meckiff. The odds were that he and Grout would be unlikely to survive Hall's last six thunderbolts.

Meckiff successfully blocked Hall's next ball. It was followed by a ball of fearsome pace down the leg side. As the ball flew past Meckiff, the alert Grout yelled to Meckiff to run, which he did like a startled rabbit. Grout himself charged down the pitch as Alexander hurled the ball to Hall, now more than halfway down the pitch. Hall turned and threw at the wicket to which Meckiff was running, but missed. As the crowd erupted, both Grout and Meckiff made their ground. Four runs were now needed, and four balls remained.

Grout, attempting to win the match with a boundary, swatted Hall's fifth ball high towards the mid-wicket area, where at least four fieldsmen converged to take the catch. Rohan Kanhai was the best placed of them, but as he positioned himself beneath the ball an excited Hall charged in, leaping with his hands above Kanhai's head. He dropped the catch, and Australia survived another heart-stopping moment. The crowd rocked in disbelief, whilst the West Indians could hardly believe their eyes. Hall slowly walked back to his mark in disgrace. The scorers added another run—just three more needed!

Meckiff, trusting his luck, took a lusty swing at Hall's next ball, and seemed to have struck a match-winning four to the square leg boundary. The crowd roared! But the outfield grass in the deep square leg area had not been mowed, and the ball slowed noticeably on its way to the boundary. Conrad Hunte, the nearest West Indian fieldsman, was able to intercept the ball as the Australians completed their second run and turned for the winning third.

From a distance of some 80 metres, Hunte's throw went unerringly into wicket-keeper Alexander's waiting gloves. Had the throw arrived a metre or so on either side of the wicket, Grout would have been able to make his ground. But Alexander hardly had to move to break the wicket. The diving Grout was run out, leaving Australia with one run to win and two balls remaining. Would the high drama of the last over ever end?

Lindsay Kline now came in to face Hall's seventh ball, which he succeeded in turning towards square leg. Both batsmen charged towards opposite ends as though their lives depended upon it. From 11 metres away, Joe Solomon gathered the ball and, from sideways on, hurled it at the wicket. It was a direct hit! The players leaped in unrestrained joy, whilst the crowd roared and rose as one. The match was finally over, and was the first ever tied Test. Had Solomon's throw missed, Australia would have won.

Never before had there been a Test Match like it. Never before had the life of a nation virtually stopped for several hours for a sporting contest.

The Australians went on to win the second and fifth Tests, whilst the West Indians won the third. The fourth was drawn. Thus Australia won the series 2–1.

When the cricket was over, the good and sports-loving people of Melbourne farewelled the departing West Indians with a motorcade reception through the city centre. There were countless tributes to the achievements and sporting spirit of both visitors and hosts.

Whilst the home team won the series, the West Indians won the hearts of the Australian cricket public.

ABORIGINAL AFFAIRS

In the post-war period there was growing consciousness of the situation of Aboriginal people within the Australian community.

Numbers of Aboriginal people had served alongside white Australians during World War II, and had generally been accepted as 'good mates'. But with demobilisation, little was done to assist the serving Aboriginal people to be assimilated into the community alongside their former comrades.

During the 1950s, there were several government initiatives aimed at addressing the special circumstances of the Aboriginal people. The Federal Council for the Advancement of Aborigines and Torres Strait Islanders was formed in 1957, and was to do much useful work during the 1960s.

In 1967, following a successful referendum, Aboriginal Australians were given the right to vote. Subsequently, the government created a Portfolio for Aboriginal Affairs, and established two additional organisations: the Australian Institute of Aboriginal Studies, in 1968, and the Aboriginal Arts Board, in 1973.

An indication of public concern over Aboriginal affairs came in 1972, when four young Aboriginal activists set up a tent on the lawns in front of Parliament House, Canberra, dubbing it the 'Aboriginal Embassy'. The gesture served to highlight the Aboriginal people's continuing struggle for recognition of their traditional culture and what they considered to be their land rights. The struggle was to continue for decades to come.

From the 1960s onwards, there was increasing agitation on the part of the Aboriginal people over the 'Stolen Generation' (see pp. 346–8).

DECIMAL CURRENCY

In the early years of Federation, when the opportunity arose to introduce decimal currency, it was decided to continue with the British system of pounds, shillings and pence.

By the early 1960s, however, when the disadvantages of the outdated currency units had become increasingly apparent, the government decided to bite the bullet and switch to decimal currency. A Decimal Currency Board was established and, on 14 December 1966, dollars and cents officially became the nation's currency units.

DROUGHT

The currency decision was taken at a time of prolonged drought. Although not as severe as the country's previous major droughts, the absence of rain in many areas from 1964 until 1966 caused serious losses and unemployment, especially in New South Wales and Queensland. Millions of sheep and cattle died or were lost as many rural areas once again struggled against the hardships caused by nature's periodic and unpredictable climatic extremes.

Fortunately, the nation at that time was prospering, and the economic damage caused by the drought was minimised. Britain had remained Australia's major trading partner and source of investment funds. Australia also benefitted during the 1950s and 1960s from a stable international monetary system and expanding overseas trade. Rural products during this period accounted for more than two-thirds of the nation's export earnings, with wool continuing to contribute more than any other commodity to Australia's coffers.

THE VIETNAM WAR

The Vietnam War, which lasted from 1955 to 1975, was an unsuccessful attempt by the South Vietnam government, backed by the United States and its allies (including Australia), to resist the spread southwards of communism and to prevent the unification of South and North Vietnam—formerly French territory.

A conference in Geneva in 1954 decided that forces under French command should move south of the 17th parallel, whilst the communist North Vietnamese, the Viet Minh, would have control to the north of the 17th parallel.

A period of guerilla warfare ensued, with troops armed and trained in the north, the Viet Cong being used to infiltrate South Vietnamese areas. To help counter the increase in insurgent activity, the United States sent 'military advisers' to South Vietnam. By 1960 their number had increased to over 11,000.

In 1964, following an attack on an American destroyer by North Vietnamese patrol boats, American involvement in the conflict increased significantly. The United States' credibility was now involved as well as the maintenance of South Vietnamese independence. By 1967 there were more than 389,000 American troops in South Vietnam.

In response to pressure from the United States, Australia sent an initial contingent of 'military advisers' to South Vietnam, followed, in 1965, by a full infantry battalion. Selective conscription introduced in 1966 by the Holt government resulted in an additional 8000 Australian personnel being sent to South Vietnam in 1968.

At the beginning of that year, the Viet Cong launched a major offensive, which resulted in heavy South Vietnamese losses. This led to growing doubt in the United States that the Allied war effort would ever be successful.

By 1968 the United States had ceased bombing activity, and in the following year some 25,000 American troops, as well as some Australian units, were withdrawn. With more than half a million military personnel still in South Vietnam, the United States commenced a 'Vietnamisation' program, whereby the South Vietnamese, with full United States arms support, would gradually assume all responsibility for their military defence.

American concern over the outcome of the war was mirrored in Australia by widespread protests over the country's involvement. On 8 May 1970, at the height of the 'moratorium campaign', over 150,000 protestors marched in the streets of Australia's major cities.

At this time the war spread to areas in neighbouring Cambodia and Laos, which the North Vietnamese forces had infiltrated to use as bases from which to attack South Vietnamese and Allied areas. By the end of 1970 the number of American military personnel in South Vietnam had been reduced to 335,000, whilst only 179 Australian troops still remained. A year later, only about 160,000 American troops were still in South Vietnam. By that time, ineffective peace talks, which had been initiated by the two sides, continued to drag on.

Despite a peace agreement being eventually reached in Paris in January 1973, fighting continued as both sides accused the other of violations of a ceasefire agreement. South Vietnam's will to continue the struggle was seriously undermined in August 1974 when, in response to mounting pressure at home to terminate American involvement in the war, the United States drastically cut military aid. By that time there were few Allied military personnel in South Vietnam.

On 30 April 1975, what remained of the South Vietnamese government surrendered unconditionally. The country, under a military government, was then united with its capital in Hanoi.

American casualties during the war amounted to over 361,000. South Vietnam's casualties were estimated at nearly three times that number. The North Vietnamese and Viet Cong lost an estimated 900,000, and well over 1 million were wounded. Civilian losses in both North and South Vietnam were put at over 1 million. Australia's casualties numbered 519 dead, six missing in action and more than 4300 wounded.

Notwithstanding the fact that the war had slowed the march of communism, doubts were to linger in America, Australia and elsewhere as to the wisdom of the United States' decision to become involved in a struggle on Asian soil. In Australia, the conflict in Vietnam came to be regarded as an 'unpopular' war, and there remained lingering resentment over the official attitudes that developed towards Vietnam veterans. It was not until 1987 that Vietnam veterans were officially welcomed home to Australia with parades in the major cities.

THE SYDNEY OPERA HOUSE

At the time it was perhaps the finest piece of real estate in Australia. On a promontory named Bennelong Point (see p. 33) and surrounded by the dazzling beauty of Sydney's harbour, the setting on a sunny day or a clear starry night is magical. Opposite is Kirribilli Point, the site of the Prime Minister's official Sydney residence, with the tiny island of Fort Denison ('Pinchgut') in the foreground. On one side is the half-circle of Farm Cove and the

Royal Botanic Gardens. On the other is Sydney Cove, named after Thomas Townshend, first Viscount Sydney, then Home Secretary in the British Cabinet. Here the waters of the Tank Stream used to flow into what is now the western side of Circular Quay. On Sydney Cove's western side is the historical Rocks area, dominated from above by the southern end of the Sydney Harbour Bridge.

In 1955 the New South Wales government, having decided that an Opera House should be built on this magnificent 2.23-hectare site, launched a worldwide competition for the design of a suitable building. The competition attracted 233 entries and was won by a renowned Danish architect, Joern Utzon.

The building was originally estimated to cost $7 million. In 1973, when the Sydney Opera House was formally opened by Queen Elizabeth II, the cost had escalated to $102 million. The citizens of New South Wales, ever willing to have a modest gamble, contributed much of the money through the Opera House Lottery, which ran from 1958 to 1986.

The building's foundations were completed by 1963, the exteriors by 1967 and the interiors by 1973. Utzon resigned in 1966 over a dispute, mainly involving the payment of fees, and has never seen the finished building.

The shell roofs were designed by Utzon to be functional as well as beautiful, for they hid the projections for stage machinery. The famous shells were made from 2194 concrete sections held together by 350 kilometres of tensioned cables. The 1,056,000 cream and white shells on the roof were made in Sweden. The highest shell roof is 67 metres above sea level. The roofs weigh 27,230 tonnes.

The mouths of the shells are filled with two layers of glass, made in France, one layer being clear and the other demi-topaz tinted. In all there are over 2000 panes of glass. Extensive use was made of computer technology in the construction of the building, especially for the complex roof structure.

Distinctive pink aggregate granite, quarried at Tarana in New South Wales, was used for the facing of the exterior and interior walls, stairs and floors. White birch plywood was used for the noiseless seats in the 2690-seat Concert Hall and the 1547-seat Opera Theatre, the upholstery being magenta-coloured wool in the former and red leather in the latter.

Australian woods—white birch plywood and brush box—were used for the ceiling and wall panelling throughout the building. A feature of the Concert Hall is the twenty-one adjustable rings or 'acoustic clouds' made of acrylic and suspended above the concert platform, designed to reflect sound back to the musicians (although there is some disagreement as to their effectiveness). The Concert Hall also houses a grand organ designed and built by an Australian, Ronald Sharp. It has 10,500 pipes and is the world's largest mechanical-action organ.

In addition to the Concert Hall and Opera Theatre, the building has a 554-seat Drama Theatre, a Playhouse seating 398, a Studio seating about 300, the Dennis Wolanski Library of the Performing Arts, four rehearsal studios, four restaurants and a café, sixty dressing rooms and suites, an artists' lounge and canteen known as the 'Green Room', and numerous administrative offices. In all, the complex has nearly 1000 rooms and can seat approximately 7000 people at any one time.

The building's name is something of a misnomer, for it was originally intended to be a performing arts centre, rather than mainly a venue for opera. However, it has always been known as the Sydney Opera House, although many of the staff refer to it as simply 'the House'.

Each year, about 2 million people attend some 3000 events at the Opera House. Approximately 200,000 people annually take guided tours of the complex. It is one of the world's most famous buildings.

THE TAMWORTH COUNTRY MUSIC FESTIVAL

When about 50,000 enthusiasts get together to celebrate a ten-day cultural festival, that's quite a party. The annual celebration of the Country Music Festival has been going on since 1973, when the inaugural festival was held at Tamworth, a town in the New England area of central New South Wales, some 450 kilometres north of Sydney.

The festival is in reality one big happy family of country music aficionados who congregate at Tamworth to enjoy almost non-stop music and dancing, free concerts, and the impromptu performances by guitar-playing and singing artists, who entertain in the streets, in pubs, shopping centres, church halls, parks and just about anywhere. There are also rodeos, bushman's campdrafting demonstrations, pipe band concerts and other organised events. Festival shuttles crisscross the city to show visitors some of Tamworth's attractions, not least being the backdrop of the Great Dividing Range.

The festival's climax is on the second Saturday, when thousands participate in the massed line-dancing held in Tamworth's main thoroughfare, Peel Street. During the 2002 festival, 6350 dancers formed into lines and for five minutes danced together to recorded music. It was a record-breaking performance.

In the evening, at the 5000-seat Entertainment Centre, there is a star-studded Music Cavalcade at which the Toyota Golden Guitar awards are presented.

Two days later is the Australia Day holiday, when those remaining have a final musical fling, then pack up and go home. Many will return the following year.

RADIO ASTRONOMY

Australia's place in the forefront of radio astronomy was confirmed in 1975 when the Australian National University's Observatory at Siding Springs came into full operation, in the very clear atmosphere frequently found at the optical telescope's site near the northern New South Wales town of Coonabarabran. The observatory was established when it was discovered that the telescope at the Mount Stromlo Observatory, sited on Mount Stromlo, west of Canberra, was being affected by Canberra's city lights.

The Siding Springs telescope is a very accurate computer-controlled instrument with a 3.9-metre reflector, and is a British–Australian project. At the observatory there is also a 1.2-metre Schmidt telescope, owned and operated by the United Kingdom Science Research Council.

The Siding Springs project followed the commissioning, in 1961, of the giant radio telescope near the central-west New South Wales town of Parkes. This wholly Australian instrument played an important part in the identification of distant quasars (very remote sources of high energy).

The Commonwealth Scientific and Industrial Research Organisation (CSIRO), which had been engaged in war-time radar research, was largely responsible for much of the early post-war work on radio astronomy. The University of Sydney also operated two interferometers, one of which—located at the Molonglo Cross Observatory—proved very effective in discovering pulsars (radio emissions with regular pulsating signals). Other powerful radio-receiving dishes were brought into operation in the 1960s, whilst near Narrabri, in central-west New South Wales, a synthesis telescope used mainly for radio-astronomical research was commissioned in 1988, as an Australian bicentennial project.

Another interferometer instrument was commissioned by the North American Space Authority (NASA) at Tidbinbilla, near Canberra. This instrument, together with the Parkes facility, has been used extensively by NASA for tracking space vehicles.

A PARLIAMENTARY CRISIS

After thirteen years in the political wilderness, the Australian Labor Party, strongly led by Gough Whitlam, was returned to power at the December 1972 federal election.

A parliamentary crisis developed in April 1974 when the Senate declined to pass the Appropriations Bills, thus denying the government the funds necessary to run the country. Whitlam had little choice but to go to the electorate on the issue, deciding on a double dissolution of both Houses.

In the event, the ALP was re-elected with the loss of only one House of Representatives seat, but still without a majority in the Senate. Thus, the scene was set for the ensuing drama.

In March 1975, Malcolm Fraser had replaced William (Billy) Snedden as Leader of the Opposition. By then, many of the developed countries were wrestling with a worldwide economic crisis, exacerbated by a significant increase in Middle East crude oil prices.

In Australia, both unemployment and inflation rose to disturbing levels. The government was beset by a series of crises, the most damaging of which was the notorious 'loans affair'. It had begun with a scheme thought up by the Minister for Mines and Energy, Rex Connor, whereby substantial petrodollar loans from a Middle East country would be sought to finance projects in certain government-owned energy agencies, with the main intention of creating new jobs for the growing unemployed and to reduce Australia's dependence on Middle East oil.

In December 1974, Connor was able to secure Cabinet and Executive Council approval to raise $US4 billion external loans. It was not long before the Opposition heard of the government's plan to bypass normal loan-raising channels, and the situation became more serious when it became known that a Middle East financier of dubious character was involved in the government's continuing and hitherto secret attempts to raise the loans.

As the scandal developed, and the government became involved in a series of blunders and ill-advised manoeuvres, Fraser seized the opportunity to block supply and thereby force an election. The Senate, which was hostile to Labor, refused supply in October 1975. The government initially responded by remaining in office, despite the likelihood of running out of money by the end of November. There followed an offer by Whitlam of a half-Senate election, prompted by the hope that the government would gain sufficient support to enable the Appropriation Bills to be passed.

It was at this point that the Governor-General, Sir John Kerr (who had been a Whitlam appointee), after seeking advice from various quarters—including the Chief Justice of the High Court, Sir Garfield Barwick—resolved to remove Whitlam from office and to commission Fraser to form a caretaker government pending an immediate general election.

Parliament was duly dissolved, and when the result of the subsequent general election became known, the Liberal–Country Party had gained ninety-one House of Representatives seats to the ALP's thirty-six. Fifty-three per cent of the primary vote had been won by Liberal–Country Party candidates. Fraser thereupon became Prime Minister, whilst Whitlam was again elected Leader of the Opposition.

A period of rancour, bitterness and argument followed the months of intrigue and manoeuvring which had preceded the election. Of the central figures in the drama, Whitlam resigned from the leadership of the federal ALP following a second defeat in December 1977 after Fraser had called a snap election. He shortly afterwards resigned from parliament.

Sir John Kerr had been deeply stressed at the end of 1975 in the aftermath of the constitution events, and two years later resigned from the office of governor-general. Kerr then sought refuge in Europe, where he died in 1991.

Malcolm Fraser remained as prime minister until 1983, when the ALP was returned to office (see pp. 331–2). With Fraser's retirement, the principal players in the 1975 constitutional drama had departed from the parliamentary scene. It had been one of the greatest political upheavals in Australia's history.

Thirty years later, the former protagonists, Gough Whitlam and Malcolm Fraser, continued to demonstrate a mutual respect as they pursued their separate roles in public affairs.

THE AUSTRALIAN DEMOCRATS

In October 1980 the Fraser government had again been returned to office, albeit with a reduced majority. A feature of the election was the emergence of the Australian Democrats, founded in 1977 and led by Don Chipp, formerly a Liberal Cabinet Minister.

In the 1987 general election the Democrats won seven seats in the Senate, sufficient for the party (together with three others from outside the major parties) to hold the balance of power in the Senate.

NATIONAL HEALTH INSURANCE SCHEMES

In July 1975 the previous national health insurance scheme was replaced by the Australian Labor Party's 'Medibank', although it was to be another six months before the governments of New South Wales and Queensland agreed to state-funded hospitals. Medibank was the first attempt at providing a free national health scheme.

Medibank was accorded general public approval, although many doctors opposed the scheme. The first Fraser government, despite election promises to retain the scheme, made significant and unpopular changes. In 1984 the Hawke Labor government replaced the scheme with 'Medicare', a revamped and improved version of Medibank but which nevertheless was not entirely approved by many medical professionals.

LABOR RETURNS TO POWER

In 1983 the Prime Minister, Malcolm Fraser, decided upon a double dissolution of Parliament, claiming that it was impossible for the Liberal-

National Party (in 1982 the Country Party changed its name to the National Party) to govern due to obstruction on the part of the Senate parties.

On the day the election was called, William (Bill) Hayden, who had assumed the ALP leadership following Gough Whitlam's resignation, was persuaded to step aside in favour of Robert (Bob) Hawke, who had entered the parliament in 1980 following ten years as president of the Australian Council of Trade Unions (ACTU). The sudden change in the Labor leadership, and the prospect of a stronger Labor Party under the charismatic Bob Hawke, was sufficient to persuade the electorate that a change of government was desirable.

The result was a resounding victory for Labor, which was returned with a 25-seat majority. Bob Hawke was to score a record four consecutive Labor election victories, and to remain as prime minister until 1991.

One of the strengths of the first Hawke ministry was the 'Accord' between the Labor Party and the ACTU. The Accord was a set of social and economic policies which the Labor government would adopt in return for union restraint on wage increases and industrial militancy. The first Accord was agreed to just before the 1983 election, and was followed by six further Accords, the last being the 'Accord Mark 7', agreed to in 1993.

The working relationship between the Labor Party and the ACTU was to prove of enduring strength to the successive Hawke governments, and was marked, amongst other things, by a period of relatively stable relations between the unions and employers. During this time there was also a decline in union memberships as well as in membership of the ALP.

THE AMERICA'S CUP

The America's Cup (or the 'Auld Mug'), the most prestigious of yachting's trophies, had never been wrested from the Americans since the United States first won the trophy from the British in 1851.

Between 1962 and 1980, Australia made six unsuccessful challenges for 'the Cup'. The last three had been mounted by an Australian syndicate headed by a Perth entrepreneur, Alan Bond.

The Bond syndicate's fourth challenge was in 1983. The yacht, *Australia II*, had been designed and modified by Ben Lexcen. The crew, skippered by John Bertrand, won the deciding seventh race off Newport, Rhode Island (off the northern New York State coast), amidst nationwide excitement. Shortly afterwards, the famous trophy was taken from its time-honoured place at the New York Yacht Club and installed at the Royal Perth Yacht Club. Four years later the Australians defended the Cup against a determined American challenge, but were decisively beaten. But the disappointment did not detract from the achievement in 1983 of Alan Bond and all those associated with Australia's first-ever success in winning the prized trophy from the proud Americans.

BANKING

The first Hawke government was also notable for a fundamental change in Labor policy when the Treasurer, Paul Keating, obtained Party approval for the deregulation of the banking system.

The changed policy allowed foreign banks to operate within Australia. This brought about greater competition in the banking industry, although there were some instances of poor-quality bank loans resulting in substantial losses and defaults.

TAXATION

An innovative feature by the second Hawke government was the holding of a taxation 'summit' meeting to consider and discuss rationalisation of the country's antiquated taxation system. The central plank of the government's proposals was the introduction of a broad-based consumption tax on goods and services. The plan, which was strongly advocated by the Treasurer, did not impress the summit delegates, the general consensus being that it would be a regressive move.

The widespread outcry that followed was such that Bob Hawke withdrew his support for the proposal. This sparked ongoing bitterness between the prime minister and his treasurer, and was eventually to lead to Keating supplanting Hawke in 1991 as the Labor Party leader. It was the first time in Labor Party history that a serving prime minister had been defeated in a leadership challenge.

THE STOCKMARKET CRASH

By the mid-1980s there was growing concern over the malaise of the Australian economy. There had been huge borrowings of overseas money, much of which was used to finance unproductive corporate takeovers by high-flying and unprincipled business entrepreneurs. Their activities raised the national debt to unacceptable levels. Unemployment remained high, and when the value of the Australian dollar on overseas markets declined rapidly in 1986, with a corresponding increase in the level of debt, it became clear that a radical overhaul of the economy was necessary.

With a federal election in prospect in July 1987 there was the opportunity for the main parties to present the electorate with positive remedial plans. But neither side was able to devise appropriate measures, and with the Liberal–National Party generally supporting the government's policies, the ALP was returned for a record third time. It seemed to be a case of 'better the devil you know than the devil you don't'.

That Australia was not the only nation with economic problems became apparent in October 1987 when a worldwide sharemarket collapse suddenly occurred. Concerted action by the central banks of the developed nations gradually arrested the decline, but not before stock values generally had fallen by up to 40 per cent and interest rates on bank loans to business had climbed to nearly 25 per cent.

A discreditable feature of the period was the inevitable collapse of the largely 'paper' investment empires of a number of 'corporate cowboys', but not before the high-profile entrepreneurs concerned had raided the tills, usually transferring their ill-gotten gains into foreign banks before themselves departing to overseas destinations. The unfortunate investors in the companies concerned were left to gather the financial crumbs, and to rue the folly of responding to the lucrative temptations presented by the tycoons' seductive sales pitches and sleight-of-hand schemes.

The malaise continued into the early 1990s as investors suffered distressing losses in several government-owned banks in Victoria and South Australia. By the time interest rates settled at more reasonable levels, some companies had failed and others had had their asset values severely trimmed.

AUSTRALIA'S BICENTENARY

Two hundred years of white settlement were marked on 26 January 1988 by celebrations of various kinds in Australia's capital cities and in many smaller centres throughout the nation.

In Sydney, where it had all begun, prayers were said by the clergy; appropriate speeches were made; birthday presents to the nation were displayed, these including a sail training vessel from Britain, an ocean-going yacht from New Zealand, and an extension to the National Maritime Museum presented by the United States. Bands played; 'Advance Australia Fair' was sung with a full charge of emotion; a state luncheon was held, the principal guests being the Prince and Princess of Wales; and a couple of hundred sailing ships (popularly called 'the Tall Ships'), surrounded by countless smaller craft, made a grand spectacle in some ways reminiscent of the scene in Sydney's harbour just two centuries earlier. Fireworks were let off to make a colourful and befitting finale to a special and memorable day.

Not everyone rejoiced on Australia Day 1988, for various groups of Aboriginals used the occasion to hold peaceful demonstrations voicing their concern over issues which affected their communities.

GREAT THINGS...

Ian Kiernan, born close to the waters of Sydney Harbour, was a businessman who remains a dedicated yachtsman. He has been sailing competitively for over 40 years.

In 1986–87 Ian represented Australia in the prestigious and challenging BOC Challenge round-the-world solo yacht race, finishing sixth out of a field of 25 from 11 nations. It was a fine achievement—with an unexpected outcome.

During the course of the race Ian could not fail to notice the huge amounts of rubbish littering the waters. It was a problem he had been aware of for many years. Returning home, Ian gave thought to his experience and decided to do something about it.

He formed a committee of friends and organised a Clean Up Sydney Harbour day to be held on 8 January 1989. Volunteers were asked to come equipped with disposable bags, gloves and suitable footwear, and to gather as much rubbish as possible in their area. The bags were to be collected by their local councils. The response was overwhelming. An estimated 40,000 men, women and children gathered rubbish from the Sydney Harbour shores.

Such was the public response that Ian and his committee then organised the first Clean Up Australia Day, to be held on Sunday 21 January 1990. Once again, the public was enthusiastic: an estimated 300,000 volunteers turned out to gather rubbish their area.

The success of the event caught the attention of the United Nations Environment Programme (UNEP), which invited Ian and his team to meet and discuss the launch of a global Clean Up campaign. The days were set for 17–19 September 1993. An estimated 30 million people in 80 countries participated in the simultaneous clean-up. The campaign has since grown continually, with 35 million volunteers from 120 countries now participating.

Ian's work and leadership was duly recognised by numerous awards. In 1994 he was named 1994 Australian of the Year, and was then made an Officer of the Order of Australia (AO) on Australia Day 1995. In that year he was also awarded the prestigious Banksia Foundation Fellowship.

Great things sometimes have small beginnings.

MABO

Land rights and native title have long been contentious issues between Australia's Indigenous people, the Australian government and pastoral leaseholders. These issues were widely discussed when two cases came before the Australian Supreme Court.

The 1992 Mabo case concerned the legal rights of the Meriam people resident in the Murray Islands (in the Torres Strait) to own and use their traditional land. The claimant was a Torres Strait Islander, Eddie Mabo (Edward Koiki Mabo). He died in 1992, just months before the High Court decision: to grant the Meriam people property rights and, furthermore, to reject completely the notion of *terra nullius* (meaning that land belonged to no one at the time of British settlement).

Terra nullius was initially established when Captain Cook set foot on Possession Island (see p. 25) during his 1770 voyage of exploration. He was of the opinion that the Aboriginal people were nomadic and too small in number to be considered landowners. He was wrong, for at that time the Aboriginal population of Australia was an estimated 4 million people, grouped in several hundred nations.

Subsequent High Court decisions determined that native title may be possessed by an individual or a community dependent upon the content of the traditional laws and customs and cannot be transferred to another other than by surrender to the Crown (the country's governing power). Native title rights and interests are not rights granted by a government, but may apply to land and waters to the extent that they are consistent with other rights established over the land by law or executive action.

The Commonwealth Native Title Acts 1993 established the protection and recognition of native title, and gives Indigenous Australians the right to be consulted about, and perhaps participate in, activities proposed to be undertaken on the land. This has greatly benefited Indigenous Australians and their communities in regard to heritage protection and employment opportunities. The Australian government also provides funding to resolve native title issues arising from the Native Title Act 1993.

The 1992 High Court decision overturning the fiction of *terra nullius* was followed by the 1996 Court decision in a case launched by the Northern Queensland Wik people of Cape York. This decision stated that the grant of a pastoral lease does not necessarily extinguish (remove) native title, and that such rights may coexist with leaseholders' rights.

The Mabo judgment in no way challenges the legality of non-Aboriginal land tenure. Only vacant Crown land, national parks and some leased land can be subject to claims by Aboriginal owners.

THE REPUBLIC DEBATE

In the 1880s and 1890s, as we have seen, there had been a growing debate amongst the colonies over the issue of federation (see pp. 229–32).

A century later, the nation's mind became increasingly occupied with another debate—whether or not Australia should become a republic.

The central issue of the republican supporters was that it was inappropriate that the country's head of state (Queen Elizabeth II) was not resident in Australia, and was not an Australian.

The monarchists, on the other hand, saw no reason to change the status quo, contending that the monarchy had served Australia well for two centuries and more, and that the functions of head of state were being effectively carried out by the Queen's representative, the Governor-General.

Since Federation, the Australian system of government had been substantially based on the republican mould, with sovereignty derived directly from the people. Only three changes to the Constitution of Australia would be required for the nation to become a fully republican state.

These changes would involve establishing the office of a resident Australian head of state, setting out the powers of the head of state, and making provision for the states and territories to remain self-governing. It is the mechanisms necessary to affect these changes that is still one of the contentious issues in the debate between the monarchists and the republicans.

In 1993 the Keating government established a Republican Advisory Committee to prepare an options paper to consider the issues involved. The Committee's deliberations were published in a report at the end of the year.

In the 1997 general election the Howard government was voted into office, and decided to hold a referendum on the republican issue.

The referendum was duly held on 6 November 1999, when voters were required to give their decision, firstly, on whether to enact a proposed law to alter the Constitution to allow for the establishment of a republic; and, secondly, whether to enact a proposed law to alter the Constitution to insert a preamble. (This preamble would 'enable the Australian people to highlight the values and aspirations which unite us in support of our Constitution; contribute importantly to the process of national reconciliation between indigenous and non-indigenous Australians; and recognise at the end of our first century of federation the enduring priorities and influences that uniquely shape Australia's sense of nationhood'.)

Fifty-four per cent of the electorate voted 'no' to the first question, and sixty per cent voted 'no' to the second question.

The nation's democratic response to these questions suggests that there will be a return to the republic debate in the not-too-distant future.

CLIMATE CHANGE AND RENEWABLE ENERGY

During the 1980s, scientists began reporting that holes were occurring in the Earth's ozone layer above the Arctic and Antarctic regions.

The thin ozone layer is contained within the stratosphere, which is the second highest— counting upwards—of the Earth's five atmospheric layers (or blankets) that protect the planet from the Sun's ultraviolet radiation. The stratosphere extends from about 17 to 51 km above the Earth's surface.

The ozone holes reported by the scientists were caused by CFCs (chlorofluorocarbons), which were commonly used as pressure propellants in refrigerators, some air conditioners, in some aerosol sprays, and in the manufacture of packaging foam.

While the use of CFCs has been largely eliminated, and the size of the ozone holes correspondingly reduced, public attention had been drawn to the dangers of global warming resulting from the 'greenhouse effect'—meaning the burning of fossil fuels and widespread deforestation resulting in the increase in mean air temperatures.

The so-called greenhouse effect results from the absorption of infrared radiation by the atmosphere. Radiant energy reaches the Earth's surface mainly as visible light from the Sun, which is then re-emitted as heat.

The extensive burning of fossil fuels in the generation of electricity is one of a number of main causes of atmospheric pollution, resulting in increases in worldwide average air temperature by several degrees. This in turn causes melting of polar ice and the consequent rise in mean sea levels.

It has been predicted that by 2070 global temperature will have increased between 1°C and 6°C.

In 1997 delegates from most of the world's industrialised countries met in Kyoto, one of Japan's main cities, to discuss an addendum to the agreement reached in 1992 at the Earth Summit conference held at Brazil's capital, Rio de Janeiro. Each delegate at Kyoto agreed to reduce their country's carbon emissions by about 5 per cent by 2012. Despite fears that the Kyoto Protocol would not survive, progress was made at a subsequent meeting in Bonn in July 2001, where 178 countries agreed to a compromise involving lower targets (of around 2 per cent), enabling ratification to proceed.

Among the contentious issues was the question of how far countries could use 'carbon sinks' (e.g. forest vegetation that can absorb carbon) to meet pollution-reduction targets.

The USA refused to accept the Kyoto Protocol and withdrew in 2001, attracting much international criticism. By the end of 2002 the Protocol had been ratified by 100 countries.

In 2003 Russia announced that it would not ratify the treaty in its present form, putting the Protocol's future in doubt.

The basic problem facing governments worldwide is weighing the risk of economic market share, both nationally and internationally, against the prospect of delivering planet Earth to future generations with undesirable and irreversible climatic conditions.

In Australia, while the introduction of a national program to limit greenhouse gas emissions is yet to occur, one enterprising Australian city, Newcastle, has taken the initiative on climate change. The Newcastle City Council, having already taken steps to reduce its own greenhouse emissions, turned its attention to 20 of the city's greatest polluters and is encouraging some 11,000 businesses in the area to effectively manage their carbon and water usage.

To combat the problems of fossil fuels, several Australian initiatives are in place. The massive Snowy Mountains Hydro Electric Scheme's (see pp. 303–8) seven power stations have been feeding electricity into the nation's electricity grids since the 1950s.

In more recent times, wind-power generating farms have come into operation, producing useful, but at present relatively small amounts, of electricity.

In 2009 Australia's first water desalination plant came into operation at Sydney, to be followed by a similar plant in Melbourne.

By about 2020 a potentially very useful source of electricity—base-load geothermal power—is scheduled to play an important part in supplying Australia's future non-polluting power needs.

At depths of about 4500 to 5000 metres are fractured granite rocks with temperatures of about 280°C. Super-heated water flows through these hot rocks, and when pumped through man-made underground heat exchangers, produces electricity.

By about 2020, when extensive testing and commissioning have been completed, geothermal plants constructed with world-class technology are scheduled to be in operation in South Australia's Cooper Basin and New South Wales' Hunter regions.

These plants are already supplying neighbouring communities with electricity. They are expected to make a significant contribution to Australia's future energy needs, thus reducing dependence upon high-emission fossil fuel power plants.

THE OLYMPIC GAMES

The quadrennial Modern Olympic Games have so far been staged twenty-four times since the first event was held in Athens in 1896.

The 1956 Olympics in Melbourne was the first to be held in the Southern Hemisphere, and was also the first to have closing ceremonies. Australians, led by Dawn Fraser and Murray Rose, won eight of the thirteen swimming events. Betty Cuthbert won three gold medals in the track events, being victorious in the women's 100- and 200-metre sprints. She was also a member of the 4 x 100-metre relay team.

In 2000, Australia again hosted the Olympic Games, this time in Sydney. Australian athletes were again dominant in the swimming events, gold medals being won by Ian Thorpe, Michael Klim, Grant Hackett, Ashley Callus, Chris Fydler, William Kirby, Todd Pearson and Susie O'Neill. Australia also won gold in the Men's Trap Shooting, Men's Individual Archery, Men's Madison Cycling, Women's Under 49 kilogram Taekwondo, Women's 470 Sailing, Men's 470 Sailing, the Equestrian Three Day Team Event, Women's Water Polo, Women's Hockey, Women's Beach Volleyball and Women's 400 Metres, which was won by Cathy Freeman.

It was Cathy Freeman who carried the Olympic Torch into Sydney's 'Stadium Australia' Olympic venue at Homebush Bay. To the thunderous cheers of the 110,000 people packed into the stadium, and watched by an estimated four billion television viewers, the champion Aboriginal runner carried the torch up a giant stairway, then lowered the flame to a reflective pool to ignite around her a ring of fire as the cauldron rose slowly to the top of the stadium. The Games of the XXVII Olympiad had begun.

The Olympic flame had travelled 36,000 kilometres through thirty-six countries to begin a 100-day journey throughout Australia, commencing at Uluru (Ayers Rock) in the heart of the continent, and finally crossing Sydney Harbour Bridge on the ninety-ninth day. Carried by relays of young and not-so-young Australians, both well-known personalities and ordinary people, the special torch's epic Australian journey was conducted on horseback, by air, by rail, and even underwater at the Great Barrier Reef.

A spectacular opening ceremony had preceded the arrival of the Olympic torch, the central theme being the nation's history as seen through the eyes of black and white Australia. The two cultures were represented in seven sequences, each linked by segments by thirteen-year-old Sydney girl Nikki Webster and Aboriginal man Djakapurra Munyarryun.

A feature of the Sydney Games was the vital part played by the volunteers—some 47,000 specially trained men and women outfitted in distinctive and brightly coloured uniforms. About three-quarters of the volunteers were from New South Wales, the remainder coming from all Australian states and territories. Some of the volunteers even hailed from overseas countries.

Especially noteworthy were the volunteer drivers from country areas in New South Wales and the eastern states, some of whom brought their buses with them to augment the large fleet of Sydney buses which, together with the rail services, were used to transport the huge crowds to and from Homebush Bay.

Some of the volunteers worked 'behind the scenes' to supplement the official medical, security and other officials. But the majority of them gave their time to crowd control and other spectator services.

It seemed to be a unanimous opinion that Sydney had scored a perfect ten in hosting the 2000 Olympic Games—the 'Friendly Games'. The volunteers, with their ever-ready smiles and helpfulness, made a major contribution to the exceptionally smooth running of the two-weeks event.

BALI BOMBINGS

Bali, sometimes known as the enchanted island, came under Dutch control in the 1840s, then became a part of Indonesia when the Dutch recognised Indonesian independence in 1949.

Bali is now the home of Indonesia's small Hindu minority. The island is also the country's major tourist destination, renowned for its beaches, usually inexpensive shopping attractions and nightlife.

In 2002 Bali was the scene of a triple bombing attack by militant Islamic extremists. The first attack, in a popular and crowded nightclub was by a backpack-mounted suicide bomber. The second was by a large car-bomb and the third by a smaller device outside the nearby United States Consulate.

202 revellers were killed by the attacks, of which 88 were Australian and 38 Indonesian citizens. 240 people were injured. It was the deadliest terrorist attack in Indonesia's history, and the one in which Australians suffered the greatest loss of life.

The main perpetrators of the attacks were executed in 2008.

BEACONSFIELD MINING DISASTER

Beaconsfield is a small Tasmanian town 40 kilometres north-west of the city of Launceston, boasting a profitable goldmine.

On 25 April 2006, at about 9pm, an earthquake triggered rockfalls that trapped 17 men working at a depth of about 925 metres. Fourteen of the men escaped injury and were quickly brought to the surface.

After three anxious days, the rescue crews were able to report that they had made voice contact with two of the missing men. Sadly, the third was dead.

The two remaining miners—Todd Russell, aged 34, and Brant Webb, aged 37, were trapped under a large slab of rock, but had sought safety inside a nearby cherry-picker cage that had escaped damage.

Using explosives and drilling equipment, and taking great care not to trigger rockfalls, the rescue crews gradually bored a horizontal tunnel towards the two trapped miners. Avoiding the use of explosives for the last few metres, the rescuers finally reached the cherry-picker cage and freed the two survivors. The men carefully made their way along the narrow tunnel until they reached the main shaft and safety.

Several minutes later the two rescued men reached the surface and were reunited with their families.

WATER

Australia is one of the world's seven inhabited continents. It is also the driest. Rainfall is Australia's main source of water. The agricultural industry is the nation's main water user, constituting 65 per cent of total consumption in 2004–05.

A report commissioned by the Australian government in 2008 forecasts that Australia could experience future droughts that are twice as severe as that of 2006. Averaged over a long period, Australia's rainfall experience is three good years, followed by four average years, then three bad ones.

Australia is one of a small number of water-scarce countries that have instituted markets for trading water. Most of the trading is on a temporary basis (usually one year). One advantage of temporary transfers is that water allocations can be increased or decreased as needed.

Desalination is a practical method of making salt water drinkable. There has been strong growth in desalination plants, especially in the Middle East.

Australia at present has three desalination plants with several more in development. One such plant, at Kurnell on Sydney's coast, was commissioned in 2009 and is used to augment Sydney's water supply from the catchment dams to the south-west of the city.

Rainfall at Australia's northern and eastern regions is periodically controlled by a climatic irregularity known as the Southern Oscillation, or *La Niño* (Spanish for 'the child'). This results from warm ocean currents off the east equatorial Pacific Coast that swing across the Pacific Ocean. This phenomenon can result in droughts in Australia's northern and eastern regions, and to severe mortality to marine life. There is a corresponding effect known as *La Niña*, which occurs when water temperature is much lower than usual in the Pacific Ocean's central to eastern regions. This disrupts rainfall patterns and can contribute to flooding and cyclones in the Queensland region (see pp. 356–9).

Climatic conditions in Australia's western and southern regions are mainly controlled by Indian Ocean and Antarctic weather systems. The Murray-Darling Basin is one of Australia's largest river water divisions, covering about one-seventh of the continent, from the headwaters of the Darling River in Queensland to the Basin's southern boundary. The Basin covers 1,058,800 km^2, or about fourteen per cent of Australia's total area.

In 2007 some 93 per cent of Australian households had access to mains water. About half of them used grey water (water from a bath, laundry or kitchen that is collected or re-used). Nineteen per cent of households used a rainwater tank as a source of water.

Between 1970 and 1990, per capita water supplies decreased by a third worldwide. It is speculated that this is due to climate change. A United Nations report estimates that climate change will account for 20 per cent of the decline in water supply due to erratic rainfall and a rise in sea levels. The report further estimates that with pollution continuing, about two million tonnes of waste is dumped into the world's waters.

During the past century, the world's population has tripled, while water usage has increased six-fold. A UN population projection estimates that nearly seven billion people in 60 countries will face water scarcity by 2050.

Rainfall, or the lack of it, is the most important single factor determining land use and rural production in Australia. The absence of high mountain barriers is an important topographical feature affecting Australia's rainfall and drainage patterns.

One-third of Australia's land area drains directly to the ocean, mainly on the coastal side of the Great Divide and inland to the Murray-Darling system. Two-thirds of the Australian continent is arid or semi-arid. Good rainfalls (averaging over 800mm annually) occur in the northern monsoonal belt under the influence of the Australian-Asian monsoon, and along the eastern and southern highland regions under the influence of the great atmospheric depressions of the Southern Ocean.

The effectiveness of Australia's rainfall is greatly reduced by the alternation of wet and dry seasons, which vary from year to year, and to high temperatures and resulting evaporation.

The availability of water resources controls, to a large extent, the location and density of population settlements, which in turn influence the quality of the available water through production and disposal of waste. Most of Australia's early settlements were established where there were reliable surface water supplies.

The discovery of the Great Artesian Basin, which has become a major asset to the pastoral industry, resulted from observing the disappearance of large quantities of rainfall on the coastal ranges of eastern Australia.

Despite being the driest inhabited continent, Australia is the world's highest user of water per capita of population. More than 80 per cent of the average volume of water in the Murray River is diverted for industrial and domestic use, with irrigation accounting for much of this usage.

There are thirty big dams and 3500 weirs in the Murray-Darling Basin. Nearly three times the annual average flow in the Murray River is stored in dams and weirs.

From time to time it has been proposed that Australia's northern and eastern coastal rivers should be turned inland instead of draining into the ocean. Water experts are of the opinion that this is impracticable. Dr. John Williams, head of CSIRO's land and water divisions, has said that rather than trying to turn the rivers inland, governments and farmers should consider changing to dry-climate crops, improving the efficiency of irrigation networks and to reusing water, particularly in the cities.

'There are a number of solutions, and we need to explore them all,' Dr. Williams has said. 'Australia is a dry continent, and we will never be able to avoid droughts.

But with better policies for land and water use, a lot of the impacts would be greatly modified.'

In recent times various schemes have been put forward to make Australia more drought-proof. One plan is to use cloud seeding to increase rainfall in the Snowy Mountains area. Another is to capture the monsoonal rains of northern Queensland to fill the usually-dry bed of Lake Eyre in South Australia. Yet another suggestion is to put irrigation water into plastic pipes rather than open channels, thus reducing loss by evaporation.

Of all the world's water, only three per cent is fresh. Less that a third of one per cent is available to humans. The rest is frozen in glaciers or polar ice caps, or is deep within the Earth and beyond our reach.

HISTORIC APOLOGY TO THE STOLEN CHILDREN

In 1909 an Australian government body—the Aborigines Protection Board (APB)—was given the power to remove Aboriginal children without the need for a court order or parental consent. At the time, the Aboriginal people were regarded by some as an inferior race.

Since the early 1950s, children were taken (forcibly if necessary) from their Aboriginal parents and placed in institutions or with cooperating white families. They were taught to reject their Aboriginal culture, and were frequently brought up to be labourers or servants.

At the time, it was believed by some that Aboriginal people lived poor and unrewarding lives, and that accordingly their children could benefit by being placed in institutions or with white families. The practice of removing Aboriginal children from their families continued into the 1960s.

Most APB records have been either lost or destroyed, so many of the 'Stolen Generation' children have been unable to trace their biological families.

In the 1990s a Human Rights and Equal Opportunity Commission report found that many of the Stolen Generation children, when they had been placed in institutions or in homes, had been subjected to various forms of cruelty, including sexual and physical abuse.

Some Aboriginal and Torres Strait Islander people were unable to trace their birthplace and family until late in life; and when they did, feelings of cultural alienation sometimes arose, which tended to disturb the relationship with their adopted family.

The Human Rights and Equal Opportunity report advocated, among other things, an official apology from the Australian government. In 1997 the then Prime Minister, John Howard, declined to make such an apology, arguing that the current generation should not be held responsible for past mistakes.

Despite this, a campaign for a national apology quickly developed. On 26 May 1998 the first national Sorry Day was held, with ceremonies and meetings across the country. The celebration, known to some as the Journey of Healing Day, has been held annually ever since.

On 13 February 2008, then Prime Minister Kevin Rudd duly issued an official government apology. Members of the Stolen Generation were among guests on the floor of Parliament as the Prime Minister delivered the apology.

The speech spoke of honouring Australia's indigenous people, acknowledging and reflecting on their past mistreatment, and the hope that the first step had been taken towards healing and a new future.

'We apologise for the laws and policies of successive Parliaments and governments that have inflicted profound grief, suffering and loss on these our fellow Australians.

We apologise especially for the removal of Aboriginal and Torres Strait Islander children from their families, their communities and their country.

For the pain, suffering and hurt of these Stolen Generations, their descendants and for their families left behind, we say sorry.

To the mothers and the fathers, the brothers and the sisters, for the breaking up of families and communities, we say sorry.

And for the indignity and degradation thus inflicted on a proud people and a proud culture, we say sorry.'

BUSHFIRES

The combination of extreme heat, dry weather and vegetation that is abundant in natural oils has made Australia highly prone to bushfires.

Severe bushfires are an almost annual occurrence, caused variously by lightning strike, negligence (for example, discarded cigarettes and campfires that are not properly extinguished) and, sadly, deliberate arson.

Great loss of property and life is frequently the result, and never more so than in Victoria's tragic Black Saturday fires in early 2009.

An estimated 400 separate fires began around the state after a series of days where temperatures topped 40°C and winds gusted around 100 kilometres per hour. On Saturday 7 February, 2009, several large firestorms, particularly in the region north-east of Melbourne, destroyed around 3500 properties and resulted in 173 deaths. In terms of losses, it was the worst bushfire in Australia's history.

ALL AT SEA

Australia has been the scene of many remarkable yachting feats, with several brave adventurers—including a teenager—making solo journeys across the seas.

JESSICA WATSON

On 18 October 2009, a 16-year-old girl sailed out of Sydney Harbour in her pink-hulled yacht, *Ella's Pink Lady*, on a Southern Ocean round-the-world solo voyage.

After 100 days at sea, having sailed 21,300 kilometres, she crossed from the Western to the Eastern Hemisphere. Nine days later she passed the Cape of Good Hope, crossing from the Atlantic Ocean to the Indian Ocean and beginning the 9,300 kilometres journey towards Western Australia. As she neared the Australian mainland on 10 April, her parents flew over her in a light aircraft to welcome her back to her homeland. She passed Western Australia's Cape Leewin on 12 April.

On the frequently tempestuous Southern Ocean, her yacht was knocked down three times by swells at least 12 metres high, the mast horizontal in the water. The very rough weather continued for several days.

By 3 May, Jessica had rounded Tasmania and was on course to Sydney. She finally arrived home on 15 May—within three days of her seventeenth birthday.

During her epic voyage, Jessica attended to running repairs to *Ella's Pink Lady*—the battery monitor, the stove, the toilet (twice), the mainsail (twice), the wind generator blades and the engine's fuel pump.

Jessica's momentous journey had not been undertaken without some criticism.

Her tender age and lack of trans-ocean experience were cited as reasons why she should not attempt the circumnavigation. She had collided with a freighter some days before she embarked on her epic voyage, and this also was referred to by her critics.

Despite this, her courage, skill and determination led her to persist with, and successfully complete, the long and sometimes very hazardous journey. It was a fine achievement for someone so young, and earned her the title 'Young Australian of the Year' in 2011.

FRANCIS CHICHESTER

Francis Chichester was a remarkable man—an adventurer more interested in the satisfaction of achievement than in records.

In 1931 this restless Englishman flew solo from London to Sydney, just three months after gaining his pilot's licence. He was the second flyer to make the long journey (the first had been Amy Johnson, who in 1930 became the first aviator to fly solo from England to Australia).

Flying out of Sydney in 1931, Chichester crashed his tiny Gypsy Moth plane on Lord Howe Island. With the islanders' help he spent three weeks rebuilding the plane's smashed body.

Decades later, Chichester transformed himself from aviator to yachtsman. He arrived in Sydney in 1966 on the first leg of a round-the-world solo sailing voyage in a new yacht, Gypsy Moth V. He had travelled from Plymouth to Sydney via the Cape of Good Hope in 107 days, and then returned to Plymouth via the perilous Cape Horn in 119 days. He had been at sea for a total of 226 days, and was later knighted by Queen Elizabeth II with the same sword used to honour Sir Francis Drake in 1580.

Francis Chichester's exploits were undertaken despite periodic ill health. In 1958 his doctor told him that he had incurable lung cancer. That he was able to embark on his yachting exploits despite his illness is an indication of the adventurer's strength of character.

KAY COTTEE

The first woman to sail solo, nonstop and unassisted around the world was Sydney-born Kay Cottee. In 1988 she achieved the feat in 189 days, sailing in her yacht *Blackmores First Lady*. For this yachting record she was named Australian of the Year in 1989.

FEMALE FIRSTS

While several nations in the world have had female political leaders for many years, Australia could not make the same claim until late in the first decade of the twenty-first century.

QUENTIN BRYCE

On 5 September 2008, Quentin Bryce AC assumed office as the 25th Governor-General of Australia.

Born as Quentin Strachan, she spent her early years in Ilfracombe and various other Queensland towns, in New South Wales and several other parts of Australia. Returning to Queensland, the family settled at Belmont, where she attended Camp Hill State School. It was there that she first met her future husband, Michael Bryce.

Meanwhile, Quentin's father had purchased a sheep farming property near Tenterfield, New South Wales. In 1956 Quentin became a pupil at Moreton Bay College at Wynnum, an eastern suburb of Brisbane. After graduation she studied at the University of Queensland, where she completed Bachelor of Arts and Bachelor of Laws degrees, later becoming one of the first women to be appointed to the Queensland bar.

In 1978 Quentin joined the National Women's Advisory Council and accepted a number of official State positions, becoming Australia's Sex Discrimination Commissioner and, later, the chief executive officer of the National Childcare Accreditation Council. Her services to the community were recognised in 1988 when she was appointed an Officer of the Order of Australia. In 2003 she became a Companion of the Order of Australia and Dame of the Order of St. John of Jerusalem, and was subsequently appointed Queensland's 24th Governor.

ANNA BLIGH

Anna Maria Bligh was born on 14 July 1960 at Warwick, Queensland. She was educated at Miami State and then Nowra High Schools. She then worked in community organisations and the Queensland Public Service. In 1980 she graduated from the University of Queensland with an Arts degree.

Anna Bligh entered politics on 15 July 1995, when she became the Member for South Brisbane. After ten years she was appointed Deputy Premier, holding various portfolios. She became Premier of Queensland in 2007 following the resignation of Peter Beattie.

On 21 March 2009 Anna Bligh became the first popularly elected female Premier of Australia. She is married to Greg Withers, a senior public servant. They have two sons—Joe, born in 1987, and Oliver, born in 1993.

KRISTINA KENEALLY

Kristina Marie Kercher was born on 19 December 1968 to an American father, John Kercher, and an Australian-born mother, Catherine Powell.

She became involved in student politics at Notre Dame Academy and was an award-winning soccer player. She graduated with a Bachelor of Arts in political science, and was registered as a Democrat. In 1995 she graduated with a Master of Arts in religious studies. She worked for a year as a volunteer teacher in New Mexico.

In 1991 Kristina met her future husband, Ben Keneally (a nephew of the well known Australian writer, Thomas Keneally), at the World Youth Day in Poland.

She moved to Australia in 1994, but returned to America that year. In 1996 she married Ben Keneally in Boston. A daughter, Caroline, died at birth, but sons were born to them in 1998 (Daniel) and in 2000 (Brendan). They returned to Australia in 1998.

Kristina became a naturalised Australian in 2000, and in that year joined the Labor Party. In 2003 she was elected to the New South Wales Legislative Assembly. She was appointed as NSW Minister for Disability Services; then, in 2008, as NSW Planning Minister.

In December 2009 Kristina challenged and defeated Nathan Rees to become the 42nd Premier of New South Wales. She was the first woman, and first former American, to hold that office.

JULIA GILLARD

Julia Gillard was born in the Welsh town of Barry, in the Vale of Glamorgan, the first daughter of John and Moira Gillard. They had a second daughter, Alison, who is three years younger than Julia.

In 1966 the family moved to Australia after Julia contracted bronco pneumonia, settling at Pasadena in South Australia. There her father worked as a psychiatric nurse, while her mother worked at the local Salvation Army nursing home. The two sisters attended Mitcham Demonstration School and Julia later attended Unlay High School.

Gillard then enrolled at Adelaide University, but dropped her course. In 1983 she moved to Melbourne to work with the Union of Students. She also became Secretary of the Socialists Forum, a left wing organisation. In 1986, Gillard graduated from Melbourne University and, after a successful career with the Slater & Gordon law firm, became Chief of Staff to John Brumby, then the Victorian Opposition leader. She was responsible for drafting the Victorian Labor Party's affirmative action rules, setting a target of 35 per cent of the State's winnable seats to be taken by women. She also played a role in the Labor women's support network. One of Gillard's heroes was Aneurin 'Nye' Bevan, the renowned British Labour Party politician.

In 1998 Gillard was elected to replace the retiring Barry Jones as Victorian Member for the safe seat of Lalor. She made her maiden speech to the Parliament on 11 November 1998.

Following Labor's defeat in the 2001 Federal Election, Gillard was elected to Labor's shadow cabinet and given the Immigration and Population portfolios. Later she became responsible for Recognition and Immigration. One of her tasks was to develop Labor's Immigration policy.

From 2003 to 2006 Gillard became Labor's Shadow Minister for Health in rivalry to Tony Abbott, the Conservatives Workplace Relations Minister with responsibility for Health. At that time Gillard was lauded as a future Labor leader.

On 4 December 2006 Julia was elected Deputy ALP leader, and on 3 December 2007 became the first female Deputy Prime Minister of Australia when Labor leader Kevin Rudd won the Federal

Election. On 11 December, she became Acting Prime Minister while Rudd was overseas attending a UN Climate Change Conference.

In June 2010, Rudd was confronted by a Labor Party leadership spill. After a series of meetings between Gillard, Rudd and factional leaders on 23 June, Rudd stepped down and Gillard took the post of Prime Minister, Australia's first woman to assume the role. Shortly afterwards she announced that a General Election would be held in August 2010.

There was considerable uncertainty about the outcome of the election, in which Gillard was opposing Coalition leader Tony Abbott. The election result duly proved to be very close and resulted in a three-week-long hung parliament. After much discussion and some bargaining Gillard announced that Labor had been able to form a government with the support of three elected Independent Members and one Greens MP.

With Julia Gillard's appointment as Prime Minister on 24 June 2010, a remarkable coincidence had occurred. For the first time in Australia's history, the offices of Australia's Governor-General, Prime Minister and two state Premiers were held by women at the same time.

QUEENSLAND'S WILD WEATHER

Queenslanders are familiar with cyclonic depressions arriving from northern latitudes. These weather systems may visit at any season except, usually, during the winter months. If cyclones cross the coast, they invariably cause some degree of flooding and damage to property.

At the end of December 2010, a depression of unusual intensity crossed the Cape York coast and headed south, leaving severe damage and destruction in its wake.

The cyclone buffeted Cairns then, with growing intensity, moved southwards through the coastal cities, towns and inland areas towards

Brisbane, gathering destructive power as it went. The storm reached the Queensland capital at the end of December before continuing into the northern regions of New South Wales.

Brisbane and, particularly, its neighbouring towns and cities, were to suffer severely. Muddy floodwaters and increasing amounts of debris poured down the Brisbane River, flooding the CBD area (on its northern bank) for several days to a depth of about a metre. Properties on the city's southern regions were severely flooded, as were districts to the west.

There was little warning of the extent of loss of life, destruction and damage that the almost continuous rain and flooding were to cause. Toowoomba, 125 kilometres west of Brisbane and on the rim of the Great Dividing Range, was drenched by the flood of water that cascaded through the city's streets, resulting in nine deaths, including a mother and her son who were swept away from their vehicle. The unexpected volume and speed of water was described as an 'inland tsunami'.

At Gatton a woman's body was found under Daveys Bridge, and a man's body was later found in a creek near Lyons Bridge. At Myall Creek rescuers pulled a man's body from the water. At Marburg, a four-year-old boy fell from a boat and was swept away. In Durack, a Brisbane suburb, a 24-year-old man was sucked down a storm drain while checking his father's house.

By 13 January 2011, 43 persons had been reported missing from the Lockyer Valley and Grantham areas. Whole families there were unaccounted for.

In 1974 a major flood had caused extensive damage to the region. It was realised then that it was essential to control flood water flowing down the Brisbane River from the Toowoomba area, in order to mitigate damage to the state's capital and surrounding areas. Accordingly, the Wivenhoe Dam was constructed south of Toowoomba. It has a rated capacity of 100 per cent, but, in fact, the dam's capacity can reach 200 per cent before an emergency spillway needs to be opened.

Five gates at the dam were closed on 2 January 2011 to ensure that the flood compartment would be ready in the event of more heavy rain. On the night of 11 January, when capacity had reached 191 per cent, the dam's managers began periodically opening the gates, releasing water to the already flooded Lockyer Valley/Grantham area before it found its way to Brisbane, 80 kilometres distant.

Three-quarters of Queensland was now declared a disaster zone.

It is a feature of the Australian ethos that help is at hand at times of stress, destruction and death. In times of need, it is said, ordinary people do extraordinary things. So it was that large numbers of volunteers came forward, usually with broom and bucket, to help the many in need who had been affected by the widespread 2011 flood. Sandbags were greatly in demand, and as the authorities brought in loads of sand and bundles of bags, scores of volunteers were ready to carry the bags where protection from flood water was needed.

The Australian Defence Force quickly sent in contingents, mainly occupied with searching and removing debris left behind when the flood waters began to recede.

The NSW Government also flew in police to help with traffic and other law enforcement duties, allowing the local police to attend to work arising from reports of missing or dead persons. A special 100-strong taskforce of officers from NSW, Victoria and South Australia also arrived to support the Brisbane police.

As the flood waters began to recede, the Brisbane City Council issued the following statistics:

- 11,490 homes in Brisbane were inundated
- 14,296 homes in Brisbane were partially flooded
- 150,000 tonnes of rubbish had been collected
- 23,517 volunteers had been registered with the Council

The worst affected Brisbane suburbs were:

- Brisbane City–1359 properties
- St Lucia–1189 properties
- Rocklea–1144 properties
- Graceville–644 properties

Just as Queensland was beginning to mop up, another threat loomed on the horizon. Two tropical cyclones were seen developing to the north-east of the country, and both were headed for Far North Queensland.

The first, Cyclone Anthony, crossed Bowen on 31 January 2011. By the time it made landfall it had been downgraded to a tropical low and caused minimal damage. There was little relief for residents, however, as Cyclone Yasi was close on the previous storm's heels—and it was a monster.

By February 2, Yasi had become a category 5 and, at 500 kilometres wide, was tipped to be the most destructive and powerful cyclone to hit Queensland in recent memory.

Yasi hit Mission Beach at midnight on February 2 as a category 4, causing widespread property damage and storm surges across large portions of the North Queensland coast.

In 2006, the same area suffered from the devastating effects of Cyclone Larry. In 1974, Cyclone Tracy almost completely destroyed the city of Darwin. As with many other natural disasters, cyclones have become an expected, and reoccurring, part of many Australian's lives.

CHANGING NATION

Several significant changes occurred in Australia during the second half of the twentieth century.

The first was the marked increase in population resulting from post-war immigration policies. Between 1950 and 1980, Australia's population increased by approximately 2 million in each decade, the 1980 population being nearly 14.75 million.

In 1790, two years after the arrival of the First Fleet, Australia's population was approximately 200,000. One hundred years later, with most of the coastal and inland centres established, and with about two-thirds of the populace living in the cities and towns, Australia's population was in excess of 3.1

million. The total had reached 17.1 million by 1990, including an estimated 265,000 Aboriginal Australians.

By the 1960s the urbanisation of Australia's population was more marked than ever, with only about 14 per cent of the population living in rural areas. People living and working on farms numbered less than 10 per cent of the population.

By the 1970s about one-fifth of Australia's population had been born overseas, chiefly in the United Kingdom and in Ireland.

Unemployment in the post-war years increased proportionally with the levels of immigration. In 1960 there had been concern at an unemployment level of nearly 2 per cent. By 1982, total unemployment was in the region of 10 per cent, with youth unemployment at double that figure.

The post-war increase in migration evidenced significant changes in Australia's social patterns. Increasing numbers of 'new Australians' came from European, Mediterranean and Middle East countries and, notably from the 1970s onwards, from Asia. Cultural and religious facets of Australian society broadened in accordance with homeland customs and traditions, whilst changes also became apparent in food varieties, the increased consumption of wine, the trend towards more footpath cafés and quality restaurants, and in the broadening entertainment spectrum. Australia had increasingly become a multicultural society and, it seemed to many, was all the better for the diversity and the dilution of the hitherto somewhat top-heavy Anglo-Saxon mix.

Other trends were discernible during the march towards the end of the twentieth century and the commencement of the third millennium. Human behaviour became more relaxed and nonconformist. Many of the traditional ways of life, taboos and accepted standards of speech and of dress customs were swept aside as the process of examination of traditional values proceeded, to be replaced by new customs, fads, likes and dislikes. This trend was particularly noticeable in regard to mass entertainment, popular music and dress.

It was also noticeable that the traditional ties with Britain were weakened, as increasing numbers in the nation's multicultural society were unable to share the ties of earlier generations with the British monarchy and with family and friends in 'the old country'. The allegiances and ties of the enlarged non-British migrant element in the population gradually added to the trend towards greater independence and to all things Australian.

ACKNOWLEDGMENTS

Several years ago I visited various reference libraries, including Sydney's admirable Mitchell Library and the adjoining State Library of New South Wales, to discover various events that occurred during Australia's modern history, and individuals who contributed to the country's development. During this intensive research I chanced upon a wide range of facts, stories and word pictures of both modern Australia's early days and of more recent times. All these various scraps of information duly went into my files, and because I then had no thought about a 'potted history' or any other work, I made no record of the sources of these various notes.

I express my grateful acknowledgment to the authors of various published sources, of which I have no record, in instances where information from their works has found its way into the preceding pages. My thanks are also due to the staffs of Sydney's Mitchell and State libraries for their ready assistance, which led me down the fascinating paths of research into aspects of modern Australia's history.

I have a deep sense of gratitude to my wife, Enid, for her infinite patience and tolerance during the several years that have passed during the research and writing of this book; and for her invaluable suggestions in regard to many aspects of the text

The original manuscript of this work has undergone an almost unbelievable transformation at the hands of my publishers. I express my grateful appreciation for the advice and expertise of everyone at New Holland connected with the book's production. In particular, my special thanks go to Anouska Good and to Sophie Church, for their vision, skill and encouragement in the first edition of this book, and to Lliane Clarke and Talina McKenzie, for their ready and helpful advice in bringing to print these pages, which recall some of the memorable people and events that have enriched Australia's historical past.

BIBLIOGRAPHY

The author acknowledges with grateful thanks the following sources consulted in the course of preparing this work.

Atkinson, A. & Aveling, M., *Australia*, 1838, Fairfax, Syme & Weldon Associates, Sydney, 1987

Australia 2000, Webster Publishing, Sydney, 1999

The Australian Encyclopaedia, Vols. I to X, Chisholm, A.H., (ed.), The Grolier Society of Australia, Sydney, 1965

Bambrick, Susan, ed., *The Cambridge Encyclopedia of Australia*, Cambridge University Press, Melbourne, 1994

Bolton, G., ed., *The Oxford History of Australia*, Vols. 1–5, Oxford University Press, Melbourne, 1990

Britannica, CD 99 Multimedia Edition © 1994–1999 Encyclopædia Britannica, Inc.

Burness, P., *The Nek*, Kangaroo Press, Sydney, 1996

Cannon, M., *The Roaring Days*, Today's Australia Publishing, Victoria, 1998

Clark, M., *A Short History of Australia*, Heinemann, London, 1964

Clark, M., abridged by Cathcart, M., *Manning Clark's History of Australia*, Melbourne University Press, Melbourne, 1993

Clark, M., ed., *Sources of Australian History*, Oxford University Press, Melbourne, 1957

Clarke, F.G. Australia: *A Concise Political and Social History*, Harcourt Brace Jovanovich, Sydney, 1992

Coupe, S., (gen. ed.), *Frontier Country*, Vols. 1 & 2, Weldon Russell, Sydney, 1989

Dutton, G., *Country Life in Old Australia*, Currey O'Neil, Melbourne, 1982

Feeken, E.H.J., Feeken, G.E.E. & Spate, O.H.K., *The Discovery and Exploration of Australia*, Nelson, Melbourne, 1970

Feldt, E., *The Coast Watchers*, Lloyd O'Neill, Sydney, 1975

Fingleton, J.H., *The Greatest Test of All*, Collins, London, 1961

Flood, J., *Archaeology of the Dreamtime*, Angus & Robertson, Sydney, 1995

Guest, V., Lawrence, J. & Eshuys, J., *World War I*, Macmillan, Melbourne, 1990

Hickey, M., *Gallipoli*, John Murray, London, 1995

Isaacs, J., *Pioneer Women of the Bush and Outback*, Lansdowne Press, Sydney, 1990

Issues in Society, The Spinney Press, Thirroul, NSW

Jupp, J., ed., *The Australian People*, Cambridge University Press, Melbourne, 2001

Jupp, J. & Kabala, M. (eds.), *The Politics of Australian Immigration*, Commonwealth of Australia, 1993

King, J., *Australia's First Century*, Infosentials, Melbourne, 2000

King, J., *In the Beginning*, Macmillan, Melbourne, 1985

Lamb S. & Sington D., *Earth Story: The shaping of our world*, BBC Books, London, 1993

The Land and the People, Reader's Digest, Sydney, 1989

Liddell Hart, B.H., *History of the Second World War*, Cassell, London, 1970

Lucas, L., *Thanks for the Memory*, Grub Street, London, 1989

McCarthy, D., *Gallipoli to the Somme*, John Ferguson, Sydney, 1983

Molony, John, *The Penguin Bicentennial History of Australia: The Story of 200 Years*, Viking, Melbourne, 1987

Morrison, R., *The Voyage of the Great Southern Ark*, Ure Smith Press, Sydney, 1988

Murphy, B., *The Other Australia: Experiences of Migration*, Cambridge University Press, Melbourne, 1993

Pownell, E., *The Thirsty Land*, Hicks Smith & Sons, Sydney, 1967

Stone, D.I. & Mankinnon, S., *Life on the Australian Goldfields*, A.H. & A.W. Reed, Sydney, 1982

Taylor, P., ed., *After 200 Years*, Cambridge University Press, Canberra, 1988

Taylor, P., *Australia: The First Twelve Years*, Allen & Unwin, Sydney, 1982

Taylor, P. & Cupper, P., *Gallipoli: A Battlefield Guide*, Kangaroo Press, Sydney, 1989

Thompson, A., *Anzac Memories: Living with the Legend*, Oxford University Press, Melbourne, 1994

Walker, M. & Gleeson, G., *The Volunteers*, Allen & Unwin, Sydney, 2001

The Winners: Sydney 2000 Olympic Games, Penguin Books Australia, Melbourne, 2000

Published in Australia by
New Holland Publishers (Australia) Pty Ltd

Sydney • Auckland • London • Cape Town

1/66 Gibbes Street Chatswood NSW 2067 Australia
218 Lake Road Northcote Auckland New Zealand
86 Edgware Road LondonW2 2EA United Kingdom
80 McKenzie Street Cape Town 8001 South Africa

First published 2003 by New Holland Publishers (Australia) Pty Ltd
This edition published 2011

A record of this is available at National Library of Australia.

ISBN: 9781742571287

Publisher: Lliane Clarke
Project editor: Talina McKenzie
Proofreader: Victoria Fisher
Designer: Emma Gough
Production manager: Olga Dementiev
Printer: Ligare Book Printers, Sydney, New South Wales